# High Uintas Backcountry

A Guide and Pictorial for the High Uinta Mountains

by Jeffrey Probst
& Brad Probst

**Revised Edition!**

**New Hikes**

**More Photos**

**Updated Stats**

**Easier to Read Maps**

**Mileage & Elevation Grids**

# *Credits*

## Photography

Brad Probst
Jeffrey Probst
Robert Morris
Tom Jeffers
Robert Davidson

## Maps

Brad Probst

## Layout

Jeffrey Probst

**Special thanks to our friends who contributed their photos and shared their experiences.**



ISBN Number 0-9655871-2-6

Published by Outland Publishing, Bountiful, Utah

Printed by Publishers Press

Please send all orders, inquiries, and suggestions to:

Jeffrey Probst
Outland Publishing
122 W. 1500 N.
Bountiful, UT 84010

or

Brad Probst
4351 S. 100 W.
Ogden, UT 84405

Cover: Lovenia Lake from Notch Pass

LF-16 , Original Cover Photo

# Introduction

The High Uintas backcountry has long been a favorite haunt for backpackers, fishermen, and horsemen alike. Recreational use is heavy in some popular areas, while other remote spots may go years between visitors. Most lakes receive only light to moderate pressure. There is a lot of wilderness to go around, and you should have little trouble finding a lake that you can call your own for a few days. Maybe you'll discover your special place - one that seems custom made just for you. This book can help you find such a place; *somewhere in the High Uintas.*

Not only have we detailed a substantial number of fantastic hikes, but statistics have been compiled on each lake. The usage, camping, and horse feed have been ranked. Elevation, miles, acreage, depth, fish species, and spring water are specified as well. This book is meant to be a *trip planner.* If you have an idea of what you are searching for in a backcountry experience, this publication can serve as an excellent tool in helping you find the best areas for your particular tastes.

As you might expect, fishing in the High Uintas is lightning fast at times for those willing to venture into the backcountry. Brook trout, cutthroats, rainbows, grayling, and even a few golden trout inhabit the Uinta lakes and streams. There are over 500 lakes in this alpine mountain range that are managed for fishing. Fishing is unpredictable, but often great. There are no guarantees. A lake that was hot last year, may only be marginal this year, or vice-versa. That is why we haven't made an attempt to rate the fishing in each lake, but we will rate an area by how good the fishing prospects are in the general vicinity. Investigate several lakes. There are typically many in an area. If one lake doesn't produce, hike on to the next. That's part of the fun of alpine fishing. You get adventure mixed in with your fishing. And don't overlook the countless miles of streams. Most anglers do. The creeks are the most under utilized fisheries in the High Uintas.

In the section that describes specific hikes, we have tried to pinpoint the best camping spots, spring water, photo opportunities, and fishing holes. Sometimes we'll tell you exactly where we had the best angling, and what lure we used. But try your own methods too. Chances are good that they will work just as well - maybe better.

The High Uinta Mountains offer more than fine fishing. Solitude and grand scenery are the real attraction. Peace and quiet abound. Perhaps not in the roadside campgrounds, but certainly in the expanses of the backcountry. No motorized vehicles are allowed. You'll have to journey by foot or horseback. But if it was easily obtainable, then it wouldn't be peaceful, would it? If you haven't done much hiking here, you may be amazed how little you need to travel to lose the crowds. Quite often only a half a mile of walking puts you by yourself.

As you may have noticed, we feature 100 hikes in this guide. We hope you will seek out some of the hundreds of lakes and streams that we did not specifically highlight. Whether you wish to travel two miles, ten miles, twenty miles, or more, the High Uintas has a wilderness adventure waiting for you. You could spend a lifetime exploring its many remote drainages. But be on guard. This mountain range has an almost spiritual addiction about it. Be prepared for a powerful craving to return for more.

# *High Uintas Backcountry*

## Contents

# How to Use This Book

This book is a tool. Like any other tool, the better you know how to use it, the better you'll like the results. This book is meant to provide you with the information necessary to plan great trips into the High Uinta Mountains. It can help you plan adventures that are customized and personalized to match your tastes. Camping, fishing, solitude, and scenery are just a few determining factors. We'll also tell you how far it is, how steep it is, the elevation, and the trail conditions for each hike, so you can determine the degree of difficulty.

Backcountry data has been carefully and systematically laid out for you. We have tried not to repeat things, while at the same time providing pertinent information at your fingertips, as you need it. It is kind of like having a computerized trip planner without the computer. So let's tell you how to use it.

First, there is a section entitled **High Uintas Portfolio**. Here is a brief description of the geographical facts, terrain, wildlife, fishing, weather, dangers, restrictions, and some low-impact camping rules. Read this if you haven't visited the High Uintas yet. Hopefully, you will capture some of the flavor of this unique mountain range.

The main portion of this book details a wide variety of fantastic hikes. Whether you like long treks or just day hikes, you'll find a good selection to choose from. We have rated the important factors for you. Things like solitude (usage), fishing, scenery, spring water, campsites, and horsefeed are important when choosing an area to explore. Each hike is preceeded by a handy **Trip Planner** that summarizes these important facts and more.

Each hike has four components: a photo from the area, a description of the hike, a map segment, and a trip planner. The trip planner has two pieces of information that deserve special notation - drainage and trailhead. The drainage will tell you which corresponding map to review in the **Maps and Statistics** section. The trailhead indicates where to look in the **Trailhead Directions** section to find your way to the trailhead. You may notice that the mileage listed in this book often differs from trailhead signs. Trust the book. We have noticed many minor errors on signs.

The **Maps and Statistics** section is in order by drainage, as they occur from West to East. The more popular south slope drainages are illustrated first, then the north slope. The 100 featured hikes are also organized by drainage.

Each drainage map shows some of the topography of the land. Trailheads, trails, streams, and lakes are shown to scale. Each lake that is managed as a fishery will be named, and will also appear on the statistics chart on the opposing page. Therefore, there is no need to flip pages to find out important information about a lake. The map and the data are always side-by-side, and can be easily photocopied for your own personal use in the field.

For every 10 miles, you can probably add an extra mile to the statistics to account for hiking around fallen timber, switchbacks, river crossings, and so on.

In this revised edition, a mileage and elevation chart has been included for each drainage map. These grids graphically illustrate the difficulty of the hike by showing you the ups and downs of the main trail.

Many of the lake statistics in this book were compiled from the ten booklets that are available from the Utah Division of Wildlife Resources. This book is not meant to replace those booklets, but rather to complement them. For further information on a specific lake or drainage, pick up a copy of the appropriate booklet from the DWR.

Even though foot travel is the most common mode of transportation in the Uintas, this book does not tell you how to hike or backpack. There are other publications devoted to the subject, and unless you are a seasoned backpacker, we suggest you read one before heading to the mountains. An excellent choice is the book entitled **Backpacking $ense** by Jeffrey Probst. It was written with areas like the High Uintas in mind.

For hikers desiring a roadside base camp, this book has a **Campground Directory**. Roadside camping in the High Uintas is another issue that deserves its own book, but we felt you might at least need a summary of the campgrounds. Besides, some backpackers prefer to leave their vehicles in a campground rather than at a trailhead, for better security. Trailheads are more susceptible to theft or vandalism, but this hasn't been much of a problem yet.

Other goodies in this book include a **USGS Topo Map Directory**. On the back cover is a map of the road system for accessing the High Uinta Mountains. We purposely put it on the back so that you can set this book on your car seat or dash, and have easy viewing while driving.

We hope you enjoy using this new tool. Now, if you can just convince others that you've been "working with your tools"....

*Helen Lake (Rock Creek Drainage)*

# *High Uintas Portfolio*

The High Uinta Mountains, named after the Uintat Indians, have the distinction of being the only mountain range in the lower 48 states that runs east to west. It is the birthplace of several major rivers that make up Utah's watersheds, including the Provo, Weber, Duchesne, and Bear Rivers. There are over 400 miles of streams in these mountains, along with 1,000 ice-cold lakes and ponds. Over half of these lakes are managed to provide some of the best high country fishing found anywhere.

Most of the High Uintas lie within an official wilderness area re-established in 1984. Since then, no motorized vehicles or machinery have been allowed, including bicycles. These regulations have helped immensely in keeping a pristine environment. Livestock grazing still continues in some localized areas, but there is plenty of space where you can avoid their annoyances. Most cattle and sheep seem to be found around timberline, where they can feed on high grasses, then retreat to the shelter of the pines.

Utah's tallest mountain is nestled deep in the center of the wilderness area. Kings Peak (elev. 13,528 feet) stands between the Yellowstone and Uinta River Drainages, but is probably best reached from the North Slope via Henrys Fork Drainage. Because it is Utah's highest point, it is extremely popular among "peak baggers," and can be conquered without the aid of climbing gear. Just walk on up if you're in *good* physical condition. It's a long hike though, no matter which approach you attempt.

Blue-ribbon backpacking is abundant throughout the High Uintas. Enjoy true wilderness experiences in rugged places with names such as Spread Eagle Peak, Highline Trail, Dead Horse Pass, Hells Kitchen, Lightning Lake, Yellowstone Creek, Buck Pasture, Amethyst Lake, and hundreds more.

The western half of the High Uintas is most popular, due simply to its proximity to Utah's main population centers of Salt Lake City, Provo, and Ogden. A two hour drive from any of these cities can put you at any one of a dozen Uinta trailheads. Generally, the further east you travel by car will determine how much solitude you'll find when traveling by foot or horseback.

The terrain is characterized by large stands of pines that lead into alpine basins and cirques. Small lakes generously dot the backcountry. They can be found almost anywhere: along a stream, at the foot of a talus slope, adjoining a lush meadow, or at the bottom of a towering cliff. Encase all of this within steep rocky peaks that rise thousands of feet, and you'll have a pretty fair picture of what's in store for you.

Winter lasts a long time in the High Uintas. There isn't much hikable backcountry available until late June, and mountain passes may be snow bound until mid-July. Anytime after the middle of September you risk being caught in a serious snowstorm. As you can quickly figure, the backpacking season lasts only three months, if we're fortunate. The best time to plan a trip into these mountains is during the second half of August. Then, the days are warm, the snow is long gone, and those pesky mosquitoes have mostly died off. If you don't mind cooler temperatures, try it after Labor Day. You'll have it all to yourself.

Those familiar with mountain travel know that the weather can change rapidly. Regardless of the forecast, you should always be prepared for searing sun, pouring rain, lightning, and even snow. Wear and pack your clothes in layers. With a T-shirt, long-sleeved collared shirt, sweater, jacket, poncho, and brimmed hat, you can adjust your attire to match any weather condition.

The High Uintas vary in elevation from 8,000 to over 13,000 feet in elevation. Most likely you will be camping somewhere between 10,000 and 10,800 feet. Going any higher than this puts you above timberline, where campsites are scarce and uncomfortable. At these elevations it is essential to know the effects elevation has on humans. The most dangerous is altitude sickness. It can kill. If someone develops a hacking cough, spits up blood, or seems irrational or confused, then he/she may have altitude sickness. The *only* solution is to go down. If you have suffered from altitude sickness in the past, limit yourself to an altitude gain of 1000 feet per day. Unfortunately this may include elevation gained by your ride to the trailhead too.

Bugs are a nuisance in the High Uinta backcountry. Mosquitoes can be terrible around moist meadows and ponds, so remember that when selecting a campsite. Bring your repellent, or as suggested earlier, wait until late in the season when the "skeeters" are gone. Deer flies and black flies are pesky too. If bugs are bad, try camping in an open area where the wind can blow them down.

Giardia is a widespread problem throughout the lakes, streams, and ponds of the Uintas. This tiny parasite can cause a severe flu-like disorder about two weeks after ingestion. Spring water is safe to drink without treatment, but all other water should either be boiled, treated with iodine tablets, or filtered. If you choose to filter, be sure your filter will remove giardia. If you choose an iodine treatment, follow the instructions closely or giardia may still be alive.

Rules and regulations are minimal in the High Uintas, and if we all camp sensibly it will stay that way. No permits are needed, and the only real restriction is on group size. Keep your party smaller than fifteen people and twenty stock animals. Registers exist at a few trailheads. Please use them. They are one of the few management tools that the Forest Service utilizes here. During dry spells, certain areas may have fire bans imposed. Check with the appropriate ranger district if the summer has been dry. Fishermen should review the fishing proclamation. The limit is probably eight trout, but that is subject to change. Also, there are a few stream closures when trout are spawning.

Fishing is often superb in the High Uintas backcountry, but is also unpredictable. A lake that was fast fishing one year, might be poor the next. Winterkill takes its toll, as does fishing pressure on popular lakes. If you're serious about catching lots of fish, then opt for an area with several lakes in the vicinity. If one doesn't produce, try another one nearby. Explore remote lakes, especially those that are off the trail or tough to reach. These are the real fishing gems of the High Uintas. You may find a lake where a pan-sized cutthroat will spank your fly on every cast, or maybe you'll fool a chunky two-pound-plus brookie that has never beheld an artificial lure.

The lakes are most favored among fishermen, but don't bypass connecting streams and ponds. Fish migrate into areas you would never expect. Maybe, just maybe, a sly old lunker has been quietly living out its days in an isolated pool. You have to take a chance if you want to hit the jackpot!

Small flies are the most effective lure in these alpine lakes. That makes sense, since tiny bugs make up over 80% of their diet. Give them what they are used to. Good sizes are #18 and #16. Successful patterns include Renegade, Adams, Black Gnat, and an olive scud. Small spinners (size 0-2) are also effective, particularly on brook trout in deeper lakes. Streams are best fished with a flashy light-weight spinner or a fly.

Often times someone will hear of a great fishing hole, and they will hike in during the morning hours, fish for a few hours, and then head back home fishless and discouraged. Think about that for a moment. When did the person fish? Answer: During the least productive time of day. Some lakes are good fishing anytime, but most have their feeding times. Mornings and evenings are when the fish are active. Noon time is not lunch time for backcountry trout, *it's siesta time*. If you are day hiking, and plan on fishing, then plan your hiking around the optimal fishing hours.

Catch and release is commonly practiced by backcountry sportsmen. Keep only enough fish for your next meal. Fish don't pack out well, and will likely just end up in the trash can. Put 'em back in the water instead. This is a delicate fishery that we must unselfishly preserve.

Lastly, lets talk about low impact camping. There are a few rules that we all must follow to keep these mountains in their pristine state. This shouldn't sound like scolding or nagging, but rather an education in the basics of backcountry manners.

- Split large groups into smaller camps (5/camp).
- Camp 200 feet from water sources.
- All human waste must be 200 feet from water sources.
- Use existing camps and fire rings.
- Cut NO green wood.
- Stay on trails, especially on steep slopes.
- Burn combustible garbage, pack out the rest.
- Keep quiet.
- Park horses away from water sources and wet meadows.
- Hobble horses. Picket for no more than 30 minutes.
- Respect wildlife.

# 100 Great Backcountry Trips

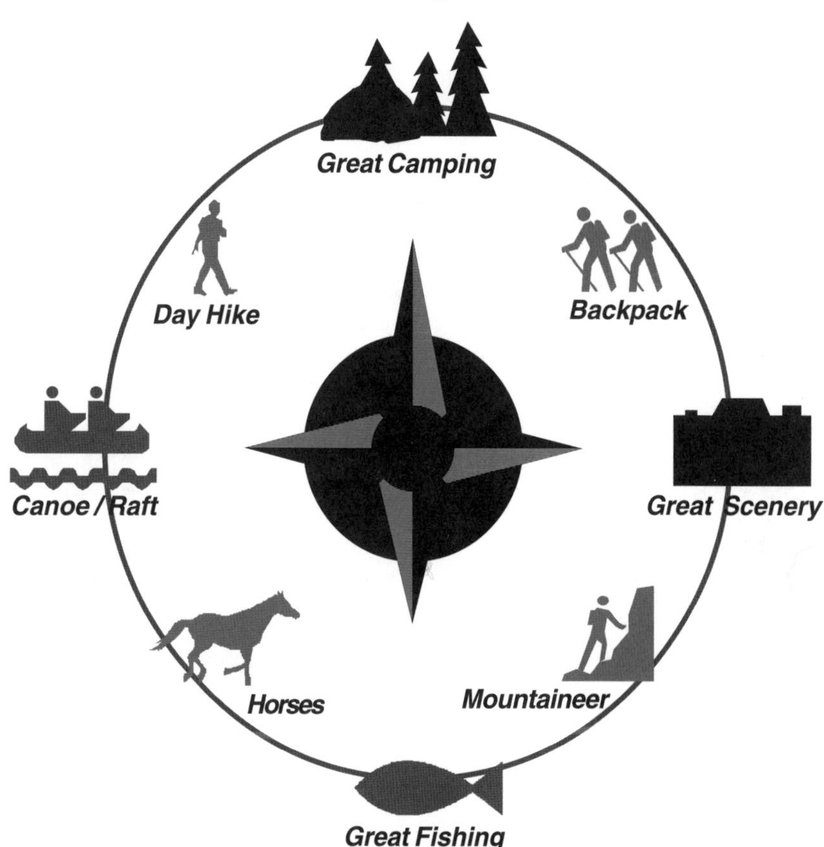

# Big Elk Lake

| Trip Planner: | | | |
|---|---|---|---|
| Miles | 1.1 | Usage | Heavy |
| Elevation | 10,020 | Campsites | Good |
| Elev. Gain | 400 | Springwater | No |
| Drainage | Provo | Fishing | Good |
| Trailhead | Norway Flats | Horsefeed | Poor |
| Near Town | Kamas | Firewood | Limited |

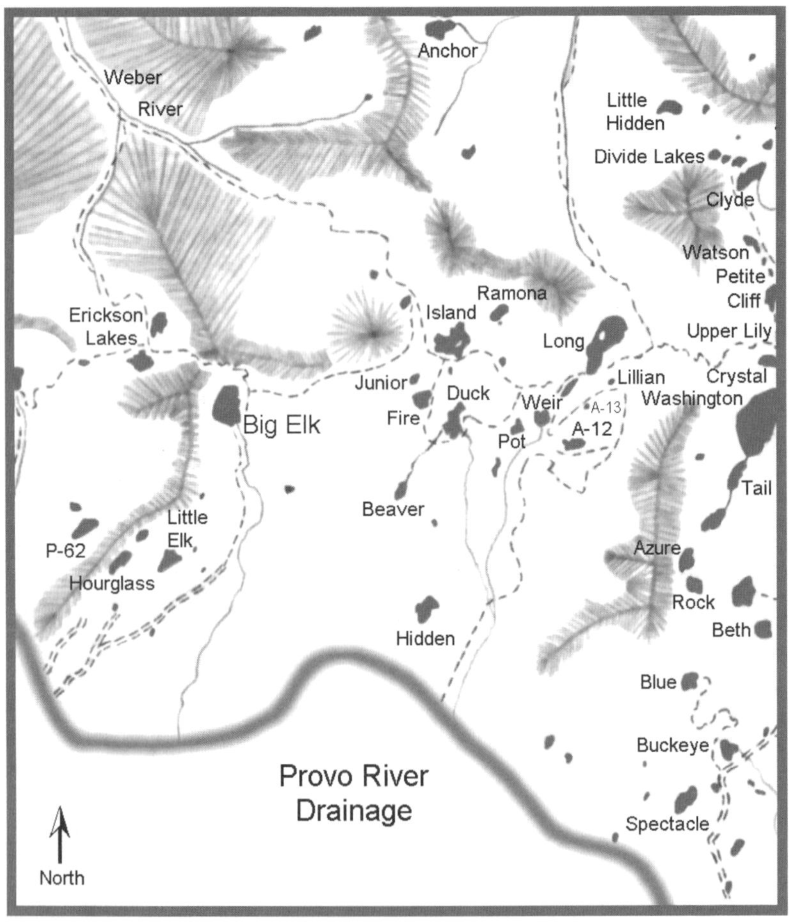

You can pack extra gear into here. The hike is just a little over a mile, so bring the lawn chairs and float tube. There is a steep incline just before the dam, but otherwise, it's an easy hike.

The hardest part about this trek is finding the right road. The Norway Flats road starts innocently enough as it turns off of U-150. But it forks several times where there are no markers and the maps don't show. Stay with the road that shows the most wear until you are about 6 miles from U-150, then a road will turn right (east). You may need a 4WD vehicle to cover the last mile or so on this road. If you stay on the road most traveled, you will end up at a beaver pond just below Hourglass Lake. This is the wrong starting place. Go back to the road that turned east and follow it down to the trailhead.

At Big Elk Lake, fishing is generally pretty good for stocked brook and cutthroat trout. A raft or canoe would be nice to escape the crowds and the bugs, but you can do just fine from shore. Fish with a small fly (#16) during the morning and evenings, and you should have little trouble catching enough for a hearty meal.

Campsites are available on the south and east sides of this deep reservoir. There are no springs around, so plan on purifying your drinking water. Big Elk receives heavy pressure, especially on weekends. Visit during the week. There might not be anybody else there. Pack out your litter, and help us keep Big Elk a clean and fun place to explore.

***Big Elk Lake***

# Long Pond

| Trip Planner: | | | |
|---|---|---|---|
| Miles | 2 | Usage | Moderate |
| Elevation | 10,100 | Campsites | Good |
| Elev. Gain | 100 | Springwater | No |
| Drainage | Provo | Fishing | Good |
| Trailhead | Crystal Lake | Horsefeed | Fair |
| Near Town | Kamas | Firewood | Limited |

Long Pond is just that - a long pond. And it is situated immediately below the outlet of Long Lake. Fortunately for you it is not a *long* hike, nor is it a long story to fill you in why we've included Long Pond in this book. While the lake receives heavy usage, Long Pond is largely ignored; even though it has better fishing and more solitude than the lake.

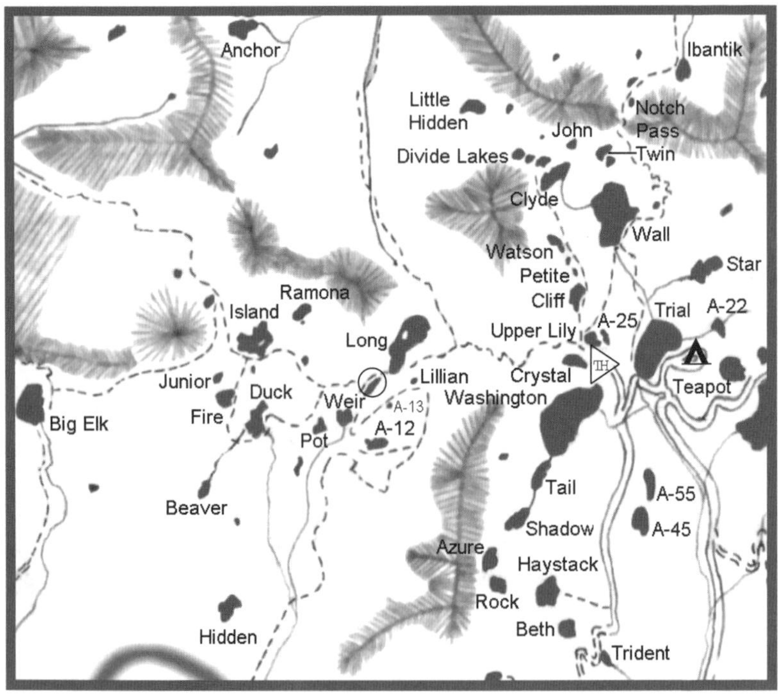

***Long Pond***

This place is fun to fish. Long Pond has a variety of trout habitat to test your angling skills. Shallows, pools, rocks, and a few deadfalls combine to give you an array of fishing challenges. This is a fairly unique body of water in these parts. It is neither stream nor lake, and it's not really a pond - at least in the way we normally envision ponds. Expect the unexpected when exploring Long Pond. The trout you'll likely catch offer variety too. Count on a mixed bag of cutthroat and brook trout. These fish migrate from Long Lake. Since it has no water flow in the winter, Long Pond is not stocked. But enough trout from Long Lake sneak into the pond to make fishing exciting. This is truely a "one of a kind" angling opportunity in these mountains.

Good campsites can be found along Long Pond. As mentioned earlier, you'll see fewer visitors here than at Long Lake. This is a good spot to camp for a small group (four or less). Usually it is a peaceful, serene place that sits just down the hill from Long Lake - out of sight and out of ear shot from the crowds at the lake. It is not a good area for horses to stop, so you can avoid them too.

# Island Lake (Provo River)

| Trip Planner: | | | |
|---|---|---|---|
| Miles | 3.5 | Usage | Moderate |
| Elevation | 10,140 | Campsites | Good |
| Elev. Gain | 120 | Springwater | Yes |
| Drainage | Provo | Fishing | Good |
| Trailhead | Crystal Lake | Horsefeed | Good |
| Near Town | Kamas | Firewood | Limited |

"Which Island Lake?" - you may ask. Just as there are many Hidden Lakes and Lost Lakes, it seems like every other drainage has an Island Lake. This one sits high on the Provo River Drainage, and can be reached fairly easily. The first mile is steep, the last half mile is steep, but sandwiched between these sections is some easy and level

***Island Lake (Provo River Drainage)***

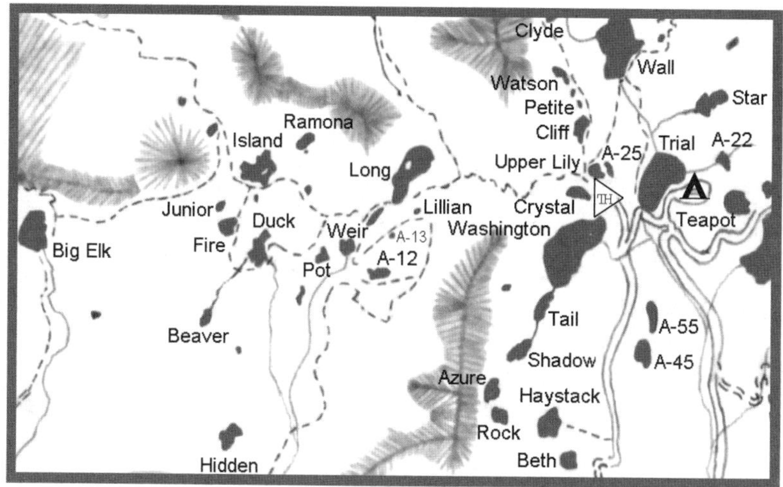


hiking. The trail is quite popular among overnighters, so expect to see a few people, especially on weekends.

Sheltered campsites are found on the east side of the lake, and spring water might be available near the northeast corner. Island Lake is picturesque with its high cliffs dropping straight down into deep water along the northern shore. Whether you are looking at these cliffs from across the lake, or standing on top of them, you'll want your camera handy.

Large wary cutthroats make fishing unpredictable. These fish are well fed by a healthy population of fresh-water shrimp, and they don't hit a dry fly as readily as trout do on other backcountry lakes. Try a pink shrimp imitation. You will only need a couple of these trout to fill the frying pan. If you are looking for faster fishing, venture over the hill about 1/4 mile to Junior Lake. This tiny lake is often overlooked by anglers, and usually provides very good fishing for small cutts. Keep going a little farther and you'll descend to Fire Reservoir where fishing can be fast at times. It doesn't get too much pressure since it is situated in steep rocky terrain, and camping opportunities are virtually non-existent. Other good fishing lakes in the immediate area are Duck Lake and Beaver Lake.

Back at Island Lake, enjoy a peaceful sunset, or stand atop the cliffs and peer into the depths of the lake for cruising trout. This lake will not satisfy true "solitude seekers," but it is a quick get-away.

# Divide Lakes

| Trip Planner: | | | |
|---|---|---|---|
| Miles | 2.5 | Usage | Moderate |
| Elevation | 10,460 | Campsites | Good |
| Elev. Gain | 440 | Springwater | Yes |
| Drainage | Provo | Fishing | Very Good |
| Trailhead | Crystal Lake | Horsefeed | Good |
| Near Town | Kamas | Firewood | Limited |

Here's a campout to take the kids on. You'll see plenty of small lakes along the way, and the trail has a good mix of uphill and level slopes. It is fairly easy to find. The trail is well marked except for the section just past Watson Lake. It looks like an avalanche wiped out a couple hundred yards of trail, but just head due north to Clyde Lake and you will easily pick up the trail again.

This hike is a great overnighter for small groups, or is a wonderful escape if you are camped at Trial Lake and want to get away from camp for a spell. You couldn't ask for a better nature trail that offers a wide variety of scenery, complete with fishing holes.

The best places to camp are at the west end of Divide #2 and right between Divide #1 and Divide #2. I would choose the latter site if the weather was guaranteed to be fair, otherwise I would seek the safety of the pines at Divide #2. Although these lakes are less than 100 yards

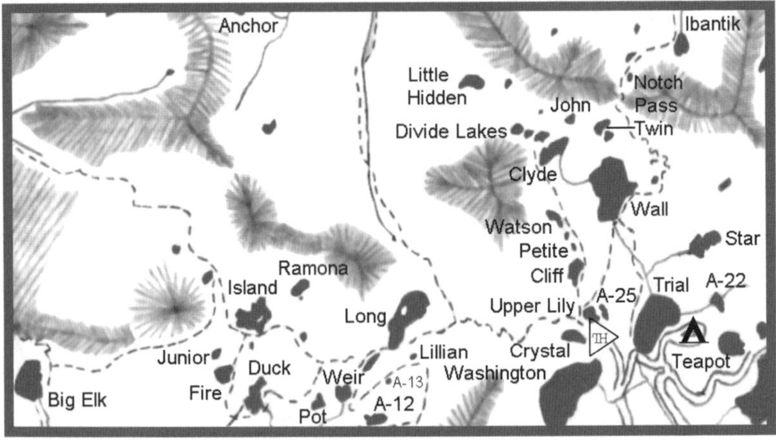

***Divide Lake #1***

apart, Divide #1 is on the Provo River Drainage, and Divide #2 is on the Weber River Drainage. There is a large rock between the two lakes, and when rain falls on it, half the water heads towards the Provo River and half towards the Weber.

Several springs are located on the west end of Divide #2. They are conveniently close to camp, and ice cold. Small lakes abound, and there is plenty to do and see without wandering too far. Nearby, Booker Lake offers fair fishing, but you'll probably do better right at Divide #1, which has a nice population of smallish brook trout. For best results, try the deeper southwest corner of the lake with a tiny fly.

If you're after bigger fish, try Little Hidden Lake on the Weber Drainage. You'll want a topographical map and a compass to find it. There is no trail to it, but stay close to the mountain to the east, and head north about half a mile. This lake has brookies ranging from half a pound to well over a pound. A #16 Renegade fly, cast in the northwest end of the lake, should put a few nicer trout in the creel. Be quiet here. The fish have learned to disappear when noisy visitors appear. As long as you're quiet, they'll keep biting. There is spring water to the northeast if you need to refill your canteen.

From Divide Lakes notice "The Notch" in the mountains to the northeast. This well known pass is a thing of beauty, especially when you're on it. From the top of Notch Pass is a spectacular view right down into Lovenia Lake. It's worth the mile trip over; or maybe you could go there on your way back to the trailhead. The Notch Pass trail returns to Crystal Lake Trailhead too.

# Twin Lakes

| Trip Planner: | | | |
|---|---|---|---|
| Miles | 2.3 | Usage | Moderate |
| Elevation | 10,410 | Campsites | Good |
| Elev. Gain | 390 | Springwater | Yes |
| Drainage | Provo | Fishing | Good |
| Trailhead | Crystal Lake | Horsefeed | Fair |
| Near Town | Kamas | Firewood | Limited |

***Upper Twin Lake***

Most people proceed unknowingly right past these lakes. It seems everyone makes the extra effort to hike over Notch Pass to see the beautiful scenery that Ibantic Lake offers. And rightly so. From Notch Pass, the country is amazing. On the other hand, Twin Lakes may make a good base camp, which gives you the serenity that no other lakes in this area can provide. Don't get us wrong, Twin Lakes get their fare share of attention, but are often over looked.

Twin Lakes offer a number of commodities. The vista is pretty, it's only a short distance from the trailhead, fishing is good for 9 to 15 inch brook trout, and other exciting excursions lie just beyond the immediate. Provisions are moderate. Springwater is only found in the early summer months, while camping areas are only fair due to rocky terrain. However, there is one excellent campsite near the northwest end of Upper Twin. This site sits on a bench, overlooking the lakes.

It's rather easy to find Twin Lakes. Even though these lakes lie off the beaten path, rock piles are displayed to show the way. Begin your journey at the Crystal Lake trailhead. Follow the trail 1 mile to Wall Lake. Here, the trail takes off to the east, then up some steep rocky switchbacks. Just past the top of all the switchbacks, rock cairns mark the turnoff. A faint trail then makes its way west to lower Twin Lake.

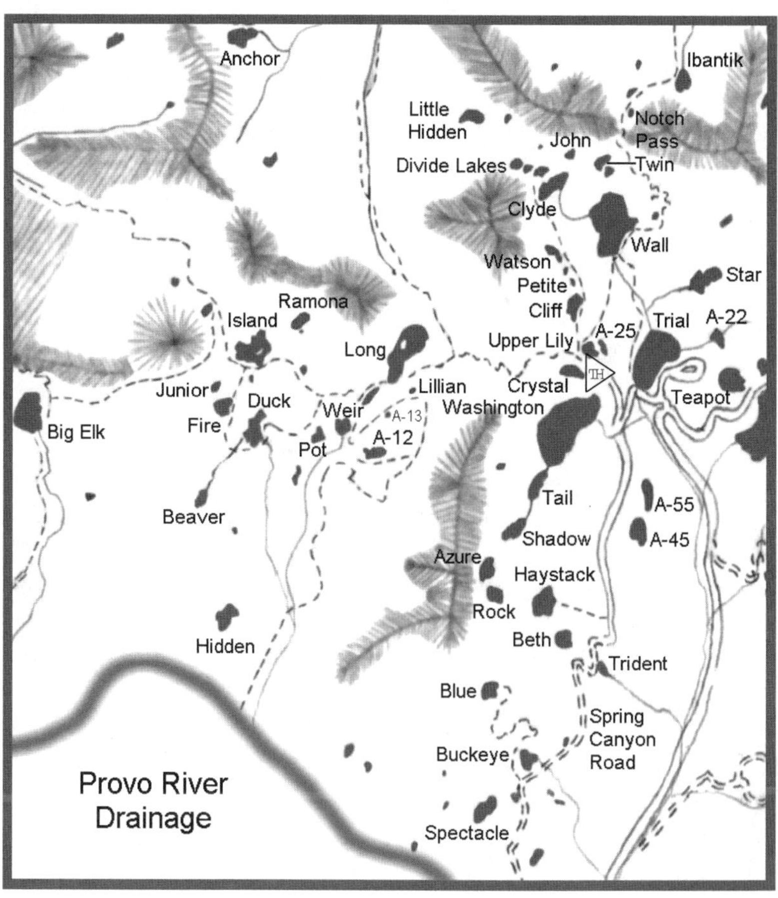

# Bald Mountain

| Trip Planner: | | | |
|---|---|---|---|
| Miles | 2.5 | Usage | Heavy |
| Elevation | 11,943 | Campsites | None |
| Elev. Gain | 1150 | Springwater | No |
| Drainage | Duchesne | Fishing | None |
| Trailhead | Bald Mtn. | Horsefeed | None |
| Near Town | Kamas | Firewood | None |

Bald Mountain - the best time investment you can make in the High Uintas. If you only have a few hours to spend, and want to experience some grand vistas, then this is the place. Just 2.5 miles of steep hiking puts you atop this well known peak, where you'll have a birdseye view of four of Utah's major watersheds. The Weber, Provo, Duchesne, and Bear Rivers all begin near here. Looking to the west

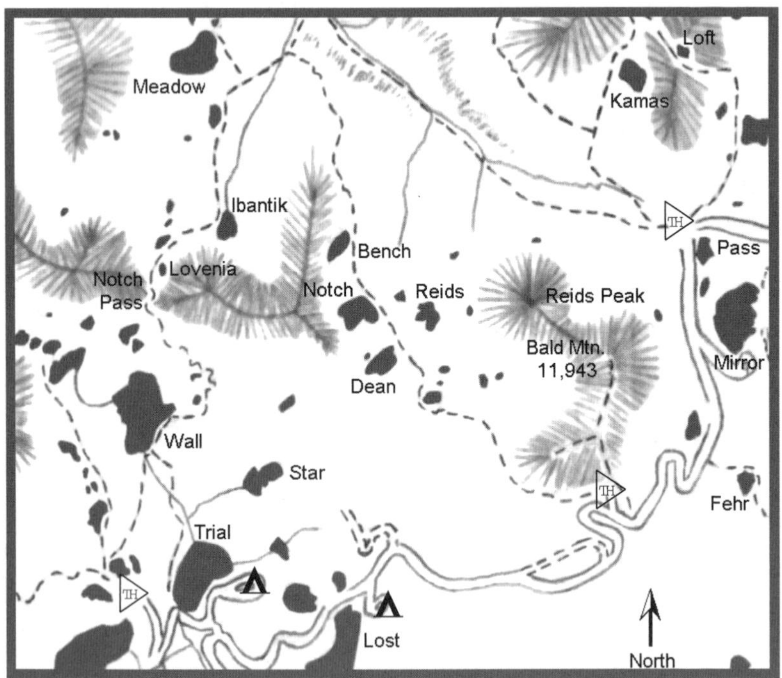

***Duchesne Drainage from Bald Mountain***

you can spot a couple of dozen lakes that speckle the upper regions of the Provo and Weber Rivers. Turn around to the east, and enjoy a spectacular view of the Mirror Lake Highway winding its way through heavy timber, past Mirror Lake, and on towards Mt. Agassiz and Hayden Peak.

This hike begins at the well-marked Bald Mountain trailhead, located at the base of Bald Mountain. You start climbing immediately, and will soon find yourself traversing a series of switchbacks on the western slope. The view is great all the way, and somehow manages to improve with every step. Near the summit, the trail follows a thin ridge with steep drops off either side. There's really no danger though if you stick with the trail, but a person with acrophobia may feel uncomfortable. Then take a natural rock stairway to what feels like the top of the world.

Take your time on this hike. It is steep. Allow about four hours for a round trip, which should give you plenty of time at the top to appreciate the views in every direction. Heed a couple of safety reminders on this hike: (1) Stay off Bald Mountain when lightning is possible. (2) Don't get too close to the cliff edges on the east side, as they can break away. Follow these rules, and your name won't be added to Bald Mountain's casualty list. OK, now don't let us scare you away. Try this hike. It is time well spent.

# Cliff Lake

| Trip Planner: | | | |
|---|---|---|---|
| Miles | .5 | Usage | Heavy |
| Elevation | 10,230 | Campsites | Very Good |
| Elev. Gain | 210 | Springwater | Yes |
| Drainage | Provo | Fishing | Fair |
| Trailhead | Crystal Lake | Horsefeed | Fair |
| Near Town | Kamas | Firewood | Limited |

You couldn't ask for a prettier setting. The stage is set with picture perfect campsites that overlook a small lake dimpled by feeding fish. A stately cliff serves as a backdrop. Grassy campsites

*Cliff Lake (Provo River Drainage)*

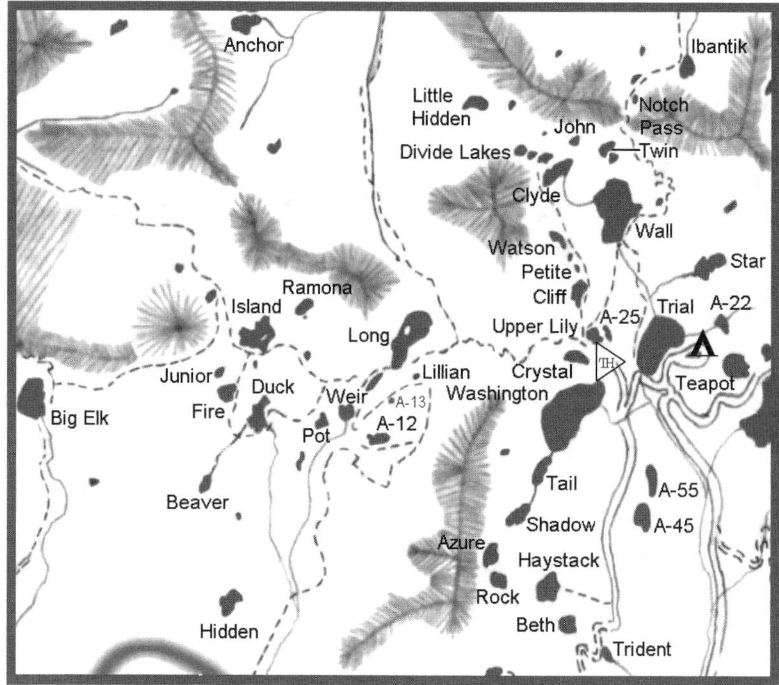


are just off the trail on the eastern shore, providing an ideal place to watch the sunset, and reflect on the finer things of life. The whole scene mirrors off the clear water.

Cliff Lake is close enough to the trailhead that you would have plenty of time to watch the sunset, and still make it back to the car before dark. It's also a great place to try out some new gear before taking on a more serious hike.

Expect to see a fair amount of foot traffic pass by this lake. Fishermen and day hikers have to pass by to get to the many lakes above. Cliff Lake is obviously not for loners, but if you're the friendly type, and enjoy a quaint little spot with a gorgeous view, then this may be for you.

A small population of cutthroat trout will keep you company. However, the fishing is likely to be only fair due to the easy access and the wary nature of these trout. Better fishing can be found by continuing up the trail another mile to Clyde Lake. Most hikers don't stop at Cliff Lake very long, but almost all remember the pleasant scenery. Try it on a weekday, and you might have it all to yourself.

# Castle Lake

| Trip Planner: | | | |
|---|---|---|---|
| Miles | .4 | Usage | Moderate |
| Elevation | 10,300 | Campsites | Good |
| Elev. Gain | -40 | Springwater | Yes |
| Drainage | Duchesne | Fishing | Fair |
| Trailhead | Butterfly Lake | Horsefeed | Fair |
| Near Town | Kamas | Firewood | Good |

This hike is thrown in for the roadside camper looking for a short diversion. Castle Lake is less than half a mile west of Butterfly Lake. Butterfly Lake has excellent campground facilities, as well as a parking area for day use anglers. There is no trail to Castle Lake, but just head due west, stay close to the base of the cliffs, and you can't miss it. There are several small ponds on the way. Don't mistake one of them for Castle Lake.

Cliffs parallel Castle Lake just beyond its northern shore. This is a quiet little place (1 acre) that can be a welcome reprieve from the public campground scene. A round trip from Butterfly Lake to

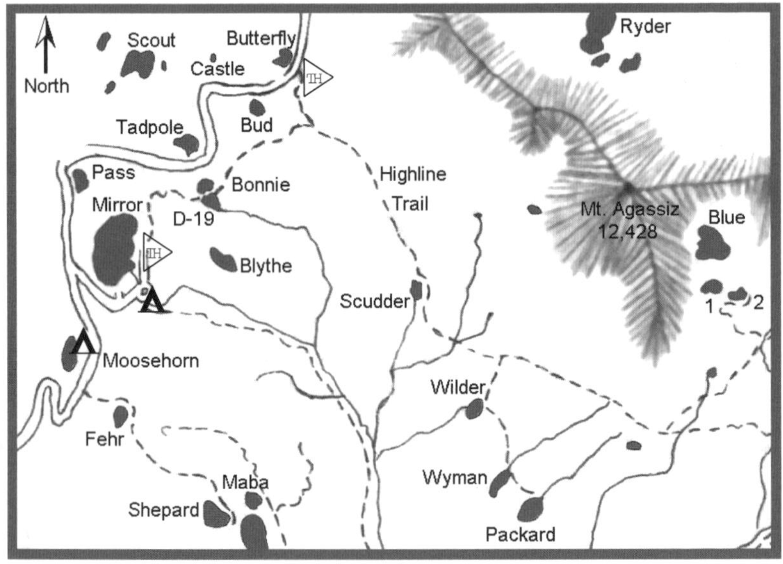

beautiful Castle Lake makes a wonderful evening stroll that should only take an hour, unless you stop to sit awhile or try the fishing.

Open shorelines make for wary trout. Castle Lake has both. Assorted size cutthroats occupy this water, but can be a real challenge to catch. Be quiet, and don't let them see or hear you. Maybe you can fool a couple of them before they know you're around.

There are a few moist areas around the lake, so mosquitoes can be a nuisance at times. Give yourself a good dose of insect repellent, and you'll breathe easier while enjoying this secluded spot. It seems further away than it is from the crowded campgrounds and the highway.

***Castle Lake***

**In every man's heart there is a secret nerve that answers to the vibrations of beauty.**
***- Christopher Morley***

# Fehr Lake

| Trip Planner: | | | |
|---|---|---|---|
| Miles | .3 | Usage | Heavy |
| Elevation | 10,260 | Campsites | Good |
| Elev. Gain | -100 | Springwater | Yes |
| Drainage | Duchesne | Fishing | Fair |
| Trailhead | Fehr Lake | Horsefeed | Good |
| Near Town | Kamas | Firewood | Good |

Even small kids can enjoy this hike. You don't have to be in good shape either. This is a mini-hike. If you only have a couple of hours to spend, you could take a leisurely stroll down to Fehr Lake, fish a bit, and still make it back in time for lunch.

The only thing difficult about this hike is locating the trailhead. There is a nice large sign indicating where to begin, but some people

*Fehr Lake*

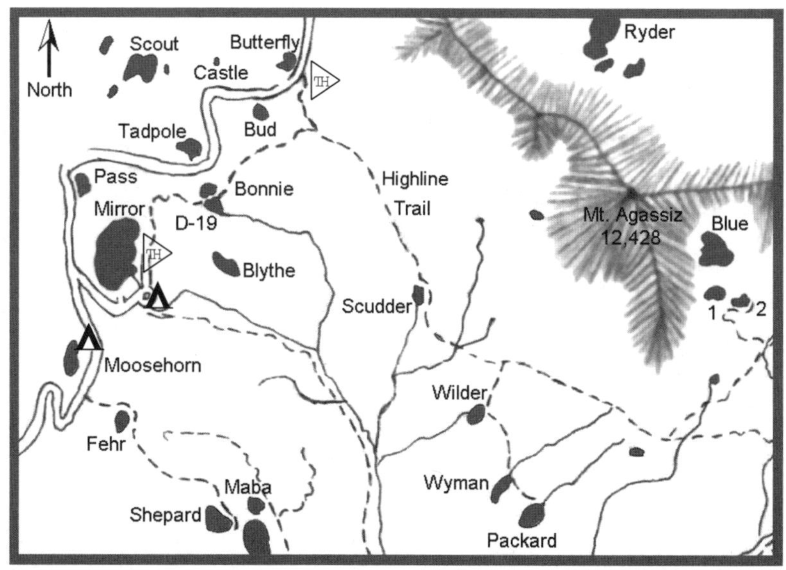


drive right past it while looking for a place to park. Look for the trailhead immediately after turning off Highway 150. You'll spot it easily, then turn left to the parking area.

The hike to Fehr is gentle and provides a variety of scenery in its short distance. You'll pass through cool groves of pines, mountain meadows, and past a small waterfall or two. It's a great place to get away from busy campgrounds. You'll feel more removed than you really are. Notice the quiet. Fehr is a natural lake (6 acres) in a picture book setting. It is surrounded on three sides by pines, and a meadow on the south. Beyond the meadow are more pines backed by a stately mountain.

Fishing at Fehr is only fair, which is probably as good as any of the roadside lakes. But you won't be crowded here. Move around and try various lures and flies, or just sit on the bank and drown a worm. The odds are you will catch a few fat brook trout - maybe even a nap. Here's a great little water to portage a canoe into, then try fishing the middle of the lake where nobody ever does.

The trail continues on past Fehr Lake. It goes down to Shepard, Maba, Hoover, and Marshall Lakes. People using this trail are just out for a hike because you could drive to these lakes on the Murdock Basin road. Try it for a relaxing day hike. It may seem a little steep on the return trip though.

# Packard & Wyman Lakes

| Trip Planner: | | | |
|---|---|---|---|
| Miles | 3.5 | Usage | Moderate |
| Elevation | 9,980 | Campsites | Good |
| Elev. Gain | 0 | Springwater | Yes |
| Drainage | Duchesne | Fishing | Fair |
| Trailhead | Highline | Horsefeed | Fair |
| Near Town | Kamas | Firewood | Good |

Wyman Lake

Packard Lake makes a great day hike for kids and adults alike. Most people begin their adventure from Mirror Lake rather than the Highline Trailhead. This is solely because better accommodations are found at Mirror Lake. The Highline Trailhead is about 1 mile shorter in distance, but from its starting point the trail descends 300 feet to the Mirror Lake trail junction. Access from Mirror Lake begins

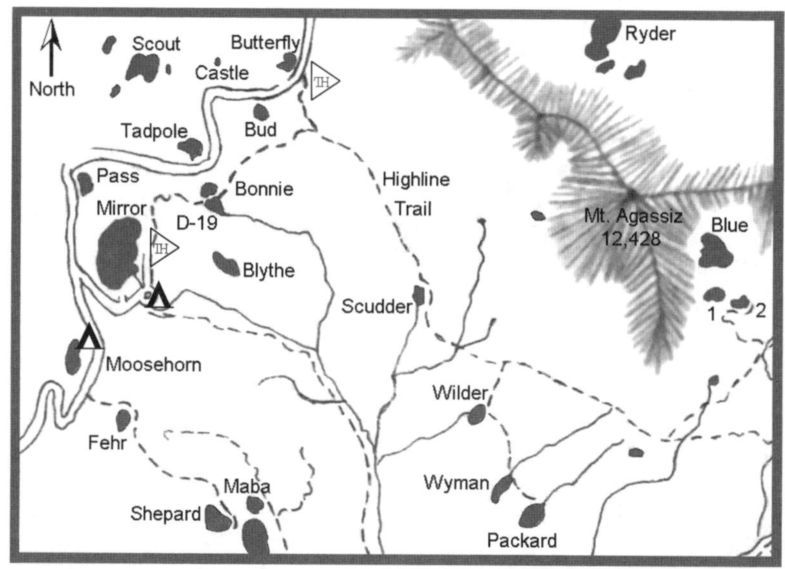


near the east side of the lake at the north end of the campgrounds. The trail makes its way 2 miles northeast then connects with the Highline Trail. From this junction, follow the Highline Trail 2 miles southeast to a posted sign on the eastern top of a ravine. Follow the Packard Lake trail 1 mile south down a steep and rocky slope, past Wilder Lake, then up and down a hill to Wyman Lake. Packard Lake is another 1/4 mile southeast of Wyman Lake.

Wyman features heavy timber and pretty lily pads clinging to the shore. Campsites are plentiful, but Wyman and Packard are located in a fire restriction area, and fuel wood may not be burned. Bring a stove if you want to cook any meals. Wyman receives heavy camping and angling use, and frequently winterkills, which usually means only fair fishing. This lake is stocked yearly.

Packard is a pretty lake located on a high ledge with a view of the East Fork of the Duchesne River Drainage. Good campsites are present, but horse feed and spring water are limited. This lake receives heavy fishing pressure, but a good supply of brook trout inhabit the lake. All lakes in this area receive heavy usage and are prone to litter. Please help keep them clean.

If there's too much company at Packard and Wyman Lakes, try going back to Wilder Lake. Surrounded by heavy timber, this small lake has nice camping, horse feed, and willing brook trout. Heck, maybe should you should just stop here to begin with, and make camp.

# Jordan Lake

| Trip Planner: | | | |
|---|---|---|---|
| Miles | 6.5 | Usage | Heavy |
| Elevation | 10,660 | Campsites | Good |
| Elev. Gain | 650 | Springwater | Yes |
| Drainage | Duchesne | Fishing | Good |
| Trailhead | Highline | Horsefeed | Fair |
| Near Town | Kamas | Firewood | Scarce |

***Jordan Lake***

Considering the heavy usage thrown upon this area, Naturalist remains a remarkably clean basin. We would like to offer our thanks and appreciation to hikers and the Forest Service for keeping this beautiful wilderness free of debris and litter. To insure this mountain range remains unscarred, fire restrictions are in effect throughout Naturalist Basin. However, campfires may be built at posted campsites at Jordan and Morat Lakes.

In scenic timbered terrain, Jordan Lake is identified by a steep boulder slope, pickled with pine trees on the northwest side. Excellent posted campsites are located west of the lake, but fuel wood is extremely sparse due to substantial camping use. Other camping areas can be found along the east side of the outlet. This wide outlet is composed of several small ponds connected by a meandering stream. A small source of spring water can be found trickling into the northwest side of the lake. Be prepared though. During dry years, only lake water will be present.

A large population of brook trout inhabit the outlet, making flyfishing a pleasure. The lake is stocked regularly. Angling can be kind of slow until dusk. Then they're jumpin' like popcorn.

The only lakes that have campsites in the Jordan Lake vicinity are Jordan, Hyatt and Everman. Shaler can be found on the Naturalist Basin trail 3/4 mile northeast of Jordan Lake. Hyatt is located on a scenic rocky shelf 1/2 mile east of Everman. Everman is in a small meadow 3/4 mile east of the Blue-Jordan trail junction and just 200 yards east of the Naturalist Basin trail. LeConte is situated above timberline 1/2 mile northwest of Jordan, over steep and rocky terrain. Faxon and Gatman do not sustain fish life.

From the Highline Trailhead, the trail descends about 300 feet to the Mirror Lake trail junction. Then follow the Highline Trail 4 miles southeast across several gentle ravines to a posted sign at the Naturalist Basin turnoff. Proceed 1.8 miles northeast to the Blue-Jordan trail junction. At this point the Jordan Lake trail crosses the river and heads east through a scenic meadow. Then it turns north up a couple of rocky switchbacks, leveling out at the lake.

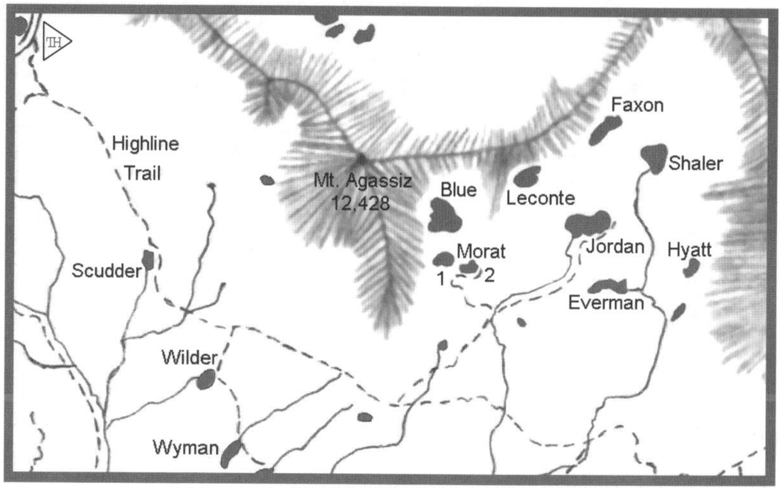

# Morat and Blue Lakes

| Trip Planner: | | | |
|---|---|---|---|
| Miles | 5.5 | Usage | Moderate |
| Elevation | 10,740 | Campsites | Good |
| Elev. Gain | 740 | Springwater | Yes |
| Drainage | Duchesne | Fishing | Good |
| Trailhead | Highline | Horsefeed | Fair |
| Near Town | Kamas | Firewood | Scarce |

***Naturalist Basin (Blue/Jordan Junction)***

From the Blue-Jordan trail junction follow the Blue Lake trail 1/2 mile west then north to Morat Lakes. The last 1/8 mile is excessively rocky and almost vertical. For trail access to Naturalist Basin, see the last paragraph of Jordan Lake information.

Morat #1 is at the base of Blue Lake ridge next to a talus slope interspersed with conifers. Morat #2 is located just east of Morat #1.

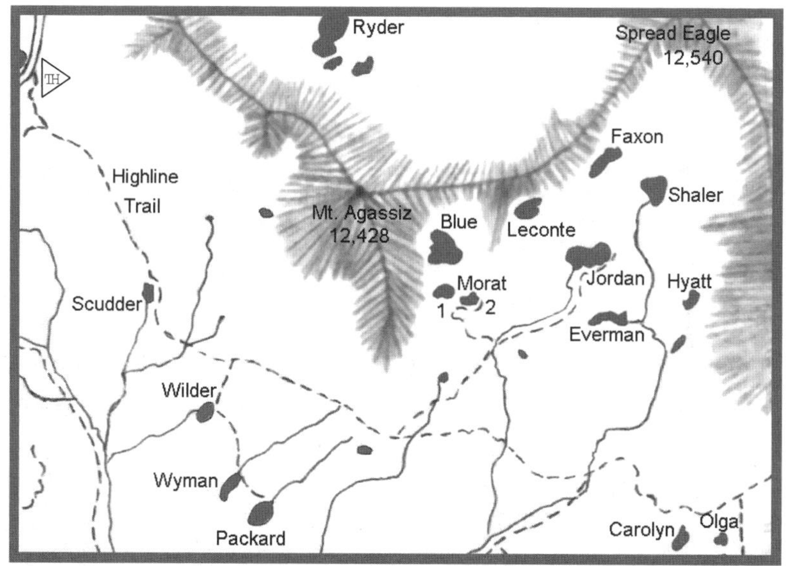


Even though these lakes sit in rocky timbered terrain, several good camping areas can be found. But remember, a fire restriction is often in effect at Naturalist Basin, and campfires can only be built at posted campsites. If your horse seems to make it up the hill that is encountered just before Morat Lakes, bring along some oats. Only limited feed is available. The only dependable source of spring water found in the Morat or Blue Lakes area is at Morat #2.

The Morat Lakes receive heavy usage from both backpackers and day hikers. Fishing pressure remains somewhat moderate at these lakes because many anglers bypass the Morat Lakes and begin to fish at Blue Lake. However, large cutthroat trout can often be netted at Morat #1. Try the west end in the early morning with a small fly, and practice your stealth. The big ones are extremely wary.

Blue Lake is located over a ridge 1/4 mile north of Morat #1. This pretty lake is characterized by a steep rocky basin at the east base of Mt. Agassiz. There are no campsites, and spring water can only be found in early summer. Fishing is usually fast for small brook trout. Blue and Morat Lakes sit in the cooler part of Naturalist Basin and are usually not free of ice until mid-July.

Near the Blue/Jordan trail junction, a couple of nice campsites exist near the main stream. This might be a good place to stay if you wanted to fish deep slow waters flowing through open meadows.

# Carolyn Lake

| Trip Planner: | | | |
|---|---|---|---|
| Miles | 6.5 | Usage | Moderate |
| Elevation | 10,460 | Campsites | Good |
| Elev. Gain | 460 | Springwater | Yes |
| Drainage | Duchesne | Fishing | Good |
| Trailhead | Highline | Horsefeed | Good |
| Near Town | Kamas | Firewood | Good |

Although Carolyn Lake is in a popular area, it is most often passed by. This small lake is in timbered country characterized by boggy shorelines and a small wet meadow. Spring water is somewhat limited, but good running water can be found on the southeast side of the lake.

One reason why we think this lake is so often overlooked is because Carolyn contains a large population of arctic grayling. This is no problem if you know how to prepare the little suckers, but most fishermen prefer high mountain trout. But if grayling are on your

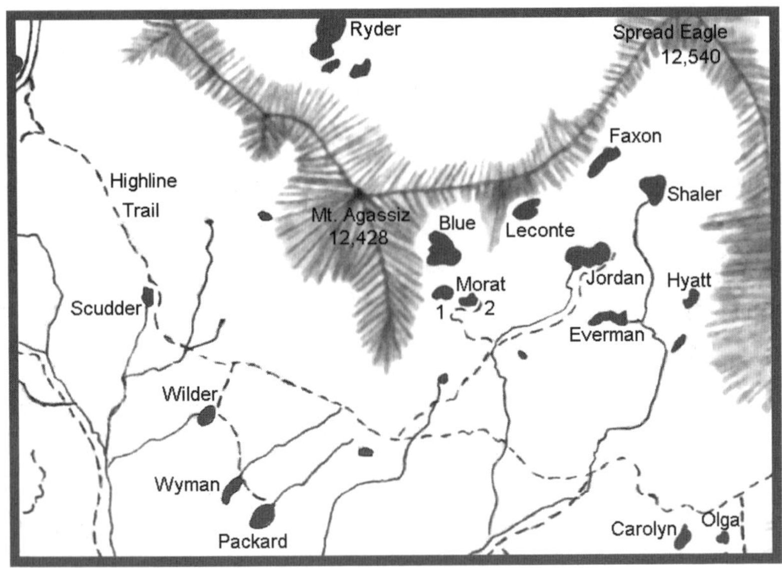

***Carolyn Lake***

menu, you should have no problem limiting out. The fish seem to be jumpin' all day long, and will smack a small colorful fly or flashly spinner.

There are plenty of good camping areas at Carolyn. However, a fire restriction is in effect in this area and only posted campsites may be used. These designated sites are located on the west side of the lake, 50 yards from shore. Non-posted camping areas exist near the south end of the lake on a little plateau. About 100 feet south of these campsites, an awesome view of the West Fork Rock Creek Drainage can be observed.

Access is 6.5 miles south then east on the Highline Trail. From the Highline Trail look for a deep rutted trail that takes off to the south and across an open meadow. About 200 yards down this trail lies Carolyn Lake. No posted signs point the direction to the lake, but the trail can be clearly seen upon arrival, if you're watching for it.

This is a great place for an overnighter that will seem more remote than it is. It is quiet.

# Joan Lake

| Trip Planner: | | | |
|---|---|---|---|
| Miles | .3 | Usage | Moderate |
| Elevation | 10,050 | Campsites | Very Good |
| Elev. Gain | 310 | Springwater | Yes |
| Drainage | Duchesne | Fishing | Good |
| Trailhead | Echo Lake | Horsefeed | Good |
| Near Town | Kamas | Firewood | Good |

It's only three-tenths of a mile to Joan Lake, as the crow flies. Unfortunately we can't fly. If you want to check out Joan Lake you will have pick your way up an extremely steep hill through loose rock, sand, and deadfall timber. There is no trail, and you'll have to choose your route carefully to avoid several sizeable cliffs. It can be done, but don't try it on a horse.

***Gem Lake***

You can start hiking from Echo Lake. To reach Echo Lake, take the Murdock Basin Road for about 5 miles to the Echo Lake turnoff, then north another half a mile. The last half mile may require a 4WD vehicle if the road is wet or rutted. You may wish to try fishing at Echo Lake for a while. It receives heavy pressure, but is one of the few lakes in the High Uintas containing Golden trout. There aren't many though.

Once you reach Joan Lake there are four good fishing prospects to check out: Joan Lake, Gem Lake, D-26 lake, and the stream connecting Gem and Joan. Take a full day, and explore the possibilities. This could be a fun-filled fishing trip for brook and cutthroat trout. Joan Lake receives moderate angling pressure, but the other locations get only light use. Don't worry if you don't see Gem Lake on your USGS topo map. Somehow they missed it. It seems a lot of other people miss it too.

A good place to camp is along the small stream between Joan and Gem Lakes. There are good campsites and spring water along the stream, and you will have quick access to most of the fishing. Litter is sometimes a problem around the lake, so how about pitching in and packing out some extra garbage when you leave. Thanks!

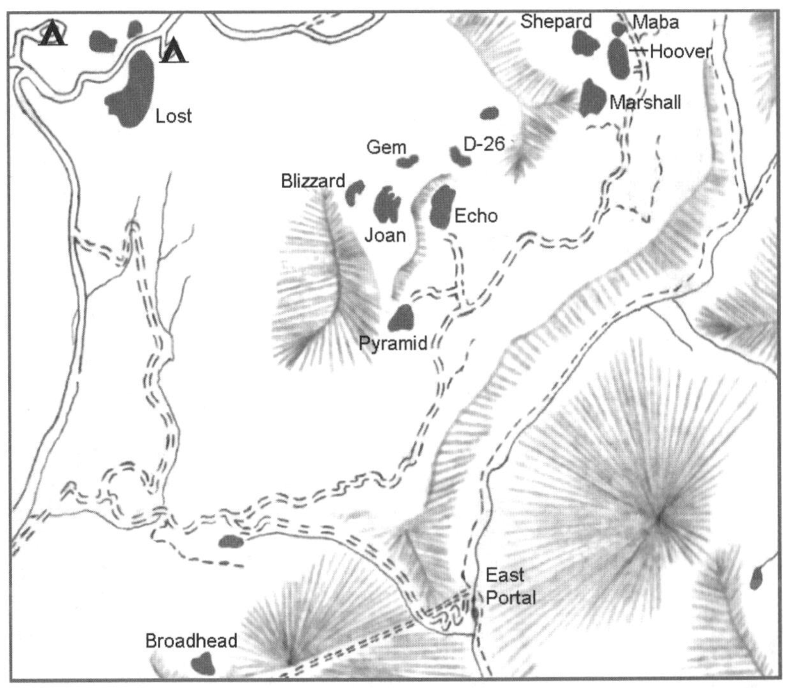

# Broadhead Lake

| Trip Planner: | | | |
|---|---|---|---|
| Miles | .8 | Usage | Light |
| Elevation | 9,960 | Campsites | Good |
| Elev. Gain | 500 | Springwater | Yes |
| Drainage | Duchesne | Fishing | Fair |
| Trailhead | Murdock Basin | Horsefeed | Fair |
| Near Town | Kamas | Firewood | Good |

Depending on your priorities, you may want to leave the backpack behind. Access is somewhat steep, and large rocks with deadfall literally litter the way. On the other hand, many people protest difficult obstructions. Which means, you should have this lake all to yourself. Broadhead Lake remains remarkably untouched,

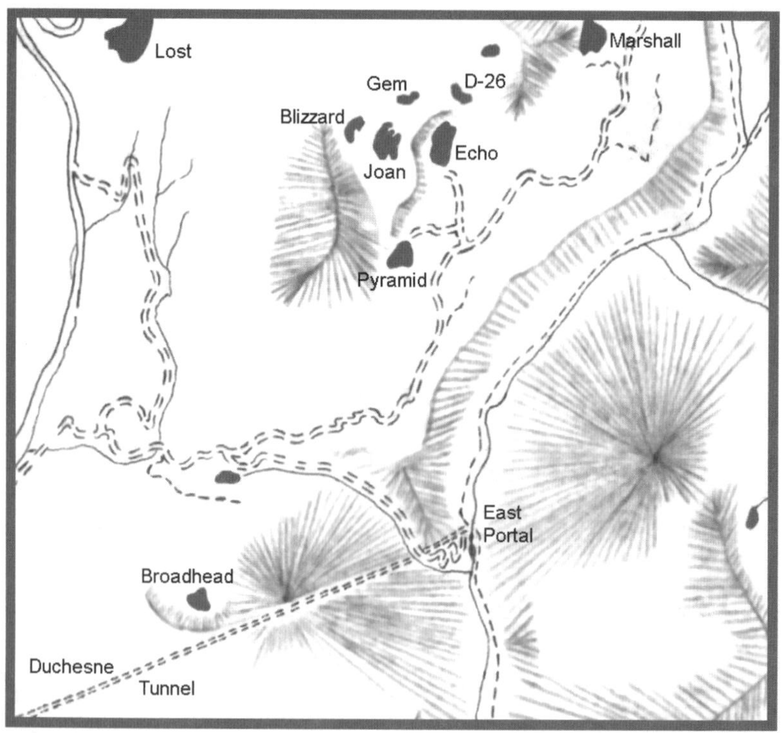

as fire rings have promptly perished (Let's keep it that way). There is no need to make a fire for the overnight camper.

Broadhead is a scenic alpine lake, nestled within a small rocky basin. Springwater flows into the lake from the west, while the outlet displays a unique waterfall. Angling is unpredictable. Broadhead was experimentally stocked with brook trout. So, if you're an avid fisherman, take a pole along. You may be in for a rewarding surprise.

According to the stats, Broadhead Lake is only just under a mile in distance. This may be true if you could walk from point A to point B. However, by the time you maneuver around deadfall and hop some rocks you can add another 1/2 mile to your adventure. The shortest route begins from the Mirror Lake Highway, about 2.5 miles up Murdock Basin Road. Look for an ATV road that turns off by a group of campsites. This ATV road has been named Buckeye Road. Follow it 1/2 mile to Green Horn Road. From here, take the Green Horn Road to almost its end. Then pick your way up the left side of a steep and rocky ravine to Broadhead Lake.

***Broadhead Lake***

# Meadow Muffin Trail (Duchesne River)

| Trip Planner: | | | |
|---|---|---|---|
| Miles | 11 | Usage | Moderate |
| Elevation | 7,550 | Campsites | Excellent |
| Elev. Gain | -2,450 | Springwater | Yes |
| Drainage | Duchesne | Fishing | Good |
| Trailhead | Mirror Lake | Horsefeed | Good |
| Near Town | Kamas | Firewood | Fair |

Most people use the Mirror Lake entry way instead of Mill Flat, solely because the trail loses elevation starting from Mirror Lake. Usually two vehicles are used to support this trip. One vehicle transports the trekkers to Mirror Lake while the other is left behind at Mill Flat. Another alternate route can be obtained by a branch off of the Murdock Basin Road. This 4WD road takes you to the east portal of the Duchesne Tunnel.

Start your adventure at Mirror Lake, on the West Fork Trail of the Duchesne River Drainage. After a slight incline, the trail descends rapidly to the Pinto Lake - Mill Flat junction. Following the trail to Mill Flat, a deep river gorge begins to emerge. Spectacular views of plummeting cliffs soon appear, as mystic scenery stimulates the soul.

Near the east portal of the Duchesne Tunnel, the gorge widens to a ford. This is also where the trail crosses the river. Due to high water, it is not feasible to cross the river until after the month of July. The gate of the east portal remains closed, 'til water is needed down stream in the Provo River. Water is then diverted through the Duchesne Tunnel. When this occurs, the Duchesne River drops to expose a makeshift trail which runs along the top of a dike.

Excellent campsites can be found before and after the ford, and springwater exists all along the trail. However, the presence of cows make drinking water hard to find. Angling is best upstream from the portal. The fish are small, but they can prove to be exciting. ( That's if you don't mind stepping in a cow pie or two). The trail upstream from the portal is plagued with cow tainted mudholes. If not careful, one of these stench-pots can suck your boot right off.

After the portal, the trail becomes rather relaxing. Vistas of a deep river gorge are seen nearby, and an excellent trail reclines on down the mountain. The last couple of miles of this trek can be a little confusing. A hit-n-miss trail winds through dense vegetation as it crosses lots of tiny streams. In any case, you'll soon know when you are on the right track. The friendly service of our courteous cows will leave a trail of meadow muffins for you to follow.

***Waterfall near east portal of Duchesne Tunnel***

# Grandaddy Lake

| Trip Planner: | | | |
|---|---|---|---|
| Miles | 3.2 | Usage | Heavy |
| Elevation | 10,310 | Campsites | Very Good |
| Elev. Gain | 500 | Springwater | Yes |
| Drainage | Rock Creek | Fishing | Good |
| Trailhead | Grandview | Horsefeed | Good |
| Near Town | Hanna | Firewood | Scarce |

Grandaddy Lake - the name implies that it is the largest and best of all the lakes. Is it the largest? Yes, it is easily the largest *natural* lake in the High Uintas. Is it the best? Judging solely by the number of backcountry visitors, the answer is yes. Usage is very heavy at this well known lake, but it seems to handle the pressure well. The crowds can scatter to numerous campsites around Grandaddy's irregular shoreline. Litter can be a problem, so please clean up your mess, leaving a spotless campsite for the next guests.

It's not a long hike to Grandaddy Lake, but it is a strenuous one. A well traveled trail climbs over 800 feet in just two miles to the top of Hades Pass. There you'll have a "grand view" of Heart Lake, Grandaddy Lake, and countless acres of the pine covered hills of the Rock Creek Drainage.

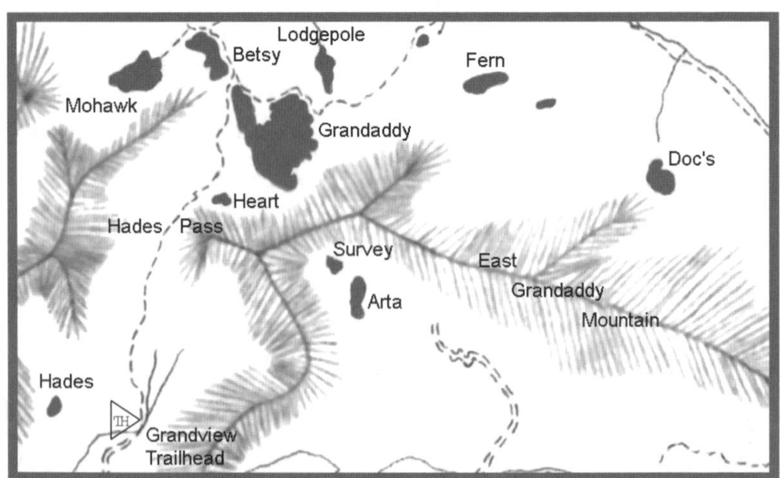

***Grandaddy Lake***

When selecting a campsite at Grandaddy, please use one of the existing sites. There are lots of them, and building new camps will only further burden the fragile environment. It may be a long walk to a spring from your camp, so you may be wise to bring along something to purify your drinking water. Firewood is extremely scarce. A stove is highly recommended if you're planning on cooking any meals.

Cutthroat and brook trout provide fair to good fishing. These trout are not stocked. Replenishment is by natural reproduction only. Catch and release angling is encouraged here, especially for larger fish that might be next year's spawners. Keep the smaller ones for dinner, and the let the parents go to raise more young.

Many other angling and camping opportunities are nearby. Betsy Lake and Mohawk Lake are practically right next door, and Lodgepole Lake is just a few hundred yards northeast of Grandaddy. Heart Lake is up a steep hill, just south of Grandaddy. You'll pass it if you go to Grandaddy Lake via Hades Pass.

There's a lot happening in this basin. Any fan of the High Uintas will enjoy seeing this area, whether you are camping here or just passing through - even if it's just for the reason of being able to say that you visited the largest and most popular backcountry lake in the High Uintas.

# Fern Lake

| Trip Planner: | | | |
|---|---|---|---|
| Miles | 5.7 | Usage | Moderate |
| Elevation | 9,890 | Campsites | Fair |
| Elev. Gain | 100 | Springwater | Yes |
| Drainage | Rock Creek | Fishing | Good |
| Trailhead | Grandview | Horsefeed | Fair |
| Near Town | Hanna | Firewood | Good |

***Betsy Lake***

Take a right at Betsy Lake, follow the West Fork Rock Creek Trail past Lodgepole Lake a couple of miles to LaMarla Lake, then cut cross-country southeast another 1/2 mile. Fern Lake is nestled at the base of East Grandaddy Mountain below a steep boulder-strewn slope. The terrain is rough. Rocks and deadfall timber are prevalent, making travel a little slow around the immediate area.

This hike is a pretty one, but it seems like it's uphill both ways. You'll rise over 800 feet traversing Hades Pass, and then you'll give almost all of that elevation back as you descend to Fern Lake. So, even though the elevation gain is a mere 100 feet in just under six miles, level ground is unheard of. If you're not forging up, you're dropping down.

The main attractions at Fern Lake are solitude and fishing. It can be hard to find an unoccupied lake in this basin. Fern may be your best bet if you are searching for a quiet secluded spot. There are a few comfortable campsites for setting up your wilderness abode. Ice cold spring water is located on the west side of the lake. There is also plenty of firewood about - a rarity in this busy basin. In all, it's a pretty good place to just settle back and let the world pass you by.

Fern Lake has been known for some darn good fishing in the past too. And they might be big ones. Fat brookies up to two pounds have been known to succumb to a well presented fly or lure. Don't plan on fish for your meals though. If they are not biting, there are no other lakes nearby to count on. Of course, you could plan a trout dinner, but bring some extra beef jerky; just in case.

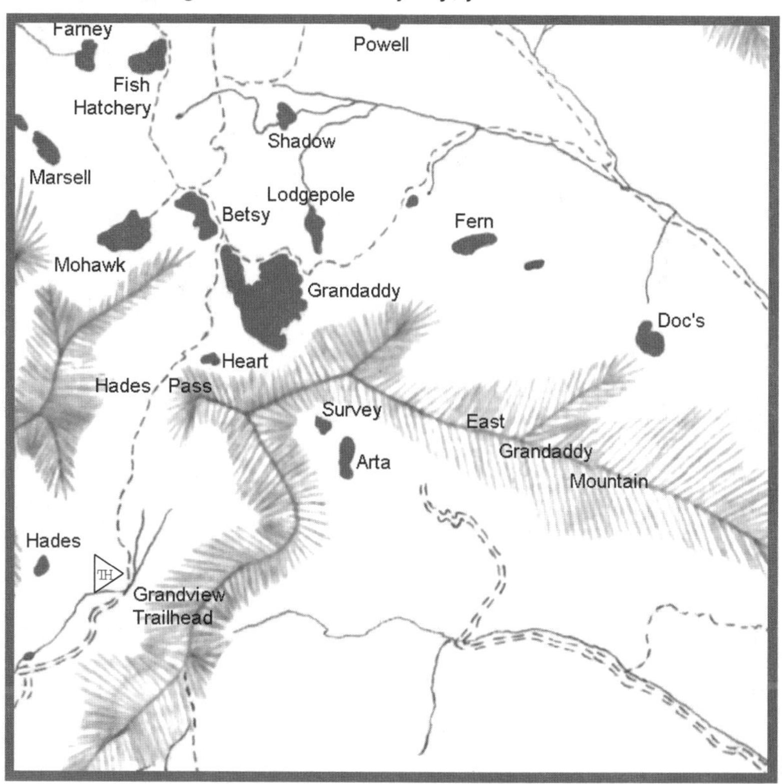

# Arta Lake

| Trip Planner: | | | |
|---|---|---|---|
| Miles | .5 | Usage | Light |
| Elevation | 10,450 | Campsites | Fair |
| Elev. Gain | 250 | Springwater | No |
| Drainage | Rock Creek | Fishing | Poor |
| Trailhead | none | Horsefeed | Poor |
| Near Town | Duchesne | Firewood | Good |

Long drive; short hike; and solitude pretty well sums up this day trip. No matter which way you come from, you will probably be in for a long drive before you start hiking. But if you would rather spend more time driving through scenic country than hiking it, then this hike may interest you, especially if you're looking to get away from other people.

It is only a half mile trek to Arta Lake, but it seems longer. A faint trail begins where the road ends, but disappears after a couple hundred yards. Then you are left to pick your own route around lots of deadfall timber. Just keep heading due west, and you will soon run into Arta Lake. Although attractive and quiet, this lake doesn't offer much in the way of good overnight campsites. The ground is strewn with boulders and pines. Water can be found on the northwest side where it drains down a steep hill from Survey Lake, but you will need to purify it.

If you've come as far as Arta Lake, we suggest that you make the extra effort to hike the short steep hill up to Survey Lake. The vista from the top of the hill overlooking Arta is magnificent, and on the other side of the hill lies Survey Lake in a great little alpine cirque (more pristine solitude). If you're really feeling ambitious, trek up the mountain behind Survey Lake, and look down on Grandaddy Lake - what a view!

Fishing was lousy when we visited these lakes, as they probably experienced winterkill. We didn't catch anything, and the only sign of life was large schools of tiny minnows at Arta Lake. You never know though - fishing could improve after periodic stocking, or maybe the thousands of minnows that we saw will grow up. It would at least be worth a try if you're making the trip anyway.

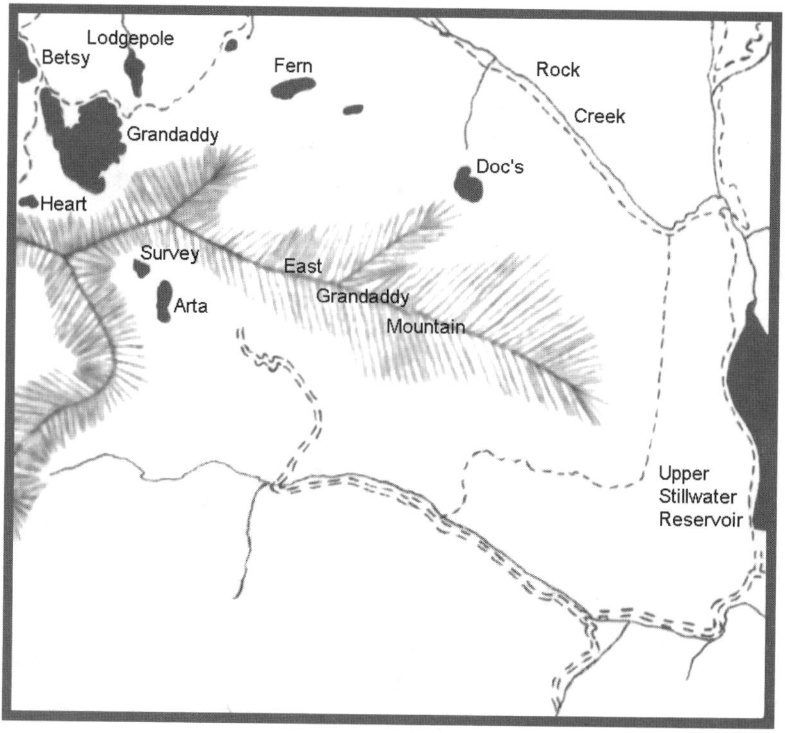

Lodgepole
Betsy
Fern
Rock
Creek
Grandaddy
Doc's
Heart
Survey
East
Grandaddy
Mountain
Arta
Upper
Stillwater
Reservoir

***Arta Lake***

# Pine Island Lake

| Trip Planner: | | | |
|---|---|---|---|
| Miles | 6 | Usage | Heavy |
| Elevation | 10,300 | Campsites | Good |
| Elev. Gain | 500 | Springwater | No |
| Drainage | Rock Creek | Fishing | Fair |
| Trailhead | Grandview | Horsefeed | Fair |
| Near Town | Hanna | Firewood | Limited |

***Pine Island Lake***

It's no wonder why this lake is popular among Scout groups - it is gorgeous. If aesthetics and a nice campsite are important to you, then check out Pine Island Lake. It is the gem of the West Fork of Rock Creek. Small pine covered islands rise peacefully out of the clear blue waters of this large natural lake. There is something especially appealing about islands on a wilderness lake. In the background, a steep talus slope adds to the alpine atmosphere. You can easily just sit in camp, munch granola bars, and enjoy the view.

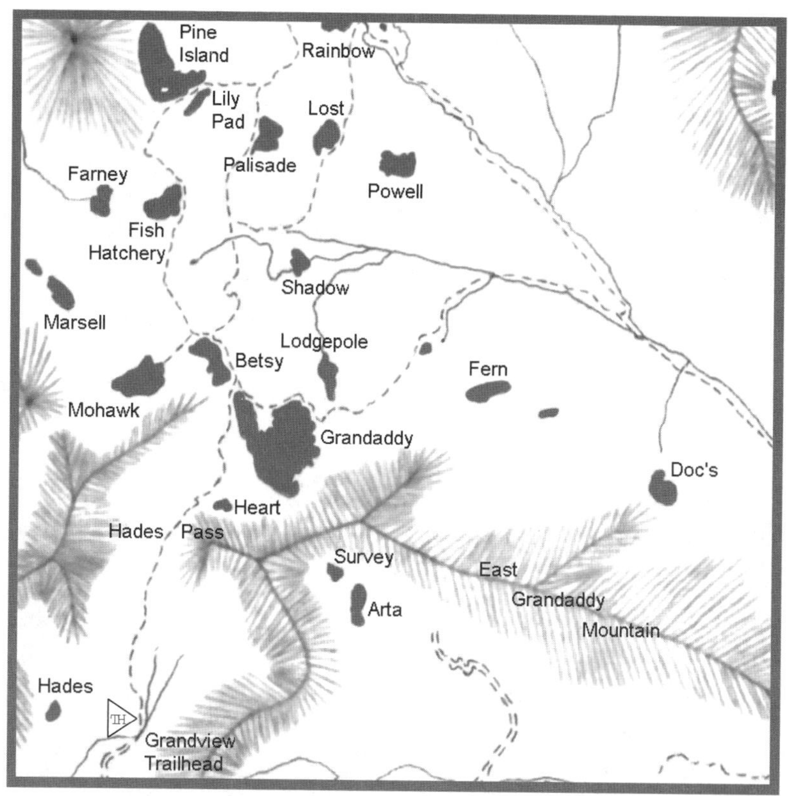


A few spacious campsites are found along the southeast shoreline, just off the main trail. There is plenty of level ground for a large group to setup several tents, and large flat boulders are conveniently located to serve as tables or benches. Fire pits are numerous, so please don't build any more. On the negative side, firewood is limited and spring water is non-existent. Be prepared to purify all of your drinking water.

As expected, fishing pressure is moderate to heavy, and unpredictable. You may have good luck, but you should have a backup plan if you are planning fish for dinner. Brook trout are stocked on a regular basis, and a few cutthroats still remain. Lily Pad Lake offers similar angling, and is just 200 yards southeast. Give it a try if Pine Island doesn't yield the kind of fishing you want.

If you have horses to carry your load, a rubber raft could be a lot of fun at Pine Island Lake. Paddle out to the islands and fish around them. Remember the life jackets. These icy waters are as dangerous as they are beautiful.

# Governor Dern Lake

**Trip Planner:**

| | | | |
|---|---|---|---|
| Miles | 7.8 | Usage | Moderate |
| Elevation | 9,990 | Campsites | Excellent |
| Elev. Gain | 200 | Springwater | Yes |
| Drainage | Rock Creek | Fishing | Good |
| Trailhead | Grandview | Horsefeed | Very Good |
| Near Town | Hanna | Firewood | Limited |

A lot of horsemen use this area, and rightfully so. Between Governor Dern Lake and the Pinto Lake area there are lots of places to graze your horses, and plenty of roomy campsites. Once you get past Hades Pass, the journey is a gentle ride through the pine forests of the West Fork of the Rock Creek Drainage. Or you can avoid the steep pass and reach Governor Dern Lake from the Highline Trailhead. It is a couple of miles longer this way, but may be easier on the animals.

***Governor Dern Lake***

Spring water is present on either the north or east shores of Governor Dern Lake. The lake is shallow for its size, but is still very pretty and easily fished. It is stocked periodically with brook trout, and a cutthroat may show up in the creel from time to time. Try a small fly in the mornings and late evenings for best results.

Nearby Pinto Lake is more popular, but it doesn't have any more to offer than Governor Dern Lake. In fact, Governor Dern is more scenic. Given that Pinto Lake is more crowded, Governor Dern seems like the better choice. Rainbow Lake is less than a mile away (south). It is also worth a look, whether looking for a camping spot, a different fishing hole, or just taking a horse ride.

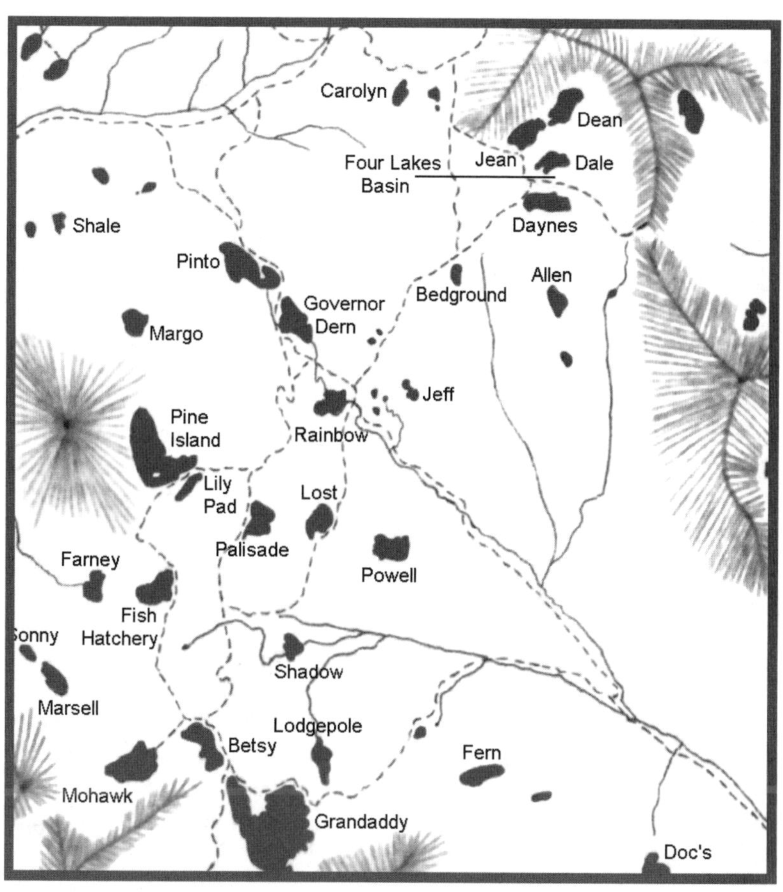

# Four Lakes Basin

**Trip Planner:**

| | | | |
|---|---|---|---|
| Miles | 9 | Usage | Heavy |
| Elevation | 10,700 | Campsites | Very Good |
| Elev. Gain | 300 | Springwater | Yes |
| Drainage | Rock Creek | Fishing | Good |
| Trailhead | Highline | Horsefeed | Very Good |
| Near Town | Kamas | Firewood | Limited |

Four Lakes Basin is 9 miles from either the Highline Trailhead or the Grandview Trailhead. We suggest using the Highline Trailhead since the hike has less than half the elevation gain as the hike from the Grandview Trailhead does. The Highline Trailhead is also closer and easier to reach if you are coming from the population centers of Utah (Salt Lake City, Provo, Ogden).

Jean, Dean, Dale, and Daynes Lakes comprise Four Lakes Basin. The best places to stay are at Dale or Daynes. Campsites, horse feed, and spring water are plentiful at both lakes, and there is plenty of space for horses. Backpackers might opt for a little more solitude at Dean Lake, which is not as suitable for horses. There is spring water at Dean Lake, but it is on the extreme northern shore (a long walk from the campsites).

Fishing pressure is heavy at all four lakes except Dean Lake. It receives moderate pressure. If you take the time to walk to the back side of Dean Lake, you'll find that hardly anyone else has been there. You might have your best success there. The predominant species in these lakes is brook trout. An occasional cutthroat may be caught, and Daynes Lake has a few arctic grayling to spice up your fishing. Fly fishing works best, but a surprising number of fishermen use worms here. You don't find many lakes in the High Uintas where bait fishermen are as successful as they are at Four Lakes Basin.

Photographers can find plenty of subject matter in this basin. Jean and Dean Lakes provide spectacular alpine scenery. Keep your camera handy as you ride or hike around. For a breath-taking view, take a hike to the top of Cyclone Pass where you can see the vast regions of the Rock Creek Drainage on either side of the pass. Daynes Lake is especially pretty from Cyclone Pass.

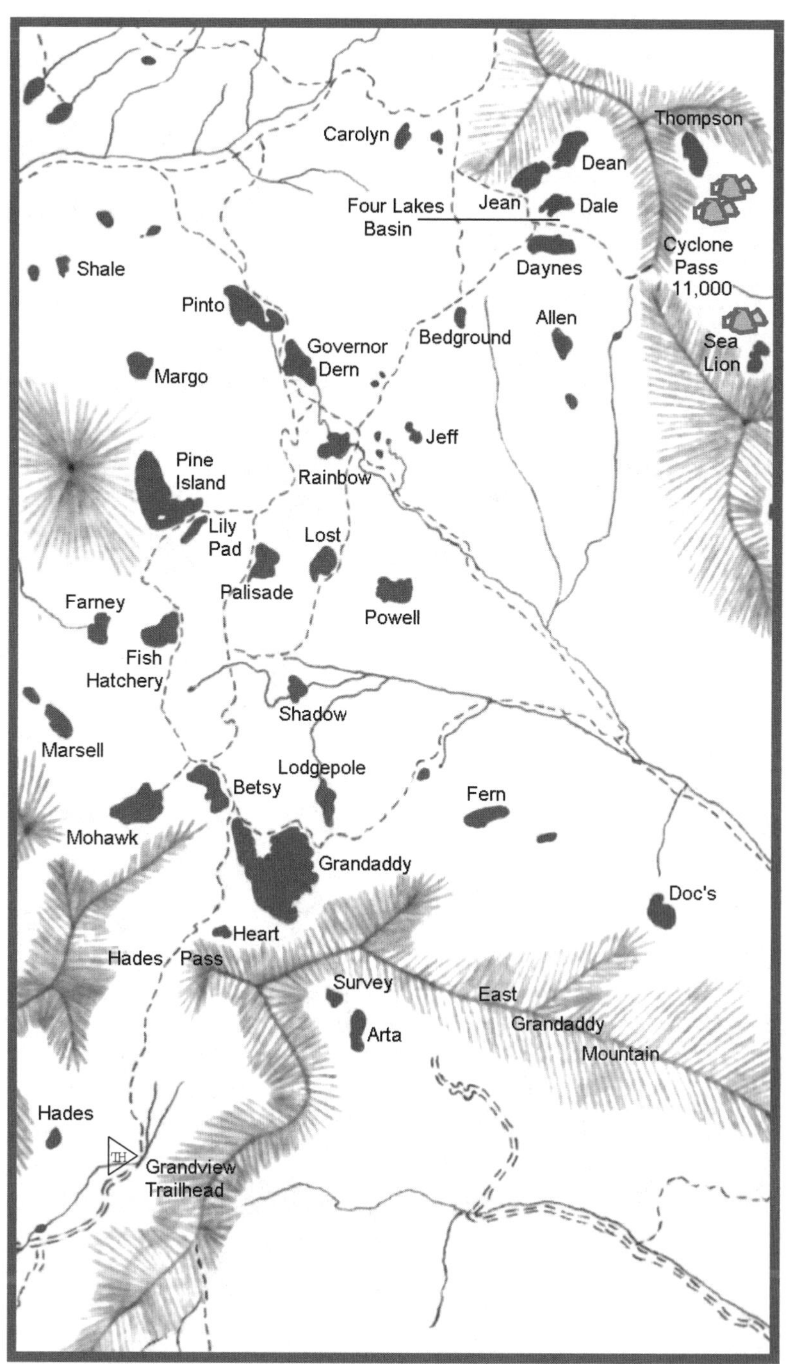


See Photos on next page

*Sea Lion Lake from Cyclone Pass*

*Daynes Lake from Cyclone Pass*

*Jean and Dean Lakes in Four Lakes Basin*

*Dale Lake*

# Allen Lake

| Trip Planner: | | | |
|---|---|---|---|
| Miles | 9.3 | Usage | Light |
| Elevation | 10,390 | Campsites | Very Good |
| Elev. Gain | 580 | Springwater | Yes |
| Drainage | Rock Creek | Fishing | Good |
| Trailhead | Grandview | Horsefeed | Excellent |
| Near Town | Hanna | Firewood | Good |

Allen Lake was named in honor of Floyd Allen, an on-duty ranger who was killed by lightning. A wooden monument still stands as a solemn reminder of the man and the awesome powers of nature. We arrived at Allen Lake on August 26, 1993 - the same day of the year that Mr. Allen met his fate in 1938. The coincidence left us wondering how he might of looked and how isolated the High Uintas were back in 1938. We checked the sky for storm clouds.

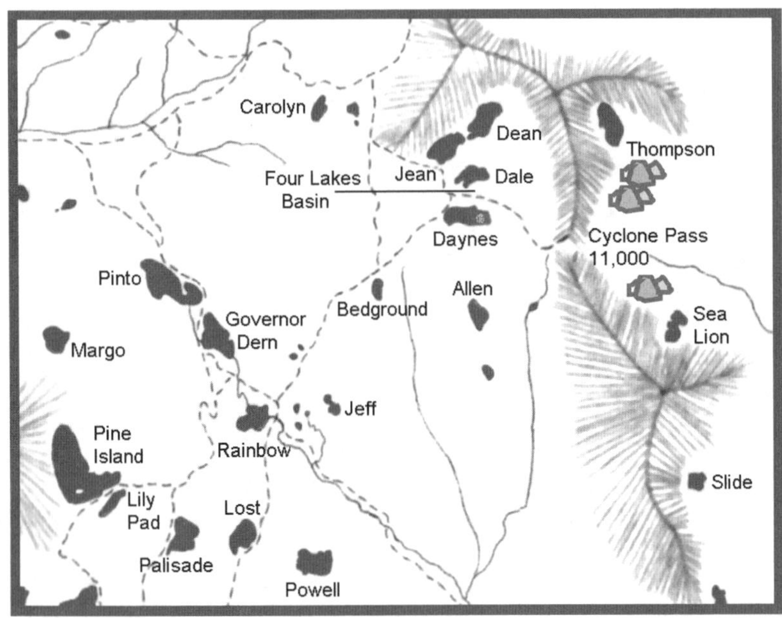

***Allen Lake***

Situated in a large grassy meadow, Allen Lake can be located by traveling due east from Bedground Lake about 3/4 mile. A hit-n-miss game trail takes off from the northeast side of Bedground Lake, so get your compass out and follow it religiously. It is easy to get turned around in this heavily timbered terrain.

Allen Lake is ideal for horses. There is lots of horse feed and water, and places to picket or hobble the horses. Spacious campsites make it easy to watch your stock from camp while still receiving shelter from large pines. The best camps dot the western side of the lake. There is also one small campsite on the eastern side that can accommodate one tent. Good drinking water can be found along the eastern shore where several springs emerge.

Anglers seeking large arctic grayling must visit Allen Lake. Grayling over one pound are caught regularly, which is pretty close to the Utah state record. A record breaker should come from Allen Lake, since it boasts the fastest growing grayling in the High Uintas. Even a one-pound grayling would make an impressive mount with its huge dorsal fin. A few big brook trout inhabit this lake too. You won't catch a lot of fish at Allen Lake, but what you catch will be sizeable. Fishing pressure is light, so the fish have a chance to grow large.

Watch out for lightning.

# Thompson Lake

| Trip Planner: | | | |
|---|---|---|---|
| Miles | 11.2 | Usage | Very Light |
| Elevation | 10,690 | Campsites | Poor |
| Elev. Gain | 900 | Springwater | No |
| Drainage | Rock Creek | Fishing | Good |
| Trailhead | Grandview | Horsefeed | None |
| Near Town | Hanna | Firewood | Limited |

We don't recommend this hike. One word can describe it - inaccessible. Thompson Lake just might be the most inaccessible lake in the High Uintas. Because of this distinction, we have included it in this book. If you're in for some serious mountaineering and some truly remote fishing, you might like it.

The only feasible access is via Cyclone Pass from Four Lakes Basin. There is a steep trail that goes all the way over Cyclone Pass and ends up in a massive boulder field on the other side. The boulders continue all the way to Thompson Lake. You can avoid

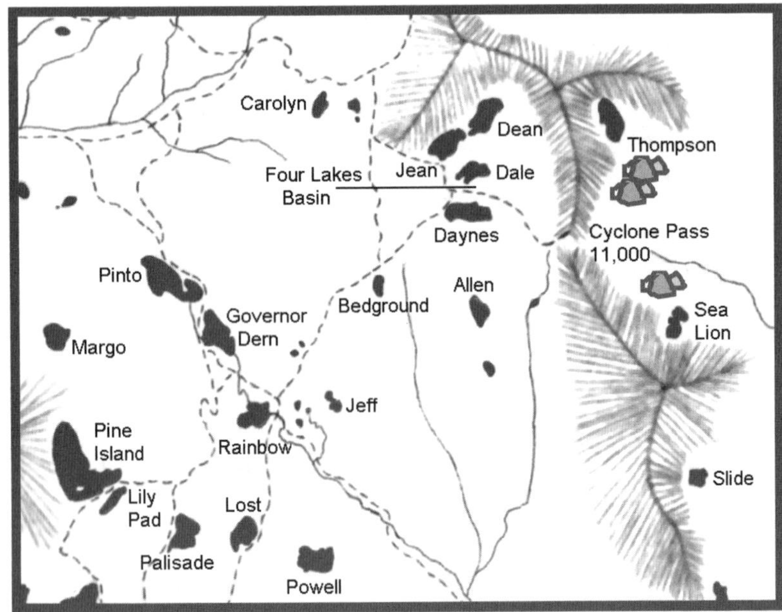

some of the boulder field by leaving the trail about half way down the eastern slope, and traversing the mountainside on an obscure game trail. It is easier walking than on the brutal boulders. Eventually you will still have to cross the rocks - and lots of them. Plan on about an hour of tricky boulder hopping. Do not attempt this hike with full packs on. It is treacherous without packs and downright foolish with.

Literally thousands of GIANT SPIDERS reside throughout the boulders that must be crossed to reach Thompson Lake. These arachnids sit virtually still in the middle of their radial web in search of prey. Upon human arrival, a most peculiar display attracts your attention. When maneuvers are made toward their domain, a skittish shake of the web mimics a vicious assault. We think this action is not to strike out at intruders. Instead, it is a plea of "please don't destroy my web."

Thompson Lake is surrounded by boulders too. There are no suitable campsites or spring water in this glacial cirque. It would be mighty uncomfortable to spend the night here, so leave yourself plenty of time to get back out. If a storm approaches, get out fast. Wet boulders are much more dangerous than dry ones, and Cyclone Pass is no place to be when lightning is brewing.

Crazy fishermen might try to reach Thompson Lake. Big brook trout roam these waters, and will savagely attack a fly or lure. You'll have a fight on your hands when one of the these brookies slam your lure. Average size is well over a pound, and who knows how big some of the old monarchs are. This is a true wilderness experience that should only be attempted by the hardy, or the fool-hardy.

# Ouray Lake

| Trip Planner: | | | |
|---|---|---|---|
| Miles | 11.6 | Usage | Light |
| Elevation | 10,380 | Campsites | Good |
| Elev. Gain | 40 | Springwater | Yes |
| Drainage | Rock Creek | Fishing | Very Good |
| Trailhead | Highline | Horsefeed | Excellent |
| Near Town | Kamas | Firewood | Good |

It doesn't look like much at first glance, but give it a chance. This is a good place to establish a base camp, or just hide out. At the north end of the lake is a great little campsite, complete with rock tables, and nearby a couple of springs enter the small streams that feed Ouray Lake. Horsemen particularly like this spot because it is situated in a box canyon with plenty of horse feed.

The quickest way to reach this area is via Rocky Sea Pass. It is easy to determine how this pass got its name, as rocks are everywhere. Watch your footing as well as the scenery. The view of the Rock Creek Drainage is awesome from atop the pass. Plan on

***Reconnaissance Lake***

stopping awhile to soak up one of the grandest vistas in the High Uintas.

Fishing at Ouray is excellent at times, and good most anytime. The east side of the lake is the deepest, and harbors most of the fish. Flies or a small spinner will take a limit of brookies and cutthroats in short time. Don't forget to fish the main stream that flows into Ouray. The fish are there if you're cautious enough and lucky enough.

If you are up to some hearty day hikes, there are plenty of other fishing opportunities in the area. Lightning Lake to the northwest is fun. It's not lightning fast, but there are enough feisty fish to keep you interested for quite a while. If it's fast fishing you want, try Doug Lake to the northeast. Small brook trout will smack a fly on just about every cast. It's hot anywhere on this tiny lake! Next to Doug Lake is Boot Lake. It is much larger and deeper, and is a good place to experiment with various lures and flies. While there, snap some photos of picturesque Triangle Mountain. Or, hike on over to remote Reconnaissance Lake and feel all alone.

If you like the area but have a large group, try camping at Black Lake. It is popular with Boy Scouts, and has nice camping. Both Black and Ouray are down from the trail, and sheltered by pines - an important factor in this wind-swept region of upper Rock Creek.

***"The Heart" of the High Uintas***

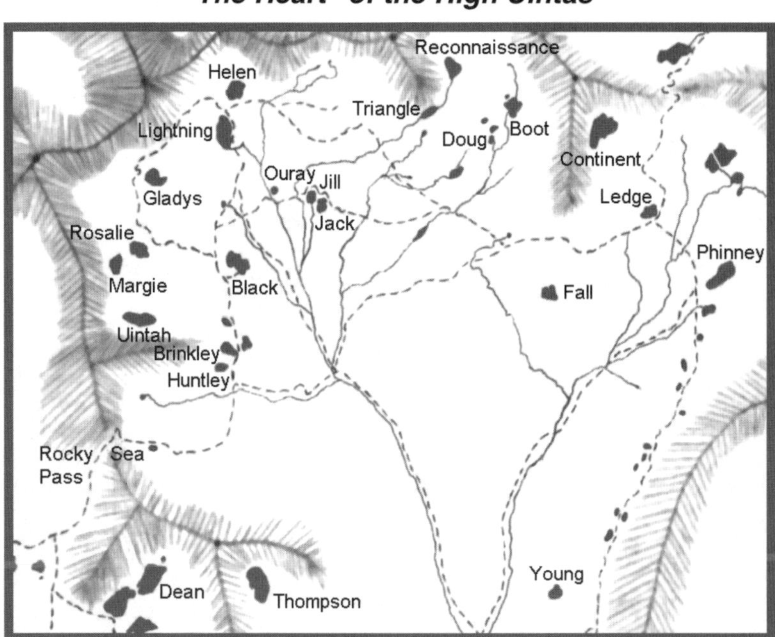

# Ledge Lake

| Trip Planner: | | | |
|---|---|---|---|
| Miles | 14.4 | Usage | Moderate |
| Elevation | 10,845 | Campsites | Good |
| Elev. Gain | 2,850 | Springwater | Yes |
| Drainage | Rock Creek | Fishing | Excellent |
| Trailhead | Stillwater | Horsefeed | Very Good |
| Near Town | Hanna | Firewood | Good |

Geologically, this area is the oldest in the High Uintas. Some refer to it as the backbone of the Uintas, while others call it the heart. After all, the upper basins of Rock Creek are shaped somewhat like a heart. Ledge Lake is a haven in this vast heart, providing everything one could want in a camp. Spring water is abundant, so is horsefeed, but also are mosquitoes around the waterlogged outlet. The fishing may be surprising. Brook trout weigh in at well over a

*Ledge Lake*

pound, and seem to prefer an olive-green scud fly for dinner. The problem is finding out what time dinner is served.

This basin houses some of the best quality fishing holes in the whole mountain range. Continent Lake, about two miles northwest, commonly surrenders brookies in the two pound class and cutthroats over sixteen inches. But you'll have to work for them. Work a green spinner deep, or a #14 Black Gnat just under the surface. The northeast segment of the lake may be the best place to start. Southeast from Ledge Lake are Phinney and Anderson Lakes. They offer fast fishing for smaller trout (1/2 pound). They'll hit anything that moves. One guy in our party caught a fish on a piece of dried apricot, but I'm sure you will have even better success on flies.

Ledge Lake gets its name from the tall ledges behind its northern shore. It is easy to find, but there is no easy way to it. It's almost fifteen miles from the Stillwater Dam Trailhead, and seems twice that long with the tremendous elevation gain. There are two other trails that may prove less taxing on the body. Both trails start at a higher elevation, but both also require traversing a steep mountain pass. It's about twelve miles to Ledge Lake coming from Blacks Fork over Dead Horse Pass, and about fourteen hilly miles via the Highline Trail over Rocky Sea Pass. Use Dead Horse if by foot, Rocky Sea if by horse.

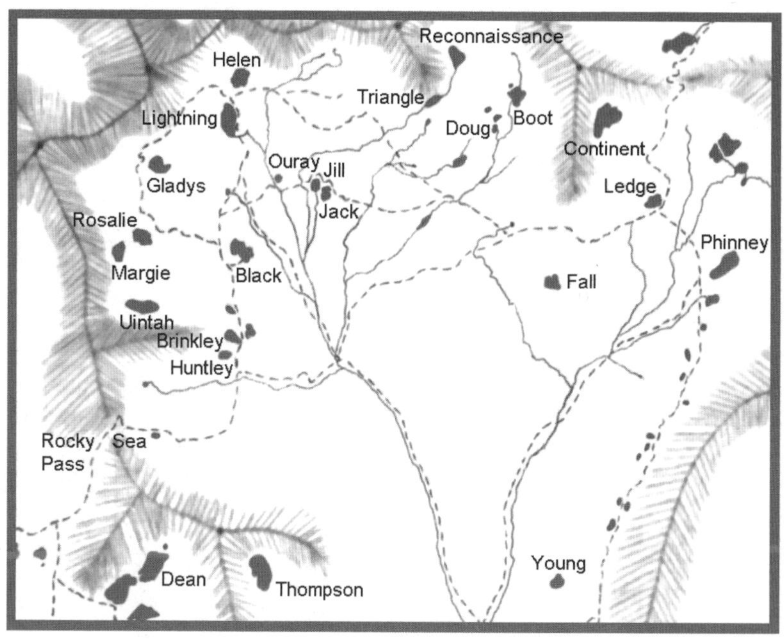

# Squaw Basin

| Trip Planner: | | | |
|---|---|---|---|
| Miles | 9 | Usage | Moderate |
| Elevation | 10,400 | Campsites | Good |
| Elev. Gain | 2,400 | Springwater | Yes |
| Drainage | Rock Creek | Fishing | Very Good |
| Trailhead | Upper Stillwater | Horsefeed | Good |
| Near Town | Hanna | Firewood | Good |

A compass is a must in this heavily timbered area. It's easy to get headed in the wrong direction as the trails twist, turn, intersect, and sometimes disappear in Squaw Basin. Getting into the area is not a problem, but finding your way around Squaw Basin can be confusing. Keep your map and compass handy, and keep your group together.

A popular camping location is at Squaw Lake, which features plenty of spring water and horse feed. Backpackers using the

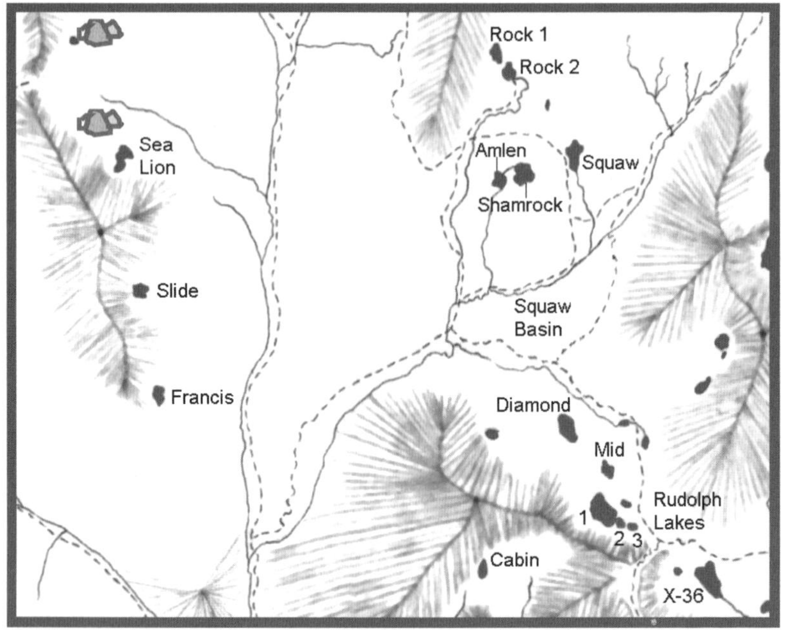

## *Cleveland Pass, Lake, and Peak*

Highline Trail find this a convenient spot to spend the night before hiking over Cleveland Pass or Tworoose Pass into the Lake Fork Drainage. If you are one of these long-trekkers, let us suggest Cleveland Pass if you have the time. It offers an unsurpassed view of the upper regions of the Lake Fork Drainage, and is well worth the extra effort.

If you are looking for a little more solitude, pitch your tents at Amlen or Shamrock Lakes. These lakes are only a few hundred yards apart, and between the two lakes you should find excellent campsites and spring water, but only fair horse feed. There is no trail to these lakes for the last half mile. Cross-country access is easiest from the southwest.

Fishing prospects are good to excellent throughout this large basin. Take a short hike up to Rock Lakes. These lakes see few visitors, and house large populations of brook trout. The southern section of Squaw Basin could have some real fishing holes too. Diamond, Mid, and Rudolph Lakes are just far enough off the beaten path to sustain good fisheries with only light to moderate pressure.

Squaw Basin is a good area for horsemen. The elevation gain is huge if you're starting at the Upper Stillwater Trailhead, and can quickly turn legs into rubber. Letting a horse do the heavy work is a great idea. Once into Squaw Basin there is lots of room to roam and explore, and a good steed can be a real leg saver and a time saver. Horse feed is abundant near most suitable campsites, and of course, water is everywhere.

# Rudolph Lakes

| Trip Planner: | | | |
|---|---|---|---|
| Miles | 12 | Usage | Moderate |
| Elevation | 10,470 | Campsites | Good |
| Elev. Gain | 2,300 | Springwater | Yes |
| Drainage | Upper Stillwater | Fishing | Good |
| Trailhead | Moon Lake | Horsefeed | Good |
| Near Town | Duchesne | Firewood | Good |

***Rudolph Lake #3***

There are three different routes to Rudolph Lakes. One trail begins at Moon Lake via Brown Duck trail - total distance 11.5 miles. Another starts at the Bear Wallow - Dry Ridge Road. Total distance is 10 miles. Or the most popular of the three begins at the Upper Stillwater - Rock Creek trailhead. Total distance is 12 miles.

From Upper Stillwater follow the Rock Creek Trail 5 miles north to the East Fork trail junction. At this point the trail goes 4 miles up several steep switchbacks to the turnoff of lower Squaw Basin. Follow this trail east then southeast another 3 miles.

Rudolph Lakes lie in an alpine ravine at the base of several talus

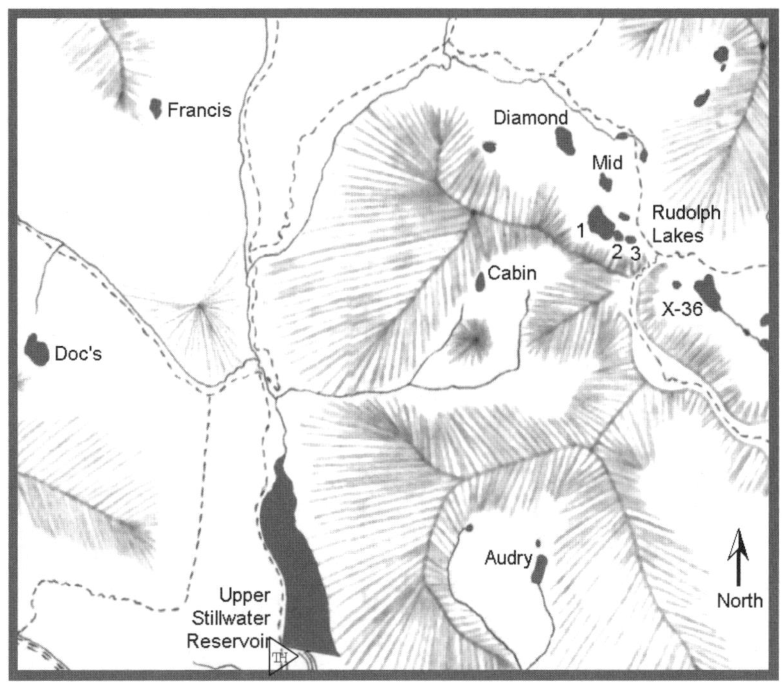


slopes. No permanent trail exists to the lakes, but a posted sign clearly points the way. Campsites can be found on the east side of #2 & 3, while spring water is located on the south side of #1. These lakes receive light to moderate usage, and anglers should have no problem limiting out. If by chance Rudolph Lakes don't produce, try Mid or Diamond. These small lakes sit in heavy timber and are off the beaten path. Angling pressure is almost nil, and fishing should be fast for brook and cutthroat trout.

Another angling trip worth checking out is Cabin Lake. It is located 1 mile southwest of Rudolph #1. Follow an old sheep trail over the saddle of Rudolph Mountain, then on through several boulder fields. The picture on the opposite page shows the saddle you'll have to cross. The saddle creates no difficult problems, but afterwards rugged boulder fields make travel tiring and time consuming.

Cabin Lake gets very little usage. This isolated lake sits all by its lonesome in its own little basin. Campsites are undesirable due to rocky and heavily timbered terrain. However, camping areas can be found near the open meadows to the north. If angling is what you're after, you're in luck. Tall tales of this lake speculate that big brook trout are healthy and not too smart - our kinda lake!

# Kidney Lake

| Trip Planner: | | | |
|---|---|---|---|
| Miles | 9 | Usage | Heavy |
| Elevation | 10,267 | Campsites | Good |
| Elev. Gain | 2,100 | Springwater | Yes |
| Drainage | Lake Fork | Fishing | Good |
| Trailhead | Moon Lake | Horsefeed | Good |
| Near Town | Duchesne | Firewood | Limited |

***Kidney Lake***

Topping out at 190 acres, Kidney Lake is one of the largest reservoirs in the High Uintas backcountry. Just try walking around it, and you'll become a believer. Because of its "kidney" shape you don't really see all of it at any one time, and it is even bigger than it looks.

There is a lot of room to spread out, so despite heavy pressure you should still find some solitude. This area is attractive to horsemen because of the large campsites that are available, and a good supply of horsefeed. The eastern shoreline has the best accommodations, including a limited supply of spring water. The area is popular with backpackers too, but they might be happier at more isolated lakes nearby - like Tworoose Lake. Tworoose is another mile up the trail from Kidney, but doesn't see many campers.

The streams linking Kidney, Island, and Brown Duck Lakes have good flow, and should provide an opportunity for some good stream fishing. Try a flashy spinner in the ripples and pools. These lakes and streams are fun to fish because of the variety of opportunites that exist. Fish the lakes for a while, then check out one of the streams for a change of pace. Cutthroat trout are stocked throughout the region, but an occasional brook trout may show up. Please release any brookies; they may reproduce.

Kidney Lake is also a convenient stop-over place for hikers continuing on into the Rock Creek Drainage. Spend a night near the trail at Kidney Lake, then you'll be fresh the next day to tackle Tworoose Pass (about 2 miles west).

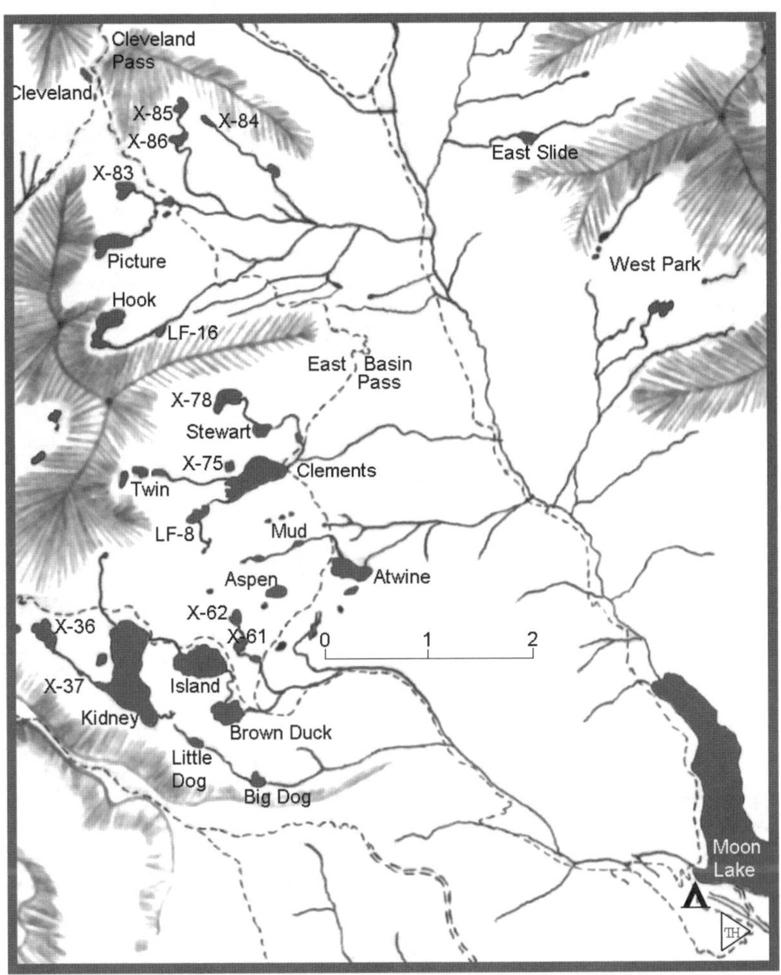

# Clements Reservoir

| Trip Planner: | | | |
|---|---|---|---|
| Miles | 10.4 | Usage | Heavy |
| Elevation | 10,444 | Campsites | Good |
| Elev. Gain | 2,250 | Springwater | Yes |
| Drainage | Lake Fork | Fishing | Very Good |
| Trailhead | Moon Lake | Horsefeed | Good |
| Near Town | Duchesne | Firewood | Limited |

*Clements Reservoir*

After a long steep climb, Clements Reservoir will look mighty good. Sheltered campsites are abundant along the northern shoreline, and you can easily imagine what it would be like to have a cabin overlooking the lake. The setting is rustic, yet peaceful.

The trail from Moon Lake starts out easy. An old road is now a wide clear trail for the first few miles. Then the going gets tough as the trail rears its ugly head, and you find yourself picking your way through the steep and rocky path. The @$%#& rocks are relentless, and don't give you a break until you reach Clements Reservoir. Level ground never looked so good as it does here.

Spring water is available, but it's a long walk to the back side of the lake to get any. It would probably be easier to purify some water from the lake or its outlet. Because of heavy use, firewood is scarce near the campgrounds. You'll have to walk a little for this commodity as well.

Fishing might be excellent at Clements. This relatively large lake can withstand heavy pressure, and frequently provides fast fishing for fat cutthroats averaging 13 inches. Fly-fish right off the dam about an hour before the sun sets, and you'll likely catch all you want. If you want to get away from the people at Clements, there are three other small lakes nearby that offer fishing. Who knows what you'll find. Southwest of Clements is LF-8. Head west to X-75, or another mile to Twin Lakes. A short journey north to Stewart Lake may prove rewarding. Any of these lakes might produce the "mother-lode" of fish you're looking for. There are no trails to any of these lakes, so be prepared for some rough cross-country travel that includes hopping over a lot of deadfall and boulders.

For spectacular scenery, hike up the trail one mile to East Basin Pass. From there you can view the entire upper region of the Lake Fork Drainage, including such sights as Mount Lovenia and Squaw Pass. Although East Basin Pass isn't as high as most passes, it provides one of the most panoramic vistas in the High Uintas.

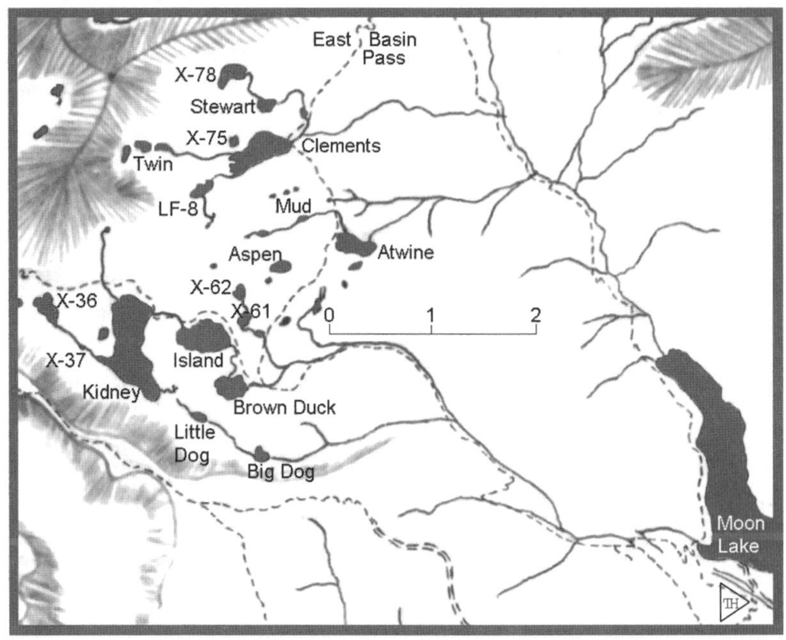

# Picture Lake

| Trip Planner: | | | |
|---|---|---|---|
| Miles | 17 | Usage | Moderate |
| Elevation | 10,731 | Campsites | Good |
| Elev. Gain | 2,530 | Springwater | Yes |
| Drainage | Lake Fork | Fishing | Fair |
| Trailhead | Moon Lake | Horsefeed | Fair |
| Near Town | Duchesne | Firewood | Good |

"Thar's gold in them thar hills." This may be your first impression upon arriving at East Basin Pass. From here you'll have an inspirational view of the whole Upper Lake Fork drainage. It leads you to believe that no one has ever been here before. That may have been the case a couple hundred years ago, but now a variety of explorers and scout troops make East Basin a popular place.

Most groups make their base camp at the three small lakes that lie below Picture Lake. Several good camping areas exist near these lakes, and others can be found along the inlet streams. These lakes receive moderate to heavy angling pressure and most of the time fishing is only fair. Try a small spinner. With a little skill, brook trout can be hooked throughout the deep water channels. Two major inlets feed these lakes. By following the southwest inlet 1/2 mile up a timbered slope, you'll find a beautiful lake called Picture.

Picture Lake fits its name perfectly. This lake has a pretty talus slope as a backdrop, with timber mirrored waters and a large outlet cascading down the mountain side. Rocky, timbered terrain surrounds the lake on three sides, adding to its artistic value. Due to this same fact, campsites are poorly defined. Picture Lake no longer supports a fishery.

Hook Lake is located one mile south of Picture. From Picture to Hook there is no trail, and the terrain is consistently rough, rocky, and filled with deadfalls. A horse will not make it through here. However, an alternate route starting from LF-16 is much easier. From LF-16 follow the inlet stream 1/2 mile west along the base of a ridge to the lake. Hook is situated in the southwest corner of East Basin next to a glacial talus slope. Huge boulders interspersed with heavy timber make camping poor, but spring water can be found near the outlet.

Hook Lake

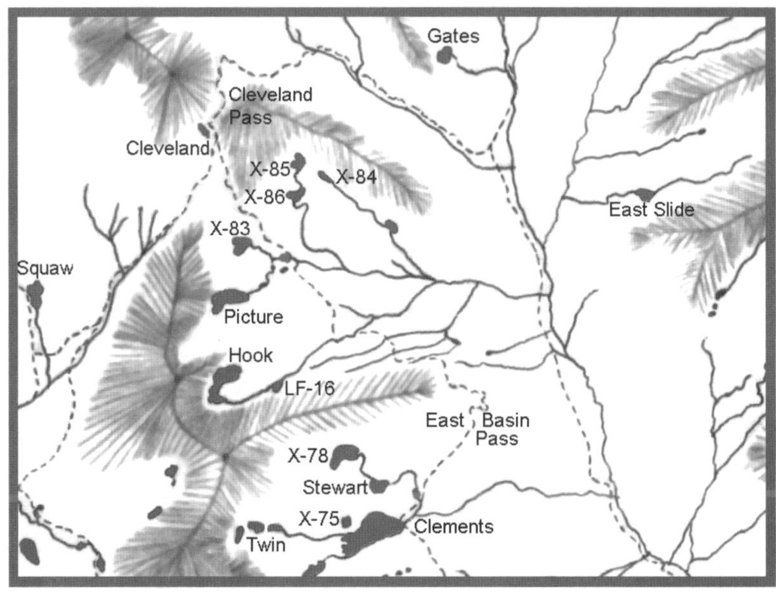

Gates
Cleveland Pass
Cleveland
X-85
X-84
X-86
East Slide
X-83
Squaw
Picture
Hook
LF-16
East Basin Pass
X-78
Stewart
X-75
Clements
Twin

# Three Lakes

| Trip Planner: | | | |
|---|---|---|---|
| Miles | 17 | Usage | Very Light |
| Elevation | 10,860 | Campsites | Fair |
| Elev. Gain | 2,700 | Springwater | Yes |
| Drainage | Lake Fork | Fishing | Good |
| Trailhead | Moon Lake | Horsefeed | Fair |
| Near Town | Duchesne | Firewood | Good |

Three Lakes are not to be confused with the three lakes that lie just below Picture Lake. Three Lakes are located in a remote area 1 mile north of the three smaller lakes next to the East Basin Trail. From the outlet of the three lakes below Picture, follow the East Basin trail north about 200 yards to where the trail levels out a bit. At this point cut cross country 1 mile northeast to the outlet of X-86.

Lake X-86 is the first of the Three Lakes you'll run into. This pretty lake is characterized by large rock shelves on the west shore and scattered timber to the east. Due to the rocky nature of this terrain, only one decent campsite exists. This campsite is found near the outlet, where you'll find good running water as well.

X-85 is the place to stay. This lake plays host to several good camping areas on the southwest side. It is also equipped with a superb spring that flows into the lake from the north. Angling usage is considered very light. X-85 should produce some fairly good fishing for fat brook trout. Access is found by following the inlet of X-86 1/4 mile to the north.

The lake that receives the least amount of attention out of the three is X-84. Like the other lakes, X-84 is in a rough alpine setting that may remind you of a desolate and far away place. Hmmm, maybe it is. Campsites and spring water are not available. Angling usage is quite light, which of course means fishing prospects may be worthwhile. Reach X-84 by following a couple of ponds that lie northeast of X-86.

***X-86 of Three Lakes***

# Ottoson Basin

| Trip Planner: | | | |
|---|---|---|---|
| Miles | 15.2 | Usage | Light |
| Elevation | 11,100 | Campsites | Good |
| Elev. Gain | 2,900 | Springwater | No |
| Drainage | Lake Fork | Fishing | Good |
| Trailhead | Moon Lake | Horsefeed | Good |
| Near Town | Duchesne | Firewood | Limited |

***Ottoson Basin from Cleveland Pass***

The easiest access to Ottoson Basin is the Lake Fork River Trail. On the other hand, the more scenic route is via the Brown Duck Trail, then through East Basin and over Cleveland Pass. From Moon Lake follow the Lake Fork River trail 11 miles north to the Ottoson Basin Trail junction. From here, go 3 miles northwest up a 1,200 foot incline to the base of Cleveland Peak. Then cut across rugged country 1.2 miles northwest to Lower Ottoson Lake.

Upper and Lower Ottoson Lakes are in open terrain in the upper west portion of Ottoson Basin. These lakes lie at the base of a talus ridge that connects Explorer and Squaw Peaks. No decent campsites are present at these lakes, but good camping areas and horse feed can be found 1/2 mile southeast of Lower Ottoson. Both lakes contain healthy populations of cutthroat trout, and fishing pressure remains mostly light. During the late summer months, sheep grazing takes place in the whole upper part of Ottoson Basin. This activity depreciates the glamour of this beautiful basin, and adds extra caution where drinking water is concerned.

The best place to make base camp is at Ameba Lake. It is just 1/2 mile north of the trail once you reach the base of Cleveland Peak. Ameba is situated in a meadow near timberline, 14 miles from Moon Lake. This lake provides good campsites, horse feed, and hot fishing for cutthroat trout.

Ottoson Basin offers one of the grandest views in the High Uintas, especially when viewed from the top of Cleveland Pass. Shutterbugs will want to be on the pass in the early morning when the sun illuminates the peaks. Mornings are also very good for fishing, but you can always find fast fishing in the evenings. If you want superb photos, choose the early hike up Cleveland Pass.

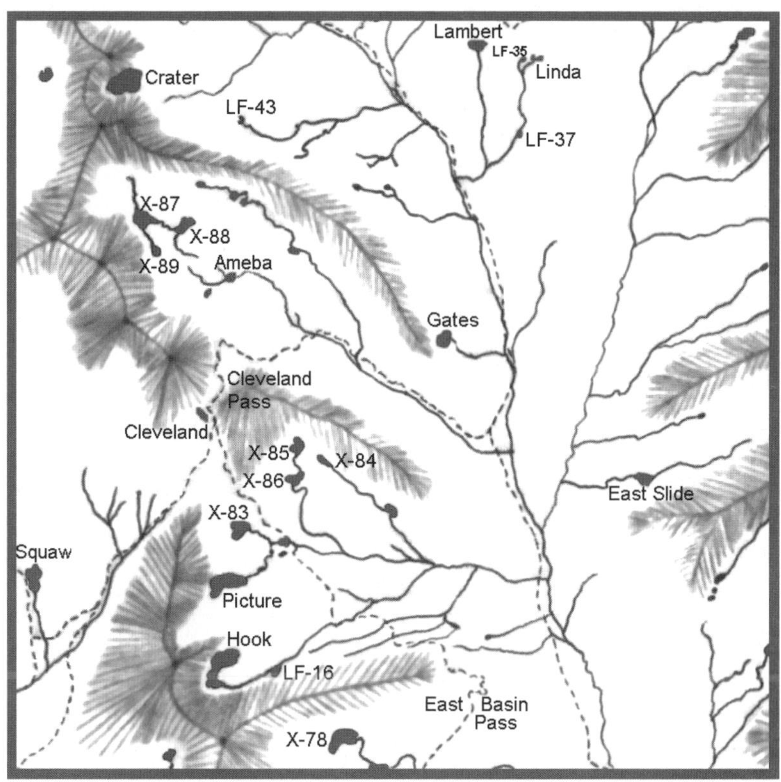

# Upper Lake Fork

| Trip Planner: | | | |
|---|---|---|---|
| Miles | 15 | Usage | Light |
| Elevation | 11,200 | Campsites | Good |
| Elev. Gain | 3,000 | Springwater | Yes |
| Drainage | Lake Fork | Fishing | Good |
| Trailhead | Moon Lake | Horsefeed | Good |
| Near Town | Duchesne | Firewood | Limited |

The upper regions of the Lake Fork Drainage display some of the finest scenery in the High Uintas. From one pass to another, grand panoramas seem to enchant the mind. Red Knob Pass grants access to two other beautiful drainages, while Squaw and Porcupine Pass branch into others. To say the least, this area is a gold mine for photographers. However, the Lake Fork Trail from Moon Lake is not as seductive as it winds through a 14 mile corridor of tall standing pines. Not much else can be seen until you get to the upper basins.

Although Crater, Lambert and Oweep Lakes are located in the Lake Fork River Drainage, they are easier reached from East Fork Blacks Fork by way of Red Knob or Squaw Pass - if the passes are free of snow. Not only is this route a mile or two shorter, it is more scenic and supports a loop trail. Be prepared for some hard work going over Red Knob Pass.

The lakes of the upper Lake Fork Drainage are as glamorous as the odd shaped peaks. Take Crater for example. This lake lies at the northeast base of Explorer Peak and is encased by a spectacular cirque basin. Steep cliffs and talus slopes abut the water from the north, west and south. Crater is known to be a mystifying lake. Some say that brook trout rise to the surface all at once, then mysteriously disappear for the rest of the day. "Where do they go?" we ask. Who knows? This lake has a depth of at least 150 feet, and no one really knows if anybody has found the bottom yet.

If you are planning to stay at Crater Lake to see if these stories are true, good luck. Due to open rocky terrain, campsites are poorly defined. Camping areas and spring water can be found 1 mile to the east. Access to Crater is 16 miles north on the Lake Fork River trail, then cross-country 2 miles west.

In the middle of the upper Lake Fork Drainage, lies Lambert Lake. Find this alpine water by following the Highline Trail. If coming from the west, keep to the trail until you get above timberline. Once you exit the pines, the lake should be south of the trail just a few hundred yards. Lambert offers good campsites and horse feed, but spring water is limited. It receives moderate usage from those hiking the Highline Trail. Fly Fishing is often great for feisty fat brook trout. The best campsite at Lambert Lake is located just above the cliffs overlooking the lake. It includes a small spring that emerges from the rocks, and rolls down to the lake.

Nearby, Linda Lake sits in a boggy meadow 1/2 mile east on the Highline Trail from Lambert, then 1/4 mile south from the trail. Campsites and spring water are limited, but a wary population of brook trout await your offerings. LF-35 is right next to Linda Lake, and may provide faster fishing. For some reason, the brookies at LF-35 preferred a flashy lure the day we stopped by.

In the eastern portion of the upper Lake Fork Drainage lies Oweep Lake. This scenic lake is at the base of a long talus slope bordering the Lake Fork and Yellowstone drainages. Surrounded by rocky terrain, camping areas are limited. Spring water is abundant, and fisherman usage is considered light. In late summer, sheep grazing occurs in the whole upper Lake Fork Drainage. Oweep Lake receives the least amount of this activity.

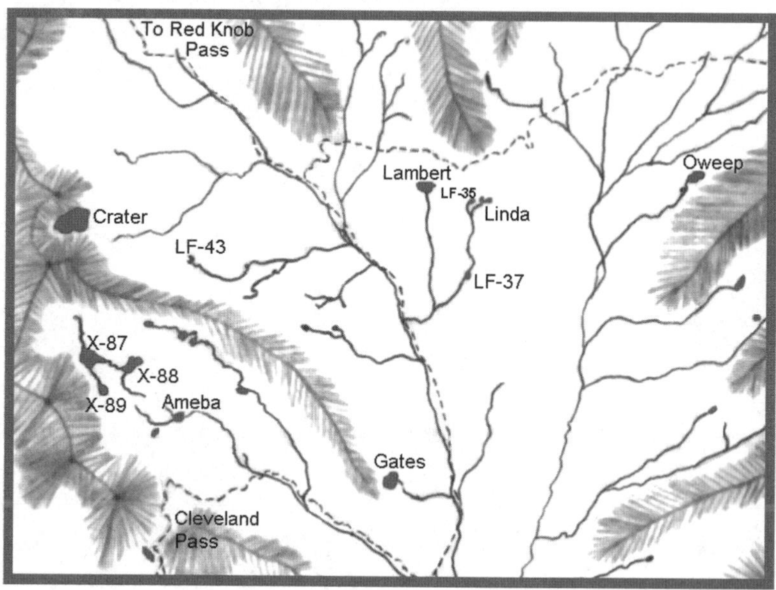


See Photos on next page.

*View from Red Knob Pass looking West*

*Lambert Lake*

Crater Lake

Linda Lake

# Toquer Lake

| Trip Planner: | | | |
|---|---|---|---|
| Miles | 3 | Usage | Light |
| Elevation | 10,470 | Campsites | Good |
| Elev. Gain | 250 | Springwater | Yes |
| Drainage | Lake Fork | Fishing | Fair |
| Trailhead | Hell's Canyon | Horsefeed | Good |
| Near Town | Duchesne | Firewood | Excellent |

This is one of those places where you go to be alone. Toquer Lake is the only body of water in the area deserving of the designation of "lake." It's not on the way to anywhere else, so very few hikers bother checking it out. But if you're looking for a short mild hike that leads to serene scenery and a great chance for some genuine solitude, then look no further.

Toquer Lake offers an exquisite setting, but better campsites can be found about 1/4 mile below the lake. Everything you need is found near the lake. A cold free-flowing spring on the north side

***A healthy population of elk roam the High Uintas.***

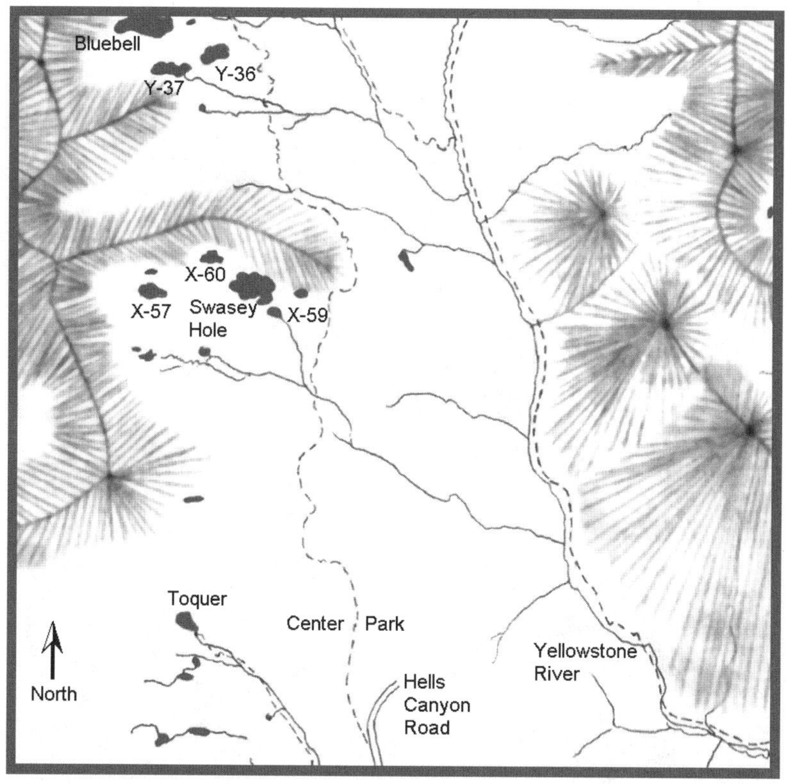


provides drinking water, and firewood is virtually everywhere throughout the heavily timbered terrain. If you're lucky, the lake will even yield a few of its brook trout for your evening meal. But don't expect great fishing. An avid fisherman would probably be happier somewhere else, and that's OK. That means there will be even fewer visitors here.

The trail from the Center Park Trailhead is a tough one to follow. It frequently disappears, and you may find yourself picking through the many fallen trees. Keep you map handy while hiking, and keep bearing northwest. You can always just find Fish Creek, and follow it up to Toquer Lake.

If you are camped at Toquer Lake, try hiking to the top of the ridge about one mile to the northeast. From there, you'll witness one of the finest vistas of Swasey Hole and the upper regions of the Yellowstone Drainage. On a clear day you can see all the way to Kings Peak. Take a camera, of course.

# Spider Lake

| Trip Planner: | | | |
|---|---|---|---|
| Miles | 7.8 | Usage | Heavy |
| Elevation | 10,876 | Campsites | Excellent |
| Elev. Gain | 600 | Springwater | Yes |
| Drainage | Yellowstone | Fishing | Very Good |
| Trailhead | Hell's Canyon | Horsefeed | Fair |
| Near Town | Duchesne | Firewood | Fair |

***Spider Lake***

Don't let the elevation gain fool you. This is a tiring hike. On paper the terrain doesn't look that bad, but you'll feel like a yo-yo upon arrival. The trail seems to go up and down endlessly. Allow yourself extra hiking time to make up for the rest stops you're bound to need. Take your time and enjoy the scenery. It is a pretty hike. You may have a tough time remembering any level ground until you reach Spider Lake. Then things get much better. The camping sites are plentiful all around the lake, and that's good because this aesthetic lake sees lots of pressure on the weekends. Be sure to clean up your mess, and practice low-impact camping.

Spider is named for its many elongated bays that offer interesting, but not particularly good fishing. However, we've rated this area as very good fishing because of the many opportunities nearby. Bluebell Lake has some nice sized brooks and cutthroats. A small fly should yield about five fish per hour on a good day; maybe more in the late evening. Or try Y-36 and Y-37 just to the south. These lakes are stocked with brook trout, and receive little attention. Head northwest from Spider Lake about half a mile, and you'll run into Drift Reservoir. Who knows what you will find here. It is out of the way just enough to keep a few secrets of its own.

Take plenty of mosquito repellent if you are traveling during bug season. There are several moist areas that produce some fair sized clouds of mosquitoes. Take that into consideration when selecting your campsite, and you'll breathe easier.

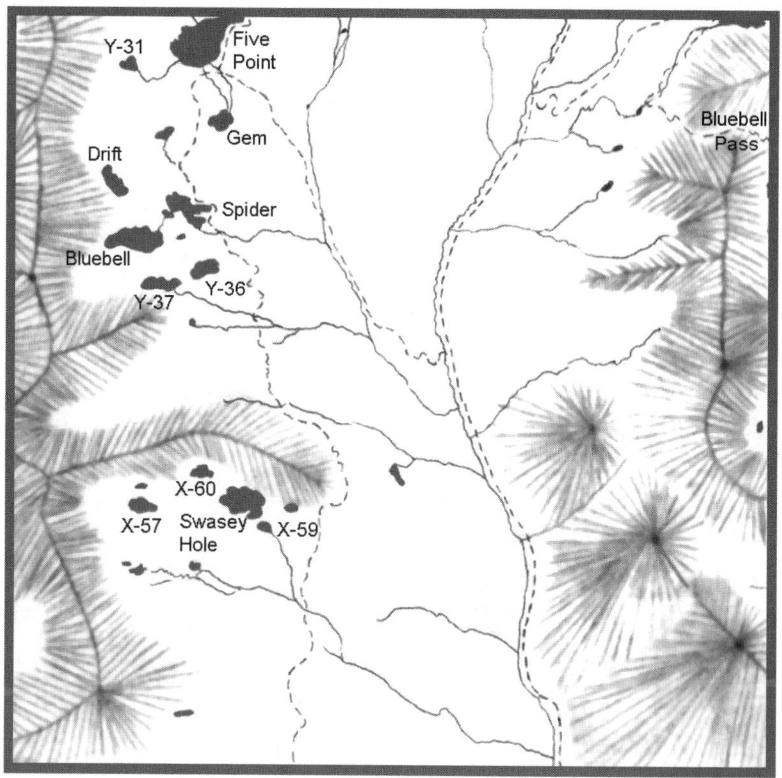

# North Star Lake

| Trip Planner: | | | |
|---|---|---|---|
| Miles | 15.5 | Usage | Light |
| Elevation | 11,395 | Campsites | Fair |
| Elev. Gain | 3,200 | Springwater | No |
| Drainage | Yellowstone | Fishing | Good |
| Trailhead | Swift Creek | Horsefeed | Poor |
| Near Town | Duchesne | Firewood | Scarce |

Of all the lakes in the High Uintas, North Star is considered to sit closest to the exact center of this mountain range. Due to this fact, access is possible from several locations. The shortest routes are found at either Center Park or the Swift Creek Trailhead. From Swift Creek follow the Yellowstone Creek Trail 8 miles to the Garfield Basin junction. Then proceed 4 miles northwest up a 1,600 foot incline to Five Point Lake. Past Five Point, keep following the Garfield Basin trail 3 miles north then northeast to the Highline trail.

*Five Point Lake*

Then take the Highline trail another 3/4 mile north to North Star Lake. Other starting points are at China Meadows, East Fork Blacks Fork, or the Highline Trailhead.

North Star is a popular stopping point for backpackers making the Highline trek. Although only a few mediocre campsites exist, it is the only decent place to make camp in the area. If you are traveling via the Garfield Basin route, you may want to pitch your tent at Five Point Lake and save North Star Lake as an exciting day hike. The upper portion of Garfield Basin is characterized by rocky windswept tundra. There is little or no horse feed, and firewood is extremely scarce.

North Star and Tungsten Lakes receive moderate angling pressure for brook and cutthroat trout. If you are looking for more solitude and more remote fishing possibilities, try lakes Y-2, Y-4, and Y-5. These lakes receive little attention and harbor an excellent supply of pan-sized brook trout. Find these lakes by following the inlet of North Star Lake 1 mile north to Y-2. Then just follow a string of lakes to Y- 4, 5 & 6. Sorry, there are no fish at Y-6.

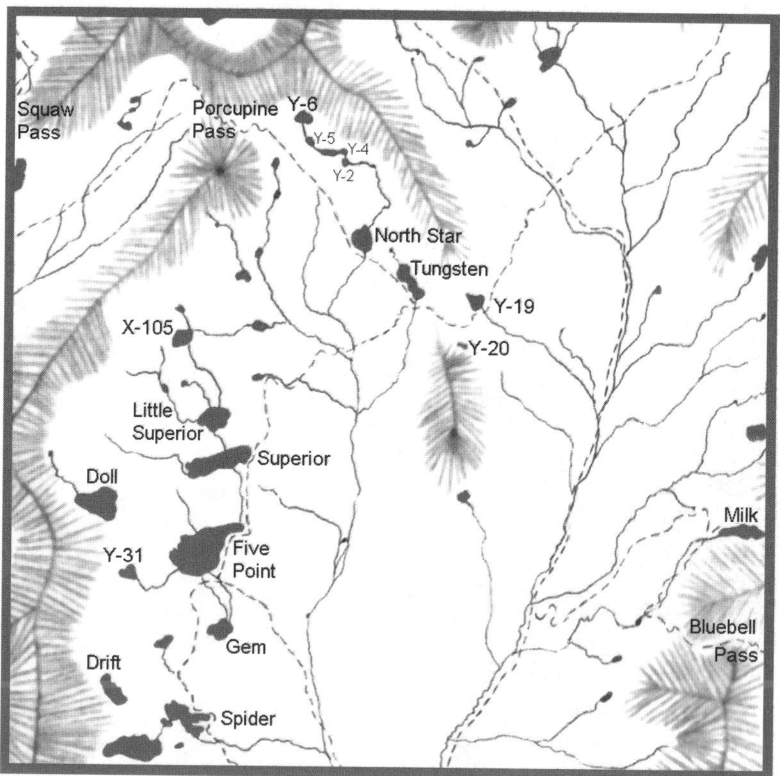

# Milk Lake

| Trip Planner: | | | |
|---|---|---|---|
| Miles | 11 | Usage | Light |
| Elevation | 10,983 | Campsites | Fair |
| Elev. Gain | 2800 | Springwater | No |
| Drainage | Yellowstone | Fishing | Good |
| Trailhead | Swift Creek | Horsefeed | Fair |
| Near Town | Duchesne | Firewood | Good |

Milk Lake is for loners. In fact, Milk Lake is a loner itself. Situated high on the east side of the Yellowstone Drainage, there are no other lakes for miles in any direction. It's a long steep hike whether following Yellowstone Creek or coming over Bluebell Pass from the Swift Creek Drainage. The Swift Creek route is shortest by three miles, and is suggested. You'll need to traverse Bluebell Pass, but it is not bad as mountain passes go, even by horseback.

If you feel alone and remote at Milk Lake it's because, well, you are. It's a great feeling. You might feel almost like an explorer in this vast country that rarely sees visitors of the human kind. This is a true wilderness experience. You should be in great

shape and confident of your skills before coming out here.

The best camping and horse pastures are located just west or south of the lake. Spring water is hard to come by, so bring along a water purification method. Giardia can be found anywhere in the High Uintas, even in high remote alpine lakes.

As for fishing, who knows what to expect. This is the type of water that could produce some quality fishing time. Stocked brook trout can live many seasons without seeing an artificial lure, and may have the chance to reach large proportions. But if the fish aren't cooperating here, tough. There's no place else nearby.

Perhaps here it is better to just relax and enjoy the quiet space. You will most certainly have earned it.

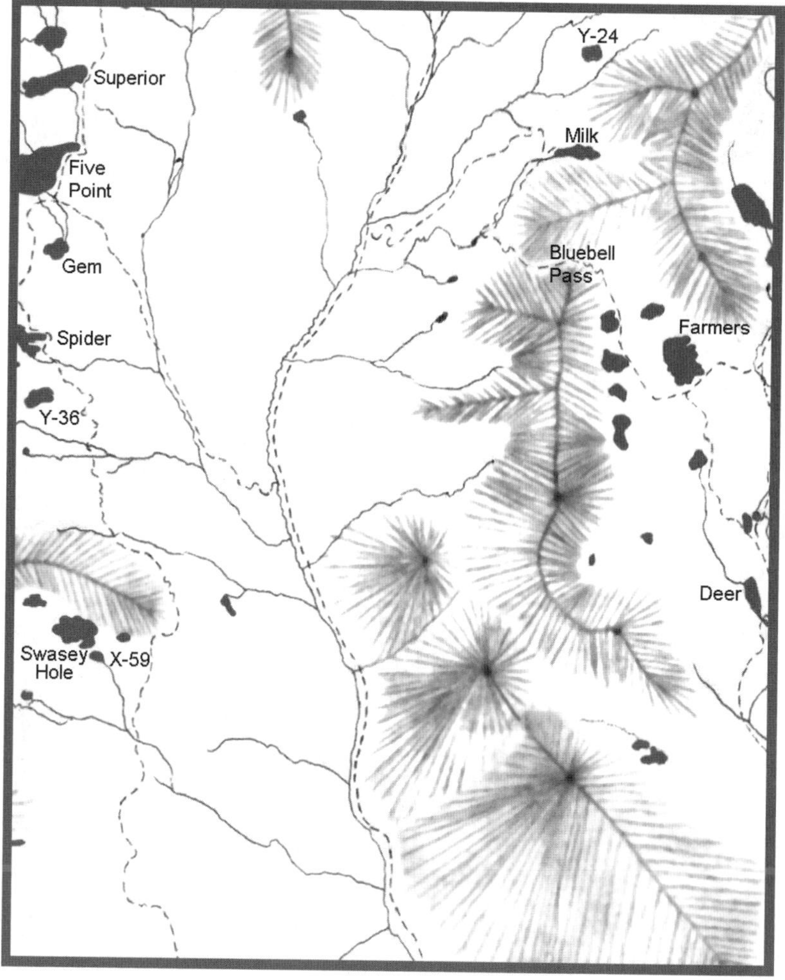

# Lily Lake

| Trip Planner: | | | |
|---|---|---|---|
| Miles | 1 | Usage | Moderate |
| Elevation | 9,346 | Campsites | Fair |
| Elev. Gain | 1,250 | Springwater | No |
| Drainage | Swift Creek | Fishing | Good |
| Trailhead | Grant Springs | Horsefeed | Poor |
| Near Town | Duchesne | Firewood | Good |

A short but strenuous day hike can put you at beautiful Lily Lake, surrounded by pines and quaking aspens that hiss in the breeze. The lake is clear and deep, except for the southern end where numerous aquatic plants grow in the shallows. If Swift Creek Campground is your base camp, Lily Lake is an excellent place to escape the crowds, and find some peace and quiet.

Start hiking at Grant Springs in Yellowstone Canyon about half a mile below the Swift Creek Campground. A good trail will lead you safely up the mountain side northeast to Lily Lake. It is quite steep, as you'll pick up over 1,200 feet of elevation in just one mile. It may seem further than a mile. Mountain miles usually do. But don't give up. You should complete the trek in about 30 - 45 minutes. The walk back down should be a lot quicker.

Fishermen like to venture to Lily Lake in hopes of finding faster fishing than they found near the campgrounds. This may or may not happen. Lily Lake is stocked with brook trout, but stocking schedules, angling pressure, and the mood of the fish will determine your fishing luck. Try to be at the lake in the early morning or the late evening. This should be feasible because of the short hike. Try a small fly (#16) around the inlet and outlet, and don't overlook the lily

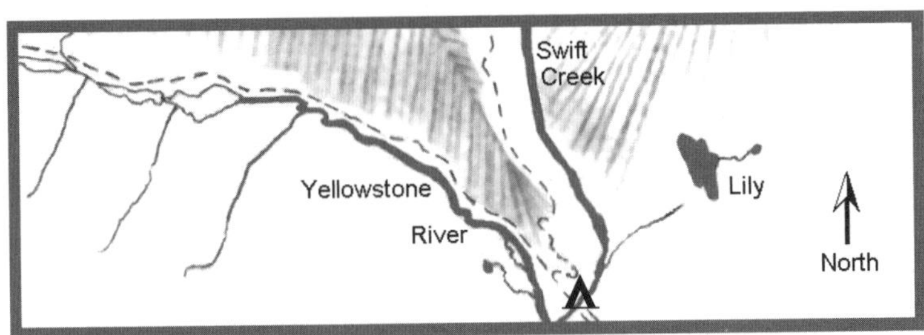

pads. Brook trout like to hang around these looking for bugs. Lily Lake is just close enough to camp that you won't mind toting a few fish back for dinner.

Lily Lake doesn't sport good camping facilities. It is not a good place to spend the night. Please don't make any new camping areas or fire pits. This area is more suitable for day use, and probably should remain that way.

# Deer Lake

| Trip Planner: | | | |
|---|---|---|---|
| Miles | 5.4 | Usage | Moderate |
| Elevation | 10,240 | Campsites | Fair |
| Elev. Gain | 2,050 | Springwater | Yes |
| Drainage | Swift Creek | Fishing | Good |
| Trailhead | Swift Creek | Horsefeed | Fair |
| Near Town | Duchesne | Firewood | Fair |

Early in the summer season, before the higher country opens up, you may find yourself wanting some alpine adventure. Here's a lake that just might provide some early relief from cabin fever. That is if you call mid-June early. Pack some warm clothes. The temperatures can still be pretty brisk during June. Much of the hike is steep, but it's not very far. Deer Lake makes an excellent *primer* hike that can easily fit into a weekend.

*Deer Lake*

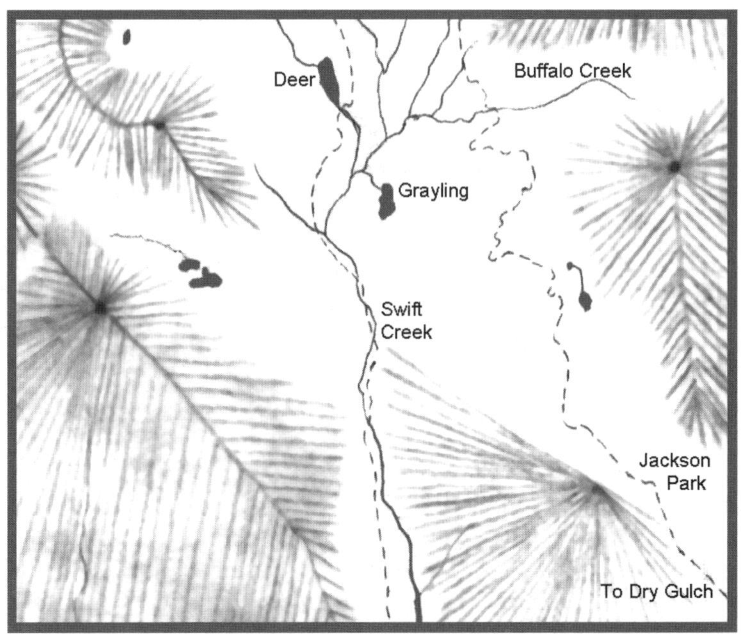


Deer Lake is probably at its best early in the season. Later on, the lake becomes less attractive as the water level drops, leaving a muddy, rocky shoreline. If you can get there just after "ice-off", you could experience some fast fishing for pan-sized brook and cutthroat trout. Other fishing opportunities include Grayling Lake (about one mile southeast), and Swift Creek. The outlet from Deer Lake joins Swift Creek about half a mile below. Hardly anyone fishes the creek. Try it with a small spinner, and you might be pleasantly surprised.

There is a twenty foot dam across the outlet. Fair campsites can be located near the dam. They are not top quality camping spots, but they will suffice. Spring water is available at the inlet, as is a small amount of horse feed. Firewood should be plentiful even though this area sees a lot of visitors. Most travelers only stop for lunch on their way to the more popular lakes above. You should have it all to yourself during the evening hours.

Shutter-bugs will enjoy the view back down Swift Creek Drainage, as well as the setting around Deer Lake. Deer Lake lies in a narrow valley, surrounded by pines on its long sides, with a picturesque cliff sealing off the back end.

# Farmers Lake

| Trip Planner: | | | |
|---|---|---|---|
| Miles | 7.5 | Usage | Moderate |
| Elevation | 10,990 | Campsites | Good |
| Elev. Gain | 2800 | Springwater | Yes |
| Drainage | Swift Creek | Fishing | Very Good |
| Trailhead | Swift Creek | Horsefeed | Excellent |
| Near Town | Mtn. Home | Firewood | Good |

If you like to get a lot of elevation gain out of the way early, then this hike is for you. Right from the start you'll traverse a long series of switchbacks that pickup 1000 feet in 1.5 miles. Then the trail levels off for a few miles before another steep ascent to Deer Lake. Deer Lake is a great place to stop for lunch, and maybe catch a few neglected brook trout.

You will pass White Miller Lake on the way. This is a tempting place to camp, but push on another mile to Farmers Lake. Farmers is a better base camp, as it sits in the middle of several good fishing

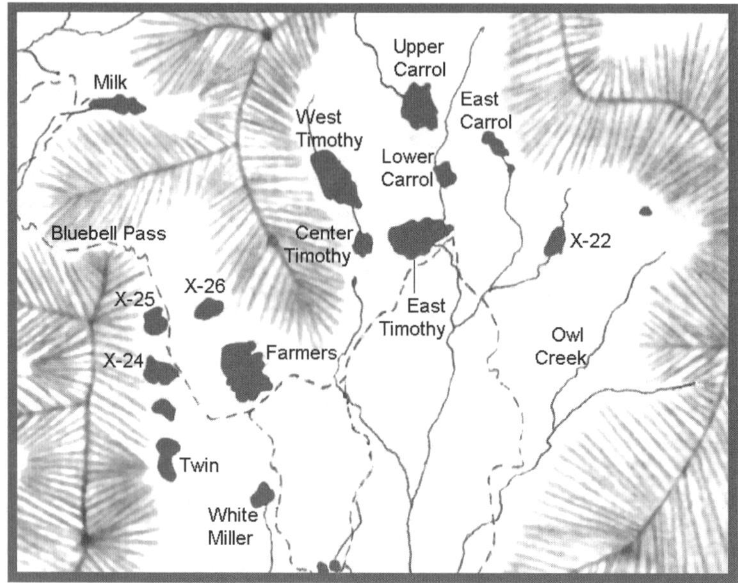

lakes, and has excellent horse pasture nearby to the west. The best campsite is about 1/4 mile below Farmers Lake. Just follow the outlet stream, and you can't miss it.

Fishing at Farmers Lake varies greatly from year to year. Some years you can catch eager brook trout on every other cast. At other times, the lake seems empty. If it doesn't produce for you, then head north over the hill to X-26. It frequently has fast fishing for pan-sized brookies. The lakes west of Farmers hold a few surprises too. Large cutthroats roam these lakes. Try the inlets with a salmon egg fly, and look out. You won't catch too many, but you'll only need a couple to make a hearty meal.

Timothy and Carroll Lakes are not far from Farmers. A short day hike of 2 to 4 miles northeast, will put you right in the middle of this open basin. Cattle graze up here, so that detracts from the aesthetics of the vast tundra; but it's still worth seeing, and definitely worth fishing. Plenty of open shoreline exists for the fly fisherman.

An interesting side-note about this hike is that at the trailhead the sign says "Farmers Lake 12 miles." At Farmers Lake the sign says "Trailhead 9 miles." When you're hiking the trail it seems that way too.

***Farmers Lake***

# Timothy Lakes

**Trip Planner:**

| Miles | 8.5 | Usage | Heavy |
|---|---|---|---|
| Elevation | 11,000 | Campsites | Good |
| Elev. Gain | 2,800 | Springwater | Yes |
| Drainage | Swift Creek | Fishing | Excellent |
| Trailhead | Swift Creek | Horsefeed | Good |
| Near Town | Duchesne | Firewood | Scarce |

Timothy Lakes offer an excellent chance for an "above timberline" experience. A grueling 8 1/2 mile hike places you in an open basin where Swift Creek originates. Horsemen and fly fishermen adore this area because of the wide open tundra. Horses have plenty of room to roam, and anglers have plenty of room for backcasting. And fishing is a primary reason for coming here. Combine the three Timothy Lakes with the three Carroll Lakes and

***East Timothy Lake***

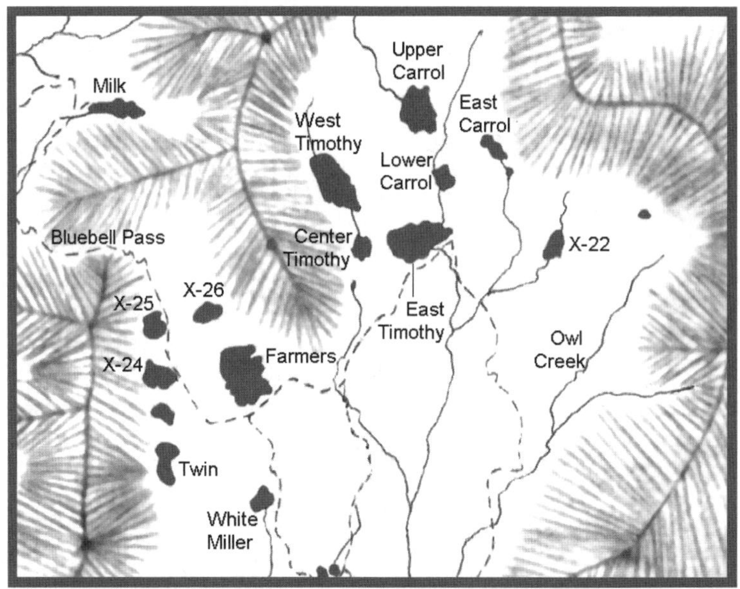


you have some of the finest fishing you can find packed into two miles.

Good camps can be setup at East Timothy or Center Timothy. At the latter you'll probably see fewer people, and will also stand a better chance of locating some spring water. But either place is a good choice. Sometimes cattle range up here, so don't be surprised if you wake up in the morning to the sound of mooing. Being above timberline, you won't find much fuel for the fire. A gas stove is a worthwhile investment if you are planning on cooking up some trout.

The trout should cooperate here. Brook trout are in all of these lakes, and cutthroats will appear from time to time. It's hard to recommend the best fishing hole. Try 'em all. If one doesn't produce, scoot over to the next lake. You're bound to find at least one lake that will yield some lightning fast fishing. Check the connecting streams too. Many trout migrate from lake to lake or simply prefer to spend their summer in the creeks. A small spinner can produce some fun action on the streams when your arms tire of fly casting on the lakes.

Farmers Lake is not too far from here, especially if you have horses. It's a nice change of scenery, and may offer some better sheltered camping. (See the story on Farmers Lake.)

# Crow Basin

| Trip Planner: | | | |
|---|---|---|---|
| Miles | 3 | Usage | Moderate |
| Elevation | 10,320 | Campsites | Good |
| Elev. Gain | 900 | Springwater | Yes |
| Drainage | Dry Gulch | Fishing | Good |
| Trailhead | Jackson Park | Horsefeed | Good |
| Near Town | Duchesne | Firewood | Good |

Good horse country. The Dry Gulch Drainage is the smallest in the Uinta Mountains, and Crow Basin forms a natural box canyon at the top of the drainage. These factors, along with abundant pasture and water make it well suited for horses. Recreational use is generally quite light, but it appears to be more heavily used than it is. Litter and well-worn horse camps take away from the aesthetics.

Crow Lake probably offers the best base camp in the basin. It features good campsites, spring water, and plenty of horse feed. Again, trash is often a problem, so it may be worth a few minutes of your time to pick up garbage. It may improve your camping

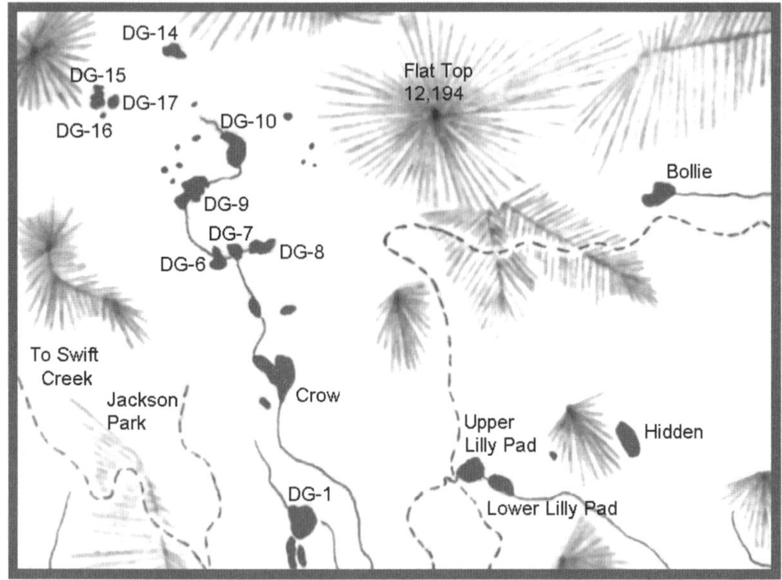

***Columbine Flowers***

experience, and will certainly enhance the natural appearance of the lake.

Fishing at Crow should be pretty good. Nice numbers of cutthroat trout patrol these waters, scooping up most anything that resembles a bug. But, as with almost all Uinta lakes, the fishing can change from year to year. If Crow Lake doesn't meet your expectations, there are several lakes close by that can be tested. Travel north about a mile to DG-6, DG-9, and DG-10. These lakes are all worth a try, and any one of them may be red-hot.

Another mile of riding northwest will put you into a cluster of lakes that rarely see fishermen (DG-14, DG-15, DG-16, DG-17). They are not fit for camping, but can provide a lot of fishing fun. Cutthroat trout in various sizes and numbers make things *very interesting.* These lakes make an excellent day hike for anyone camped at Crow Lake. There is very little horse feed up this way, and the only drinking water to speak of is from springs emerging from the talus slope at DG-14.

# Bollie Lake

| Trip Planner: | | | |
|---|---|---|---|
| Miles | 6 | Usage | Light |
| Elevation | 10,660 | Campsites | Excellent |
| Elev. Gain | 2,060 | Springwater | Unknown |
| Drainage | Uinta | Fishing | Fair |
| Trailhead | Dry Gulch | Horsefeed | Excellent |
| Near Town | Roosevelt | Firewood | Good |

Several different starting points can be used to find Bollie Lake. All access points are about the same distance, but the old logging road that ventures past Jefferson Park is the most feasible route. Access to the logging road can only be obtained by foot or horseback. The Dry Gulch Road (#122) has been barricaded about 4 miles from the turnoff of Road #119. From the trailhead, hike along an old jeep road 1.5 miles north to the trail. The beginning portion of this trail is a little hard to find and difficult to follow for the first quarter mile. Anyway, follow a hit-n-miss trail 2 miles east to the old logging road. Then follow the logging road 2.5 miles north,

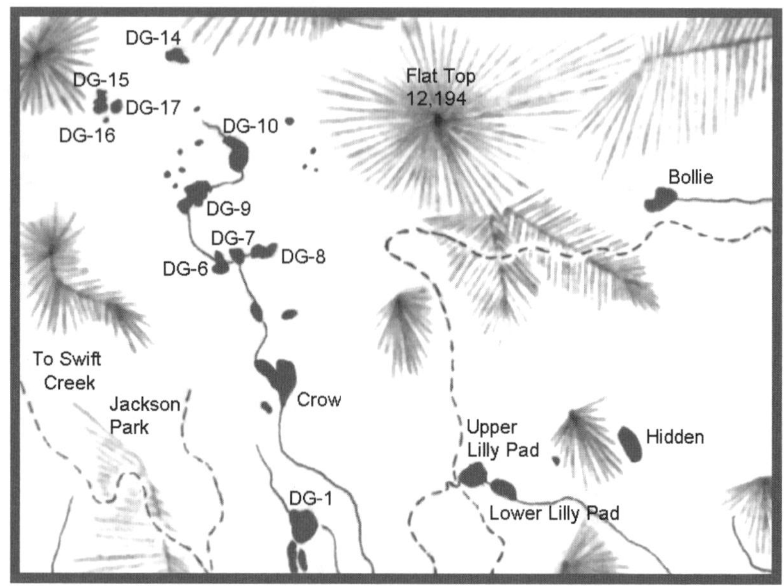

***Giant Mushroom***

passing Jefferson Park. Stay with the trail another 1.5 miles west along a canyon rim until you reach Bollie Lake.

Four wheel drive is advised for access to the Dry Gulch Trailhead. If easy car access is what you need, then the best starting point is from the Uinta River Drainage. Starting at U-Bar Ranch, follow the Uinta River trail 3 miles north to Sheep Bridge. Then take the Chain Lakes trail 1 mile west to the top of some steep switchbacks. Here an old sheep trail heads south then west 3.5 miles to the lake.

The avid outdoorsman should have great expectations of Bollie Lake. Fast fishing has been reported for pan-sized brookies, as the open picturesque shorelines make for easy fly casting. Excellent campsites and horse feed exist by the lush meadows that intersperse with the pines.

This trek also features a loop trail. If you are like us, taking the same old route back to the car can be about as exciting as breasts on a boar hog. To make things a little less boring (pun), we suggest taking the trail back that ventures over Flat Top Mountain, then past Lily Pad Lakes.

Lily Pad Lakes are in a beautiful meadow surrounded by timber. Excellent campsites are present, and horse munchies abound in the area. Upper Lily Pad Lake provides the better fishing.

# Chain Lakes

| Trip Planner: | | | |
|---|---|---|---|
| Miles | 8 | Usage | Heavy |
| Elevation | 10,580 | Campsites | Fair |
| Elev. Gain | 2,800 | Springwater | No |
| Drainage | Uinta River | Fishing | Good |
| Trailhead | Uinta | Horsefeed | Fair |
| Near Town | Roosevelt | Firewood | Limited |

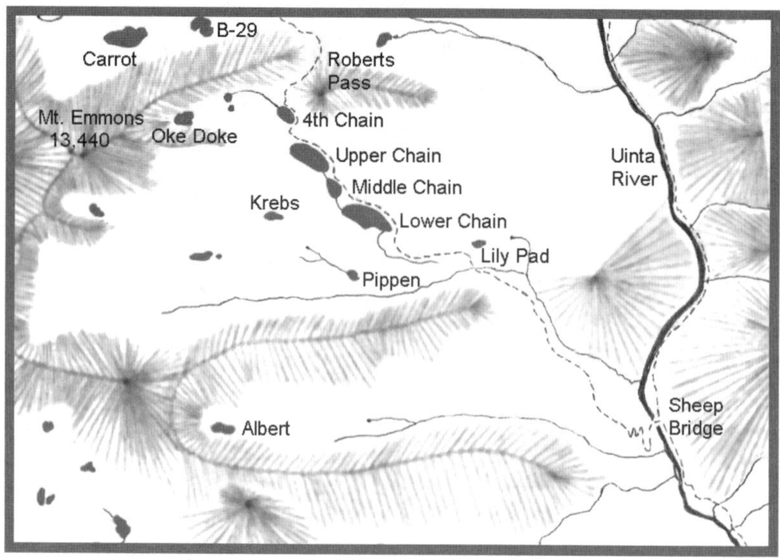


Chain Lakes are three connecting reservoirs and one natural lake. Campsites and horse feed are somewhat limited at all four lakes, but they receive heavy camping and fishing anyway. During the late summer months, the reservoirs experience serious fluctuation, and angling pressure decreases rapidly. However, from July to mid August pan-sized brookies are abundant at all reservoirs, and should produce fast fishing. Chain #4 is a natural lake located on a plateau, 9.5 miles from the U-Bar Ranch. Anglers don't utilize this lake as much as the others, but this is often the best fishing hole during late summer.

A good place to setup base camp is Pippen Lake, (or sometimes called Island). It sits in a meadow 1/2 mile southwest of Lower Chain's outlet or 9 miles from the U-Bar Ranch. Pippen is distinguished by a small island near the south end of the shore, and has excellent meadowland campsites. Plenty of horse feed dominates the surrounding terrain. Pippen is one of the better fly fishing lakes in the Uinta River Drainage, and sustains moderate angling use throughout the summer. You should have no problem filling your skillet with fresh mountain brook trout.

If you're looking to get off the beaten path, Oke Doke Lake is a good spot. This handsome lake is just 1 mile from Chain #4. From the 4th Chain Lake or Roberts Pass, head west along the south side of the ridge that extends from Mount Emmons. Oke Doke Lake is on the eastern base of Mount Emmons in a high cirque. No campsites or horse treats exist. Light angling pressure often means exciting fishing for cunning cutthroat trout.

Access to Chain Lakes begins at either U-Bar Ranch or the Uinta Trailhead. Take the Uinta River Trail 3 miles north to Sheep Bridge. Proceed east across the foot bridge and up a thousand feet of switchbacks. Catch your breath, then follow the trail northwest to Krebs Basin and Lower Chain Lake.

***Pack horses are real back-savers on long steep treks.***

# Lake Atwood

| Trip Planner: | | | |
|---|---|---|---|
| Miles | 13.6 | Usage | Moderate |
| Elevation | 11,030 | Campsites | Good |
| Elev. Gain | 3,200 | Springwater | Unknown |
| Drainage | Uinta River | Fishing | Excellent |
| Trailhead | Uinta | Horsefeed | Good |
| Near Town | Roosevelt | Firewood | Limited |

Lake Atwood houses one of the largest brook trout populations in the High Uintas. With this in mind, you just may want to throw your line in here and forget about all the surrounding lakes. Bad decision! Atwood receives most of the attention in this basin, and angling may be hampered by semi-crowded shorelines. Allred Lake and Mt. Emmons Lake, have the same problem. Although fast fishing usually occurs, so do a lot of people. This is partly because Atwood and Allred offer the best camping opportunities in Atwood Basin. Lake Atwood loses much of its appeal later in the summer when it draws down about 15 feet.

***Lake Atwood as seen from Trail Rider Pass***

Other lakes in Atwood Basin include Roberts, George Beard, Carrot, and B-29. Roberts is a typical alpine lake located in a cirque basin 1 mile southwest of Atwood. Follow a faint trail 1.5 miles west from Mt. Emmons Lake. No campsites exist in this small windy basin, so angling pressure remains light for feisty cutthroat trout.

Two miles west on the trail from Atwood, lies George Beard Lake (U-21). This lake sits in windswept terrain just below Trail Rider Pass. Most people ignore this water because there is no shelter, but this makes perfect conditions for the avid angler. That is, if there's fast fishing for wild trout - and there is. George Beard Lake contains a huge supply of native brookies. Another lake that might be worth checking out, and sits just 1/2 mile south of George Beard, is U-19. Not many fishermen make it this far.

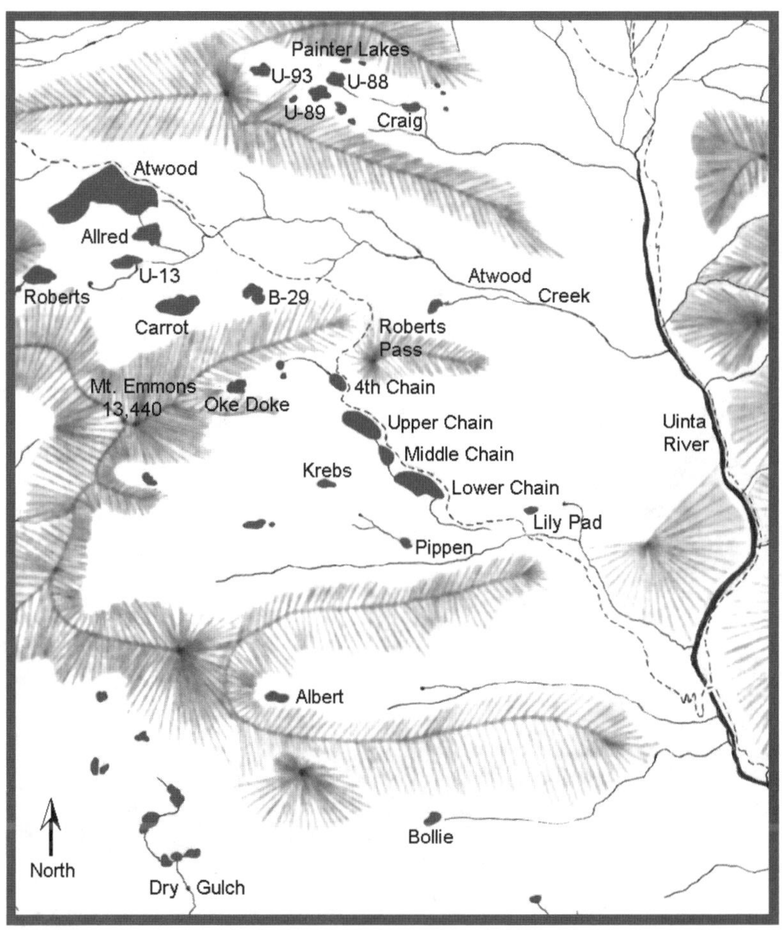

# *Kidney Lakes (Uinta Drainage)*

**Trip Planner:**

| | | | |
|---|---|---|---|
| Miles | 13 | Usage | Heavy |
| Elevation | 10,850 | Campsites | Good |
| Elev. Gain | 850 | Springwater | No |
| Drainage | Uinta River | Fishing | Good |
| Trailhead | W. Fork Whiterocks | Horsefeed | Good |
| Near Town | Vernal | Firewood | Limited |

Five different access points can be used for the Kidney Lakes area. The shortest route begins at the West Fork Whiterocks Trailhead. The others start at Uinta River, Chepeta Lake, Hoop Lake and Spirit Lake. But they are at least 3 miles longer. Excellent trails exist for each route, and stock unloading ramps are present at every trailhead except Chepeta Lake.

Several lakes comprise the Kidney Lakes Basin, and most receive substantial camping or fishing use. Kidney Lakes are no

*Kidney Lakes*

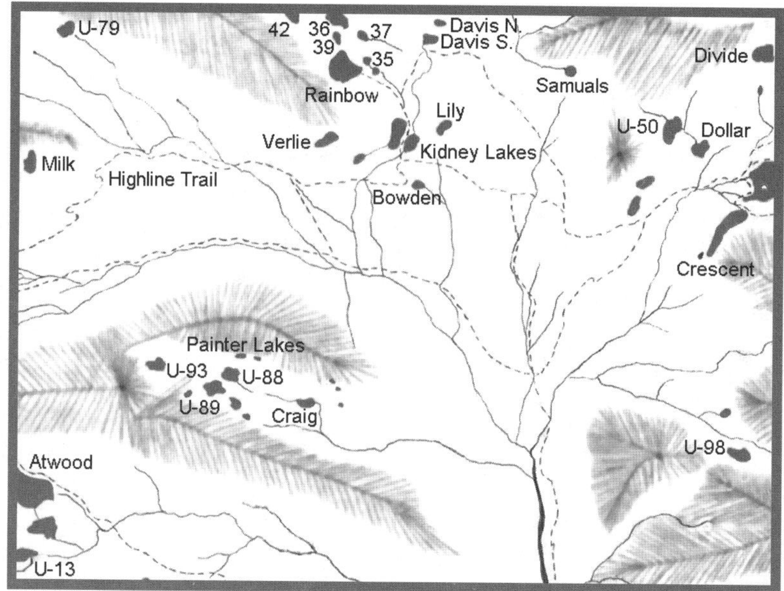


exception. Large recreational groups usually occupy both Kidney Lakes. Plenty of campsites can be found between the lakes and around West Kidney. Fishing is often good for brook trout and an occasional 1-pound rainbow. Moose are often seen feeding in the shallows of both Kidney Lakes. Be aware of these large animals, and give them their space. Although usually docile, an upset moose is extremely dangerous.

For secluded camping, try nearby Bowden or Lily Lake. Bowden has limited camp sites, but an endless supply of horse feed. Lily is a quaint little lake surrounded by yellow water lilies. Campsites with horse pastures are just west of the lake. Lily receives only light pressure even though it's only 1/2 mile from the Kidney Lakes.

Along a well-marked trail about a mile northwest of Kidney Lakes lies Rainbow Lake. The trail also leads to numerous lakes in the upper northwest portion of the basin. These lakes are in high windswept country. There are no decent camps up here. Rainbow Lake sees moderate to heavy fishing pressure, but is mostly limited to day use. Don't forget about the lakes located above Rainbow Lake. These small bodies of water may bring a nice surprise, and the ones just below are certainly worth checking out. Expect to find a good mixture of brookies, rainbows, and cutthroats.

Nearby Davis Lakes present good angling opportunities too. They are a little over 1 mile north of Kidney Lakes, and 250 yards north and south of each other. Both lakes get light use, and fly-fishing can be fast for pan-sized brookies.

# Davis Lakes

| Trip Planner: | | | |
|---|---|---|---|
| Miles | 13.8 | Usage | Light |
| Elevation | 11,020 | Campsites | Good |
| Elev. Gain | 1,020 | Springwater | Yes |
| Drainage | Uinta | Fishing | Good |
| Trailhead | W. Fork Whiterocks | Horsefeed | Good |
| Near Town | Roosevelt | Firewood | Fair |

Nestled in a high cirque, Davis Lakes offers a true alpine experience. The surrounding hills are composed of lush green grasses and scattered pines that may remind you of the Swiss Alps. Horsemen will appreciate all of the space, feed, and water for their animals, as well as the fact that horses cannot really roam any higher.

Davis Lakes are a little off the beaten path, and don't see a lot of visitors. A loop trail passes just below Davis South. It can be

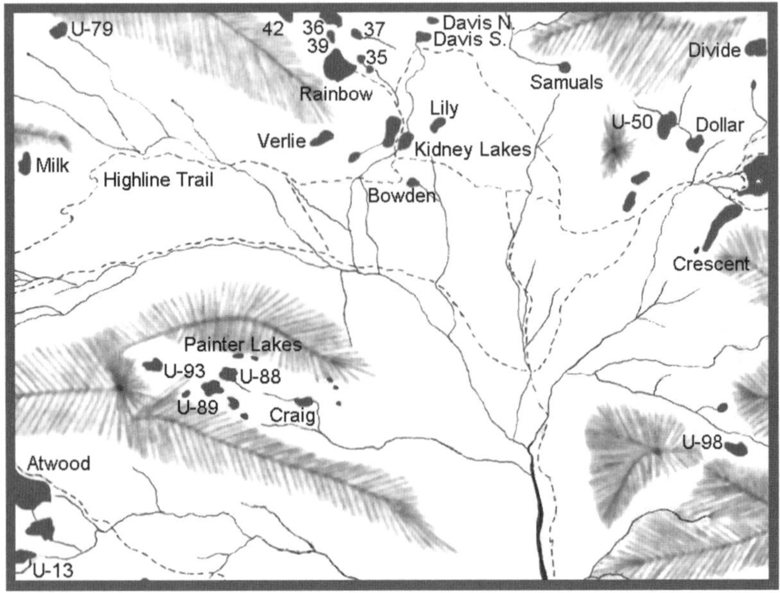

***Davis North Lake***

accessed from either Kidney Lakes, or if you're coming from Fox Lake take the Davis Lakes turnoff about two miles from Fox Lake. The turnoff is marked by a sign, and regardless of which way you take to Davis Lakes, the trail is hard to follow in places. Keep your compass and map handy, and keep pointed towards the large cirque in the mountainside.

Best camping facilities are on the south side of Davis South Lake. A spacious existing campsite should accomodate groups up to eight people. Spring water flows into Davis South along the north shore. The north shore is also the deepest, and is where most of the fish are. Plump pan-sized brookies can be easily harvested using a small fly or wooley worm. There is plenty of open shoreline where fly casters can have a ball. You won't catch big fish here, but you will probably catch as many as you want, as long you want. Small brookies also inhabit Davis North Lake, but may be tougher to fool. For a change of pace, try fishing the small stream between the lakes or the outlet stream from Davis South.

Don't be surprised to see moose in the area. There is a large herd that lives in the area between Davis Lakes and Kidney Lakes. Enjoy them at a distance, and you'll probably see them often. There are also deer and elk around, but they are much more wary.

# Painter Lakes

| Trip Planner: | | | |
|---|---|---|---|
| Miles | 15.3 | Usage | Light |
| Elevation | 11,030 | Campsites | Excellent |
| Elev. Gain | 3,200 | Springwater | Unknown |
| Drainage | Uinta River | Fishing | Excellent |
| Trailhead | Uinta | Horsefeed | Fair |
| Near Town | Roosevelt | Firewood | Good |

Painter Lakes take after their name. They are scattered about like little dabs of acrylic on a painter's palette. This beautiful wilderness is characterized by gentle rolling hills and timbered terrain. Due to the remoteness and difficult travel to this basin, Painter Lakes remain blissfully free of people and debris.

Reach Painter Basin by following the Uinta River Trail 12 miles north, then northwest to North Fork Park. From North Fork Park, follow a vague trail 2 miles south up a steep and rugged 900 foot incline next to a small creek. The first lake you'll run into is Craig.

***Painter Lakes***

Craig is the only lake in this basin with a horse pasture, and also contains a good population of cutthroat trout. Although good campsites exist at Craig Lake, better accommodations exist at Painter Lakes U-88 & U-89. Following the inlet of Craig Lake 1 mile west, you'll find the first two Painter Lakes. These lakes sit only 100 yards apart from one another. U-88 is the largest lake in the basin, so fishing may be better at this lake than any of the others. Angling pressure is almost nil, and eager Brook trout should be fighting each other to get to your lure first. But don't forget U-89. This lake fluctuates like a toilet bowl, but ya never know. A big one may be lurking inside.

Situated deep in the western part of Painter Lakes Basin is Lake U-93. It is located 3/4 mile west of U-88. U-93 is above timberline at an elevation of 11,400 feet, and no campsites or horse feed exist. Angling is unpredictable. These Cutthroats either bite or they don't. And if they do, they are small. Unless you're just out for a pleasure stroll, other lakes like U-88 and Craig will fulfill your wildest desires.

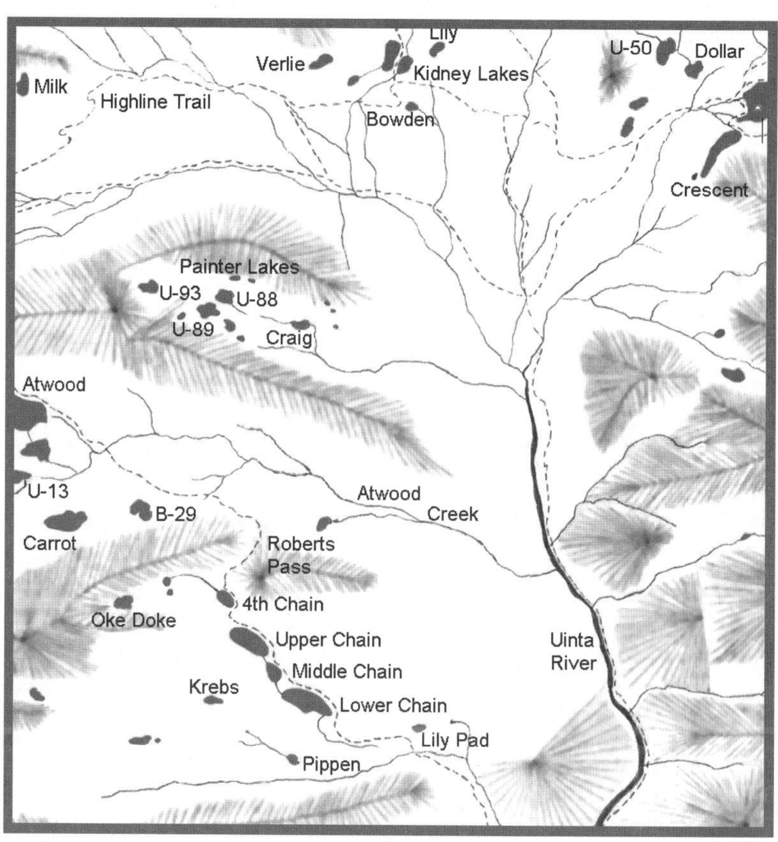

# Fox Lake

| Trip Planner: | | | |
|---|---|---|---|
| Miles | 8.5 | Usage | Heavy |
| Elevation | 10,790 | Campsites | Good |
| Elev. Gain | 800 | Springwater | No |
| Drainage | Uinta River | Fishing | Good |
| Trailhead | W. Fork Whiterocks | Horsefeed | Good |
| Near Town | Vernal | Firewood | Limited |

Although Fox is a primitive lake, it just doesn't remind you of a wilderness area. Large groups of campers bring horses loaded with all their "essentials," and begin to party. Don't get us wrong. We like to have fun just as much as the next guy, but we prefer a place that is a little less conspicuous. Fox Lake gets more than its share of *high-impact* camping.

The best access to Fox begins at West Fork Whiterocks Trailhead. Take a good Forest Service trail 8.5 miles northwest over Fox Queant Pass and to the lake. Another route that is well traveled by horses starts in the Uinta River Drainage. This trail runs next to the Uinta River for 10 miles to a three-way junction. At this point, take the trail northeast 3.5 miles up Shale Creek to Fox Lake.

Fox is a fluctuating reservoir that experiences a serious draw-down during the late summer months, and fishing success declines with the water level. Despite this occurrence, it frequently hosts large groups of boy scouts and party-goers alike. Campsites are found around the lake, while horse pastures are located north of Fox and west of Crescent Lake. Overall fishing pressure is considered moderate for brook and cutthroat trout.

Just southwest of Fox is Crescent Lake, a long narrow reservoir that only fluctuates moderately. Camping areas are all around the lake, but scouts often have them occupied during the midsummer months. Angling usage is quite heavy at times. Best results may occur in the late evening while casting off the rocks. Cutthroat trout are the main species, but an occasional brookie may show up.

Other lakes in the Fox Lake area are Dollar, Brook and Divide. Dollar Lake is sometimes called Dime Lake. This aesthetic lake is in a large meadow 1 mile northwest of Fox, and features better-than-average campsites along with a generous supply of horse feed. A good number of pan-sized brookies inhabit the lake. As with the other lakes around here, Dollar sometimes receives heavy use from large groups that migrate from Fox Lake. Your best bet to escape the crowds is Brook Lake. It lies 1 mile east of Fox near the trail. Camping areas are available, and pressure is remarkably light.

***Remains of an old cabin at Fox Lake***

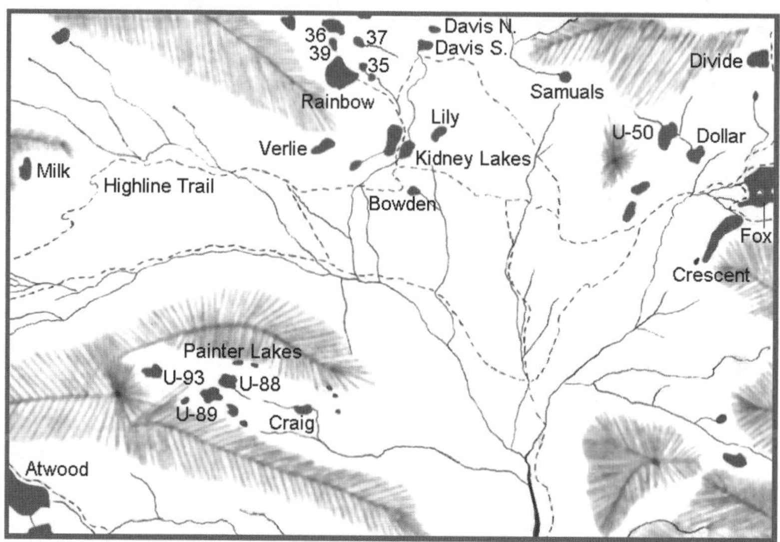

# Rock Lakes

| Trip Planner: | | | |
|---|---|---|---|
| Miles | 1.4 | Usage | Light |
| Elevation | 10,550 | Campsites | Fair |
| Elev. Gain | 350 | Springwater | Yes |
| Drainage | Whiterocks | Fishing | Good |
| Trailhead | Pole Creek | Horsefeed | Fair |
| Near Town | Roosevelt | Firewood | Good |

***Lower Rock Lake***

To Lower Rock Lake it is merely 1.4 miles. However, by the time you shuffle around all the dead fall, it will feel like two. There is no trail and lots of rocks add to the hindrance of this trek. Even though these lakes lie close to the proximity of the popular Pole Creek Campground, don't expect many people here. Obnoxious obstacles are appalling to social calls.

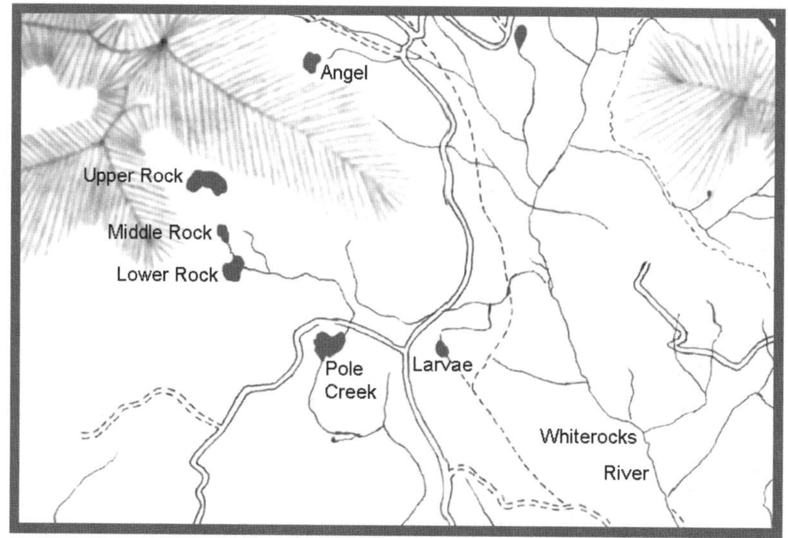


Find Rock Lakes by following the inlet of Pole Creek Lake up to a large meadow. Proceed along the south side of the meadow, then up a steep incline while embracing the outlet of Lower Rock Lake. Middle Rock Lake can be easily found by pursuing the inlet of Lower Rock, 200 yards north up a hill. Upper Rock sits across a nasty boulder field, ½ mile north of Middle Rock.

Although heavy timber and rock ledges surround Lower and Middle Rock Lakes, some open shoreline is accessible for fishing. The only decent camping areas are found near the center of a crevice on the west side of Lower Rock, and one other campsite presents itself along the east side of Middle Rock. Spring water is located on the southwest side of Lower Rock, but no other sources are known throughout this region. Angling should be best at Lower Rock Lake. Brook trout 10 to 14 inches are common. Middle Rock Lake does not receive good water circulation and is not deep enough to retain a respectable population of fish.

Upper Rock Lake sits in a shallow depression on a high flat bench. Many badgering boulders surround this lake while rock slides abut the water from the north. Open shorelines present good fly casting possibilities. But this lake withdraws fairly quickly during the summer months and most often winterkills. After all that's been said about this lake, you'll probably protest it. On the other hand, the scenery is nice, the solitude is great, and a "McDonalds" drive-in will sound rather appealing on your return trip. Well, maybe.

# Rasmussen Lakes

| Trip Planner: | | | |
|---|---|---|---|
| Miles | 1.8 | Usage | Light |
| Elevation | 10,473 | Campsites | Very Good |
| Elev. Gain | 470 | Springwater | No |
| Drainage | Whiterocks | Fishing | Good |
| Trailhead | West Fork | Horsefeed | Fair |
| Near Town | Whiterocks | Firewood | Good |

There's a lot of well kept secrets in these mountains, and here is one of them. Rasmussen Lakes offer solitude, fine camping, and good fishing. The only price you'll have to pay for all of this is less than two miles of cross-country hiking. Most likely, it's the cross-country part that keeps most visitors away. Whenever access is a little tricky, people seem to shy away. So, if you like to be alone, but don't like to hike very far, this could be for you.

To get to Rasmussen Lakes, follow West Fork Creek (starts near the trailhead), and just stay on the south side. The north bank has several inlets that will only serve to get you wet or side-tracked. After a steep rocky climb through thick pines, you will first come to Rasmussen Lake 2. You could camp here, but camping is better at Rasmussen Lake 1. Press on another quarter of a mile to the northwest.

At Rasmussen 1 there are many nice campsites to choose from, especially on the eastern side of the lake. There is no need to build a new campsite, so please don't. Horse access is possible, but there isn't much to feed them. As for drinking water, plan on bringing plenty or having some means of water purification. No reliable source of spring water exists.

Anglers will want to try both lakes. Each is stocked regularly with brook trout, and fishing pressure is light. This may be a good spot for a day hike mixed with a little fishing. It's certainly close enough to the trailhead for day use. For further adventure, check out Cirque Lake. It is only a half a mile southwest of Rasmussen Lakes, and was experimentally stocked with grayling. It may be good, or may not, but its picturesque glacial setting will certainly be worth more than the effort.

## *West Fork Whiterocks Trailhead*

WEST FORK TRAIL

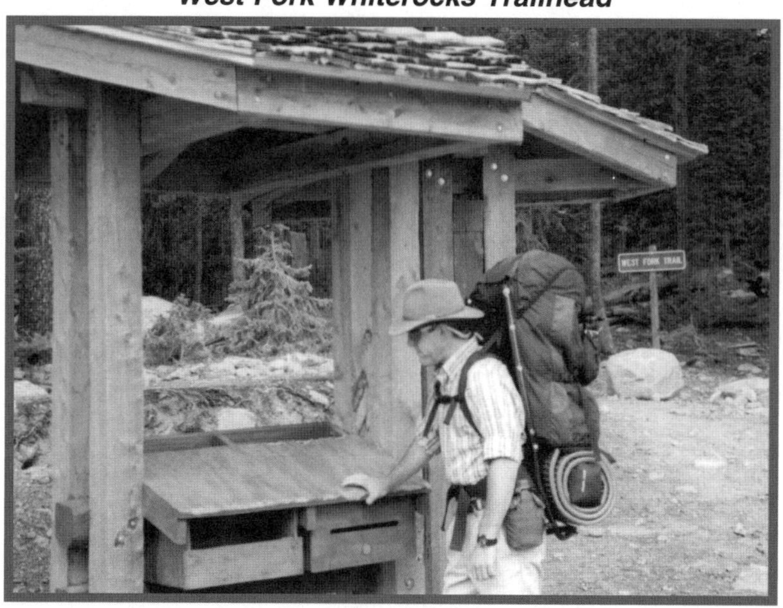

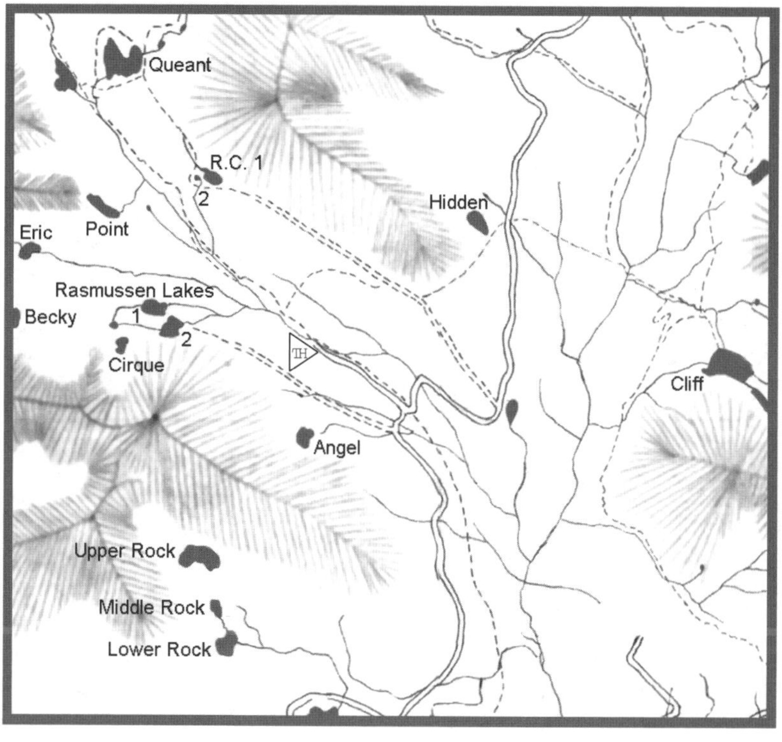
Queant
R.C. 1
2
Hidden
Eric
Point
Rasmussen Lakes
Becky
1
2
Cirque
TH
Cliff
Angel
Upper Rock
Middle Rock
Lower Rock

# Queant Lake

| Trip Planner: | | | |
|---|---|---|---|
| Miles | 5 | Usage | Heavy |
| Elevation | 10,652 | Campsites | Good |
| Elev. Gain | 650 | Springwater | Yes |
| Drainage | Whiterocks | Fishing | Fair |
| Trailhead | West Fork | Horsefeed | Excellent |
| Near Town | Whiterocks | Firewood | Limited |

A gentle hike, great camping, and a chance to get away from the masses....perhaps these are the reasons why Queant Lake is so popular. While you're likely to have neighbors here, its a whole lot better than spending the night with the RVs and roadside tenters. Besides, not all backpackers are loners. Many actually enjoy a little company, as long as backcountry etiquette is followed.

Queant Lake is big enough to handle the pressure. It's a long walk around its fifty-seven acres, and there are plenty of campsites, horse feed, and spring water. Look for the latter along the northern shore. You will have little difficulty finding a ready made camp. All you'll have to do is move in.

Queant Lake

If Queant doesn't suit your tastes, head north another 3/4 mile to Ogden Lake. It sees far fewer hikers than Queant, and offers just as many amenities. Campsites and horse feed are abundant, and a large spring flows into the north end.

Angling at Queant, Ogden, and Cleveland lakes may only be fair. This area does entertain a lot of fishermen. Plan on working a little harder here than you would on some of the more remote lakes, and stay with the basics. Small flies (#16) in the late evenings and early mornings should yield at least enough trout for a pleasant meal. There is also a good-looking stream below Queant that should produce some small trout.

Queant Lake is a great place to introduce someone to backpacking, particularly young boys. The trip is not taxing, and there is loads of room to run and explore without leaving the proximity of the lake. Everyone has to begin someplace, and Queant Lake provides an ideal setting for beginners. Hey, even us old-timers like a nice easy outing once in a while.

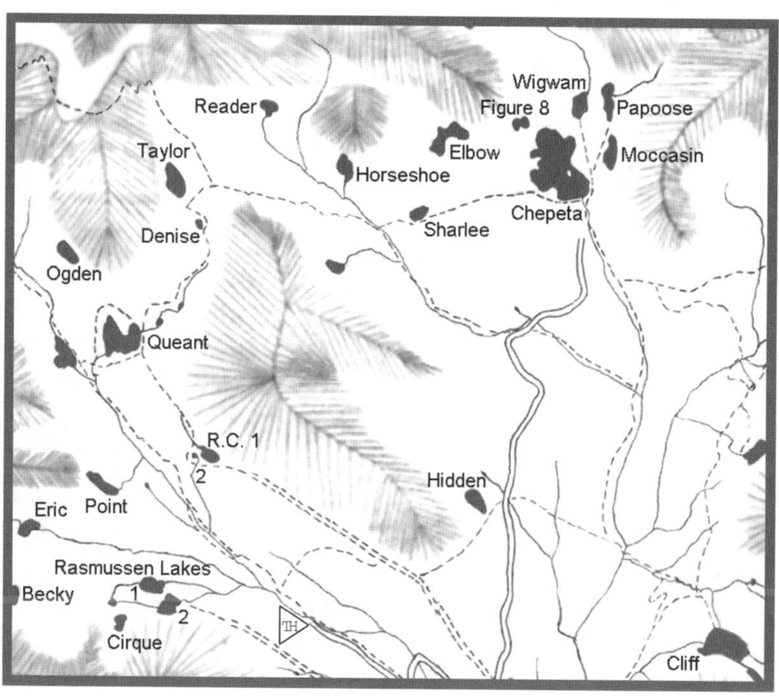

# Reader Lake

| Trip Planner: | | | |
|---|---|---|---|
| Miles | 4.2 | Usage | Light |
| Elevation | 10,960 | Campsites | Good |
| Elev. Gain | 420 | Springwater | Yes |
| Drainage | Whiterocks | Fishing | Poor |
| Trailhead | Chepeta Lake | Horsefeed | Fair |
| Near Town | Whiterocks | Firewood | Limited |

You might take a hint from this lake's name, and bring a good book to read. This is a good place to be alone and relax. Reader Lake is no longer managed as a fishery, and therefore sees few visitors. Here is a respite for the non-fishing backpacker.

Located at the head of Reader Lakes Basin, Reader Lake offers deluxe camping accommodations for the discriminating solitude seeker. Bubbling water, fresh from a mountain spring, is served up cold with every meal. The lake borders timberline and provides a wonderful alpine ambiance complete with light afternoon thundershowers and warm inviting sunsets. OK, OK, so it's not really as inviting as the travel brochure makes it sound. Reader Lake is subject to the same unpredictable weather, mosquitoes, and hazards as the other 1,000 Uinta lakes. It is better than some, and worse than others. However, it is seldom used, and is a fine place to shack out for a while and ignore the rest of the world. It's not always the aesthetic place we have described, but it might be.

To find Reader Lake, follow the Highline Trail west from the Chepeta Lake Trailhead about 2.5 miles until you reach Reader Creek. Staying on the west side of the creek, follow it northwest another mile and a half to Reader Lake. The lake is shallow and only ten acres in size. It may first appear as a large pond, but there are no other large ponds in the area to confuse it with.

As we mentioned, Reader Lake is not managed as a fishery. It has a history of winterkill. There may be a few stray brook trout that find their way up Reader Creek, so don't be surprised to see an occasional ring on the water from a feeding trout. But you'll probably be happier leaving your fishing pole in your backpack, and just keep on reading your good book.

***The results of a micro-burst, by the road to Chepeta Lake***

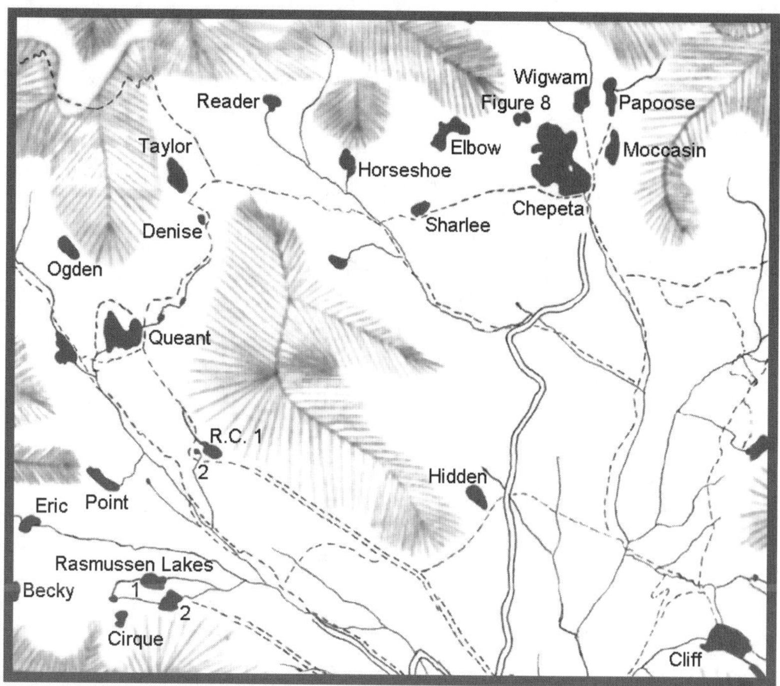

# Walk-up Lake

| Trip Planner: | | | |
|---|---|---|---|
| Miles | 3.8 | Usage | Very Light |
| Elevation | 11,114 | Campsites | Fair |
| Elev. Gain | 550 | Springwater | Yes |
| Drainage | Whiterocks | Fishing | Good |
| Trailhead | Chepeta Lake | Horsefeed | Poor |
| Near Town | Whiterocks | Firewood | Scarce |

Walk-up Lake is not as easy as its name implies. The easiest (but not easy) route is to first go to Papoose Lake, almost directly north of the trailhead. From there, hike northwest another couple of miles up steep rocky slopes and meadows. It is a little tricky picking your way through the boulders, so plan on a little extra time. You don't want to be in a hurry going through this country. It's both beautiful and treacherous.

Cirque lovers will adore this bowl carved out eons ago when glaciers ruled the High Uintas. Steep slopes drop sharply into the clear water, which reaches a depth of fifty-five feet. That's pretty

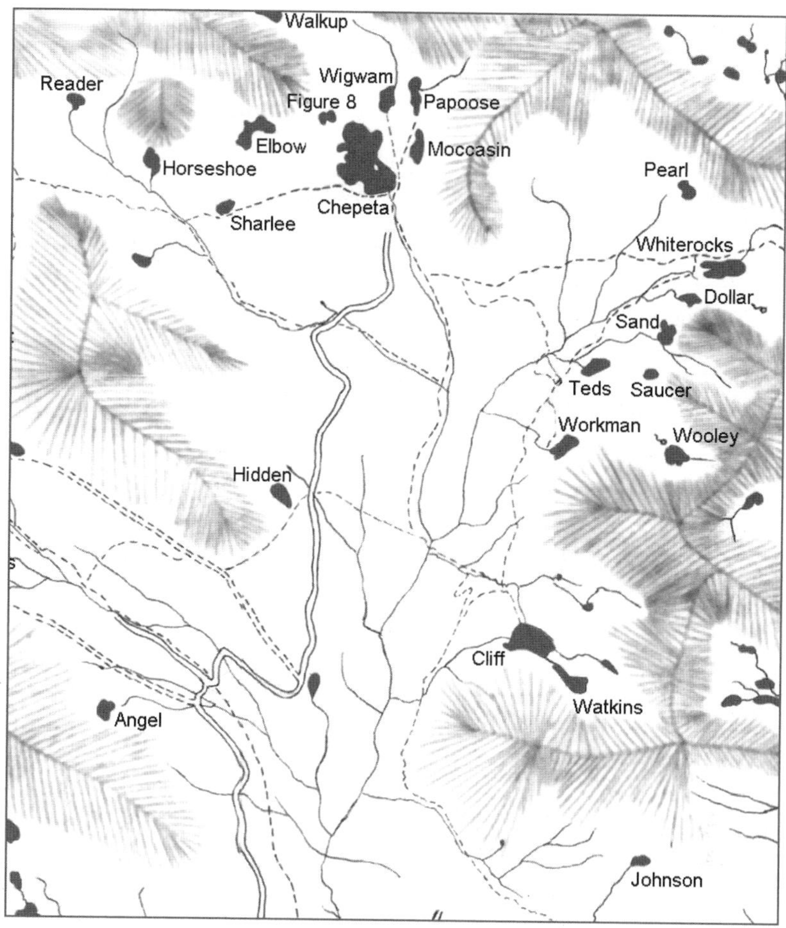


deep for a lake of only eighteen acres.

Solitude seekers should like this place. The lake sees very few visitors throughout the course of a year. You might expect it to receive considerable more pressure due to its close proximity to the popular Chepeta Lake. But its inaccessibility keeps it a quiet place. Despite its rugged access and appearance, there are some fair campsites found in grassy clearings just above the lake. Although, we wouldn't recommend this spot during a thunderstorm.

Brook trout are planted occasionally. On a lake this deep, fish are usually more selective and have more defined feeding times. Early mornings and late evenings are when you are likely to have success at Walk-up Lake. Don't expect too much if you take a day hike into here to try some mid-day angling.

# Cliff Lake (Whiterocks)

| Trip Planner: | | | |
|---|---|---|---|
| Miles | 5.6 | Usage | Light |
| Elevation | 10,348 | Campsites | Poor |
| Elev. Gain | -212 | Springwater | No |
| Drainage | Whiterocks | Fishing | Good |
| Trailhead | Chepeta Lake | Horsefeed | Poor |
| Near Town | Whiterocks | Firewood | Good |

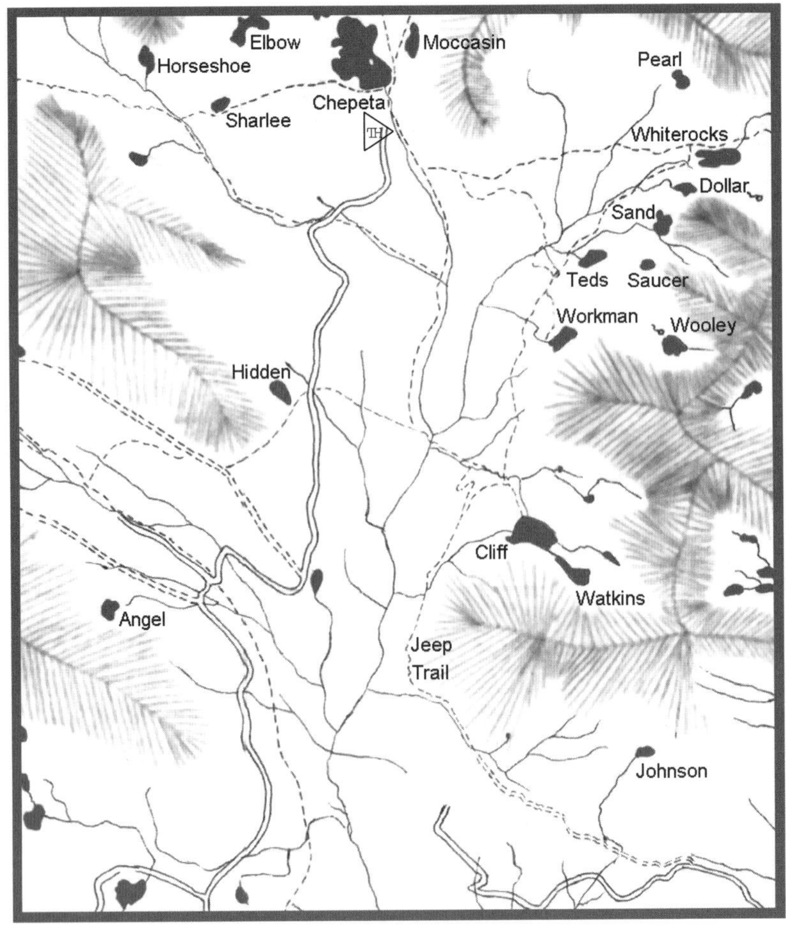

Cliff Lake can actually be reached by F.W.D. road. However, it is not advisable. Just beyond Johnson Creek, the road passes over several severe rough rock ledges. Then it circles around Dead Horse Park, only to complete its deformity at the lake. To say the least, this road will torture the toughest truck. From Paradise Park Campground, the road to Cliff Lake is graded for about 6 miles. Then the last 3 miles is considered a jeep road. Good luck!

Another alternate route can be accessed by way of Chepeta Lake. It is only 5.6 miles from here and offers more of a wilderness experience. Additional lakes can be unveiled along this trail. They are Sand, Teds, Workman, and Wooley. All of which are known to maintain excellent fly-fishing qualities and many good campsites. After you've visited these lakes, you'll wonder why go to Cliff Lake. Well, we don't know. There are no cozy camp spots and spring water is non-existent at the lake. However, Cliff Lake does get far less angling attention then any of the other lakes mentioned above.

***Cliff Lake from Cliff Peak***

# Paul Lake

| Trip Planner: | | | |
|---|---|---|---|
| Miles | 2 | Usage | Light |
| Elevation | 10,630 | Campsites | Good |
| Elev. Gain | 650 | Springwater | Unknown |
| Drainage | Ashley Creek | Fishing | Good |
| Trailhead | Paradise Park | Horsefeed | Poor |
| Near Town | Vernal | Firewood | Good |

***Paul Lake***

Fat brook trout inhabit Paul Lake, along with plenty of fresh water shrimp. The fish feed on shrimp, and grow big and finicky. You may want to try a piece of shrimp, or a small shrimp fly or scud may work better. Angling usage is light for now, but more and more people are getting good reports about Paul Lake.

The best access route follows the inlet of Paradise Park Reservoir to a small meadow. Then head north 1.5 miles up a rugged timbered incline to Little Elk Lake. From Little Elk, follow a poorly marked trail 1/4 mile north to Paul Lake. Paul is up on a level bench characterized by rugged timbered slopes and lots of rocks. Keep your map and compass handy when locating this lake. Campsites exist on the west shore, but horses won't find much to eat

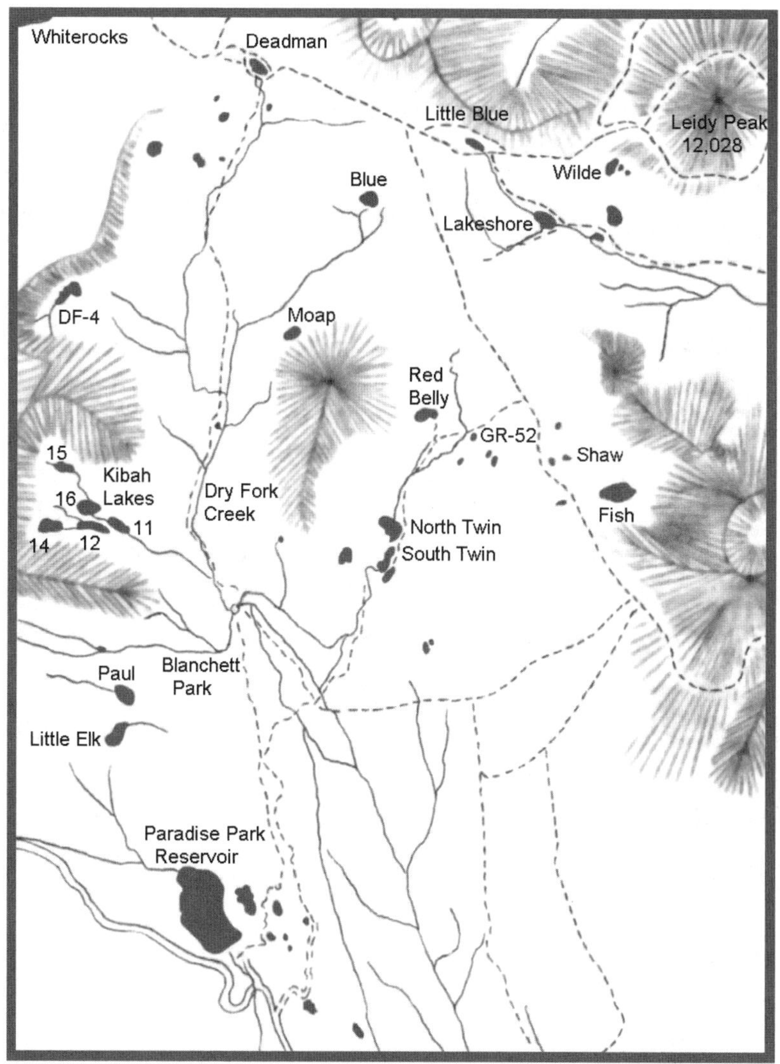


around here. This is an excellent short hike that offers great potential for fine fishing and solitude. That's a rare combination these days.

Nearby Little Elk Lake contains one good campsite at the south end. No fish or horse feed exists. But light camping use prevails due to the deluxe accommodations at Paradise Park.

For road directions, see Deadman Lake info.

# Kibah Lakes

| Trip Planner: | | | |
|---|---|---|---|
| Miles | 1 - 2 | Usage | Moderate |
| Elevation | 10,550 | Campsites | Poor |
| Elev. Gain | 450 | Springwater | No |
| Drainage | Ashley Creek | Fishing | Good |
| Trailhead | Blanchett Park | Horsefeed | Poor |
| Near Town | Vernal | Firewood | Good |

Since there are only poor campsites and horse access is nearly impossible, most people visiting Kibah Lakes are on day hikes from Blanchett Park. To reach Blanchett Park, follow a jeep road from Paradise Park Reservoir 4 miles north. Great camping areas and plenty of horse munchies are found at the park.

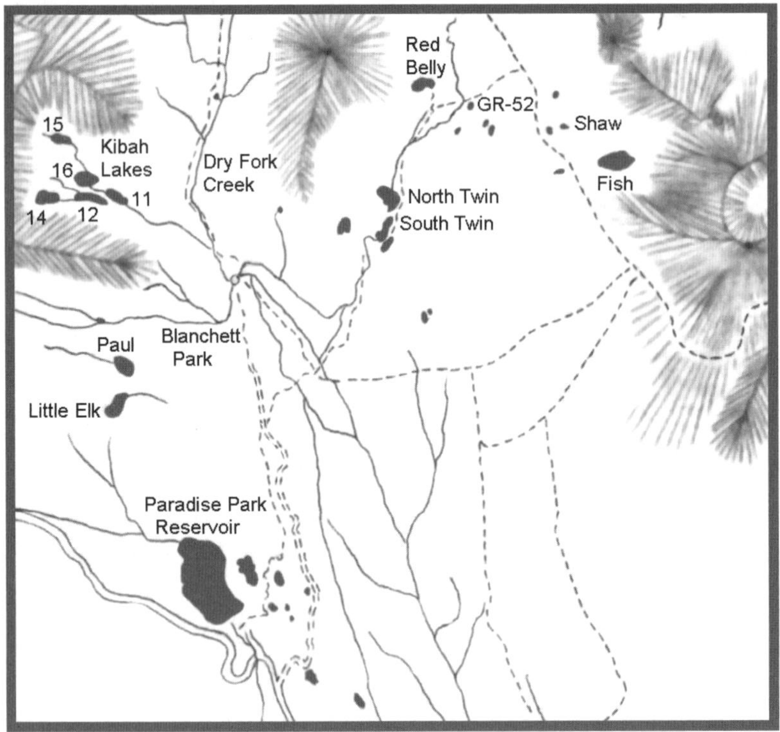

No real trail exists to Kibah Lakes. From Blanchett Park, go cross-country 1 mile northwest over some nasty boulder fields to East Kibah (DF-11). This lake is identified by a rock slide along the north shore and a wet meadow to the northwest. Fishing is spotty at times, but occasionally a large brook or rainbow trout can be netted.

Right next door to the southwest of East Kibah, sits Finger Kibah. This lake takes after its name as its shape portrays a finger. Angling should be a little faster here. Brook trout survive well in this lake, and a superb population is steadily maintained. A pan full of "finger lickin'" trout are in order here, so bring along your frying pan and stove.

***Kibah Lakes***

One half mile west of Finger Kibah, you'll find West Kibah Lake. It rests at the base of a talus slope in the southwest corner of Kibah Basin. Fishing usage is light to moderate for brook trout, and it is possible to camp overnight here utilizing a primitive campsite.

Three hundred yards northwest of East Kibah lies Island Kibah (DF-16). Surrounded by rocky timbered ridges, a small island protrudes from its shallow water. Angler use is moderate for brookies.

North Kibah (DF-15), is found about 1 mile northwest of East Kibah in the northwest corner of Kibah Basin. Because of low water levels during late summer, it tends to winterkill. However, this may be a good lake to catch some solitude.

# Deadman Lake

| Trip Planner: | | | |
|---|---|---|---|
| Miles | 5 | Usage | Heavy |
| Elevation | 10,790 | Campsites | Fair |
| Elev. Gain | 800 | Springwater | Unknown |
| Drainage | Ashley Creek | Fishing | Good |
| Trailhead | Blanchett Park | Horsefeed | Fair |
| Near Town | Roosevelt | Firewood | Scarce |

Road access for Deadman Lake is not listed in the trailhead directions of this book. So, we'll give it to you here. Begin your journey to Paradise Park at Roosevelt, Utah. Take State Route 121 north 10 miles to Neola. Keep following 121 another 14 miles east to the small community of LaPoint. From LaPoint, travel a paved road 7 miles north to a junction. Take the left-hand road 23 miles northwest to Paradise Park. You can start your trek here or drive another 4 miles to Blanchett Park via a fair 4WD road.

Deadman Lake

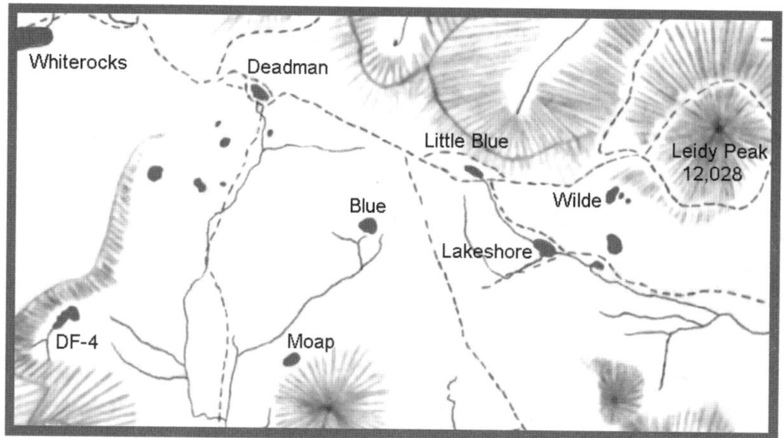


Deadman Lake can be reached from several access points, but the trail from Blanchett Park is the most feasible. This is a good Forest Service trail that splits in two different directions upon arriving at the lake. The east trail ventures over Gabbro Pass and into Lakeshore Basin, while the west trail disperses into Whiterocks, Beaver Creek and Carter Creek drainages.

Although Deadman Lake lies in unsheltered windy terrain, it gets frequent visits from scouts. A few fair campsites are found along the south shore, but horse feed is a scarce commodity. Three other lakes reside near the head of the Dry Fork Creek. From Deadman, these lakes are from 1.5 to 5 miles away.

Reach Blue Lake by traveling 1.5 miles southeast from Deadman Lake over a bald mountain. This scenic lake sits at the top of a windswept basin on the northeast side of Dry Fork. No campsites exist. Blue Lake contains an excellent supply of hungry brook trout. Watch out for sheep dip here. In the mid-summer months rotational sheep grazing depreciates the aesthetic value of this beautiful basin.

From Blue, another scenic lake is easily reached - Moap Lake. It is just a little over 1 mile south of Blue Lake at the base of a steep talus slope within a small cirque. No fish exist, but it's a beautiful spot for solitude seekers and hermits.

If remote fishing is what you're after, then DF-4 is your kind of lake. Find this lake by following Reynolds Creek 1 mile to its spring source. Then head 1 mile over rough boulders into a cirque basin. Due to the rugged terrain, no camping areas exist. Angler utilization is very light, and fishing is often hot for feisty cutthroat trout. Allow yourself plenty of time to get back to base camp before dark!

# North & South Twin Lakes

| Trip Planner: | | | |
|---|---|---|---|
| Miles | 5 | Usage | Heavy |
| Elevation | 10,300 | Campsites | Good |
| Elev. Gain | 300 | Springwater | Yes |
| Drainage | Ashley Creek | Fishing | Good |
| Trailhead | Paradise Park | Horsefeed | Good |
| Near Town | Vernal | Firewood | Fair |

***North Twin Lake***

Two different starting points can be used for reaching Twin Lakes. Blanchett Park is closer, but adventurers without a 4WD vehicle prefer the Paradise Park Trailhead. On the other hand, Blanchett Park offers great campsites for day hikers making the trek to Twin or Kibah Lakes. From Paradise Park, follow the Dry Fork trail 3.5 miles north to Dry Fork Creek. The Twin Lakes trail then heads 1.5 miles northeast to the lake. After the first mile past Paradise Park, the trail crosses several logging roads. During this two-mile stretch, the trail and rock cairns are difficult to locate.

Twin Lakes are in marshy terrain characterized by open meadows interspersed with timber. Although these lakes receive heavy usage, many camping areas are available, especially around South Twin Lake. However, spring water can only be found at North Twin. Horse feed is present at either lake, but South Twin has more. During the summer, angling usage remains steady, and fishing is usually good for brook and cutthroat trout.

If heavy pressure crimps your camping style, try Red Belly Lake. It receives a little less usage, but gets some day use from hikers staying at Twin Lakes. Red Belly is located 1 mile north of Twin Lakes on the Dry Fork trail. Campsites and horse feed are on the southeast side of the lake. Angling pressure is considered moderate for healthy cutthroat trout.

Another nice excursion from North Twin is Fish Lake. Begin near the east inlet of North Twin Lake. From the inlet, follow a hit-n-miss Forest Service trail 2.5 miles east to Fish. This pretty lake is at the foot of steep talus slopes on the west side of Marsh Peak. Meadows scattered with timber surround the outer portions of Fish Lake, along with good campsites and spring water. Heavy usage is usually encountered throughout July and August. However, natural reproduction enables cutthroat trout to survive the heavy pressure.

All of the lakes mentioned above are plagued by litterbugs. Please practice low-impact techniques, and leave this area better than you found it.

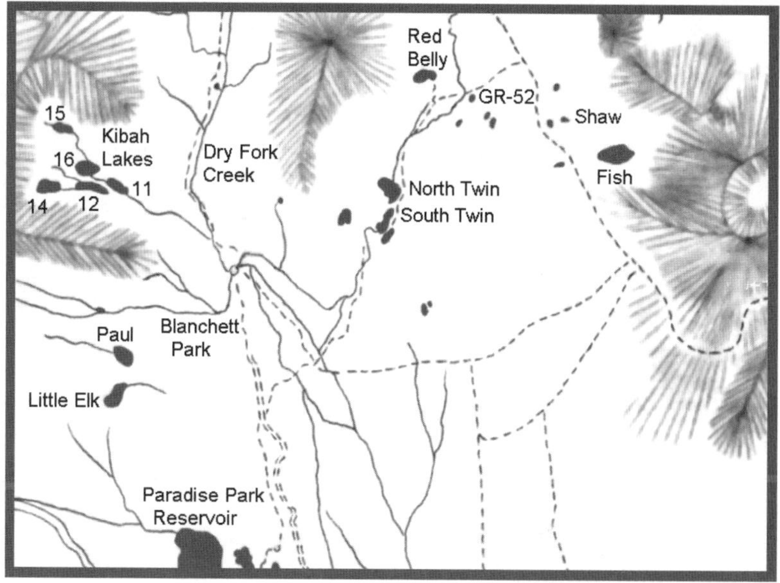

# Lakeshore Lake

| Trip Planner: | | | |
|---|---|---|---|
| Miles | 4.5 | Usage | Moderate |
| Elevation | 10,792 | Campsites | Good |
| Elev. Gain | -200 | Springwater | Yes |
| Drainage | Ashley Creek | Fishing | Fair |
| Trailhead | Hacking Lake | Horsefeed | Excellent |
| Near Town | Vernal | Firewood | Limited |

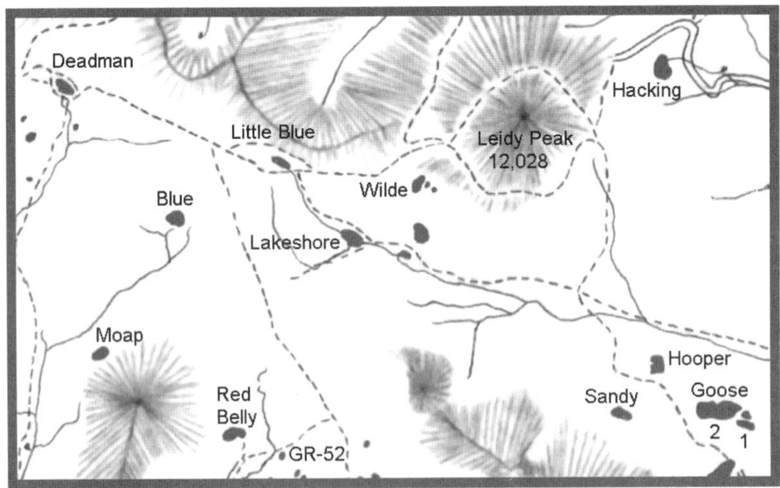


If sight-seeing is on your agenda, then Lakeshore is a great place to visit. This picture-perfect lake rests in a meadow encased by partly timbered slopes and rolling tundra. It reminded us of the scenery in the musical "The Sound of Music." You should have seen Brad running down the hill much like Julie Andrews.

The shortest route begins at the Highline Trailhead above Hacking Lake, while the other starts at Ashley Twin Lakes. Both trails are well marked, but the trail from Hacking Lake is difficult to follow as it goes around Leidy Peak. The Hacking Lake route is at least a mile shorter, and can be reached by car. Ashley Twin Lakes can only be reached by Jeep, after figuring out your way through a maze of brutally rocky roads. Take our word on this one - use the

Highline Trailhead by Hacking Lake.

Lakeshore Lake is named after the basin it's in. It is just off a good Forest Service trail in the upper end of Lakeshore Basin. Good campsites are present, along with an abundant supply of horse feed and spring water. However, sheep grazing can foul up the surrounding watershed. It would be a good idea to take precautions where drinking water is concerned.

Known as a decent fishing lake, Lakeshore holds a good population of small brook and cutthroat trout. Bring your frying pan. You should be able to catch enough for a tasty shore lunch.

Another lake in Lakeshore Basin is Little Blue. It is a cirque lake that sits on the trail one mile northwest of Lakeshore Lake at the base of Gabbro Pass. Do you like wind? You can have as much as you want here. During unsettled weather, the wind blows constantly and continues to blow even when you least expect it. No campsites or fish exist, but several springs pop up around the lake.

There seems to be plenty of confusion as to which lake is really Wilde Lake. The USGS maps name the lake we call Little Blue as Wilde Lake, as do the signs you'll encounter. But the DWR booklet describes it as we have in this book. We've gone with the DWR on other inconsistencies, so we will stick with them on this one too. They have been right more than wrong.

Take your time as you explore this wonderful wilderness - and definitely take your camera.

***Lakeshore Lake***

# North Erickson Lake

| Trip Planner: | | | |
|---|---|---|---|
| Miles | 2.8 | Usage | Moderate |
| Elevation | 10,020 | Campsites | Excellent |
| Elev. Gain | 200 | Springwater | Yes |
| Drainage | Weber | Fishing | Good |
| Trailhead | Upper Setting | Horsefeed | Fair |
| Near Town | Kamas | Firewood | Good |

North Erickson Lake sits at the head of Smith and Morehouse Creek in Erickson Basin. It can be reached from the Smith and Morehouse Trailhead, but it is easier to start hiking from the end of the Upper Setting Road in the Provo River Drainage. From there it is less than three miles to North Erickson on a good trail. You have to go over the mountain, but it's not very steep (as mountain passes go). Stay with the trail, or you might walk right past the lake. It is in a bit of a hole surrounded by pines.

The best campsites are on the west side of the lake, just off the trail. Springwater is plentiful around the lake. If you camp on the west side as suggested, there is an ice-cold spring that feeds into the southwest corner of the lake that will serve your water needs nicely.

South Erickson is just a hop, skip, and a jump to the south (1/4 mile). This pretty alpine lake abuts a talus slope, and provides some excellent photo opportunities, but camping and fishing are better at North Erickson Lake. Large slick rock formations are prevalent between the two lakes. It is worth the hike over to South Erickson just to experience the unique terrain.

Back at North Erickson, the fish await. Actually, you'll probably do most of the waiting. The fish seem to feed mostly at dusk and dawn, especially the big ones. Brook trout exceeding 18 inches in length and two pounds in weight can be caught if you're patient enough, and lucky enough. Try casting a small fly (#16 with a bubble) as far as you can. Be sure to use fresh supple line. Being able to cast long distances may make the difference of getting skunked or catching a few alpine lunkers. There aren't many lakes in the High Uintas capable of yielding trout as big as North Erickson Lake does, while requiring such a short, easy hike.

## *North Erickson Lake*

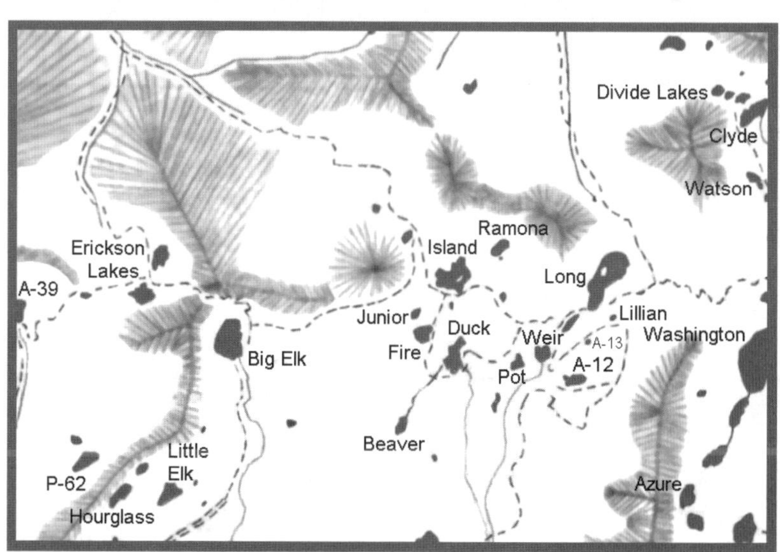

# Anchor Lake

| Trip Planner: | | | |
|---|---|---|---|
| Miles | 5.8 | Usage | Light |
| Elevation | 10,380 | Campsites | Good |
| Elev. Gain | 1,500 | Springwater | No |
| Drainage | Weber | Fishing | Very Good |
| Trailhead | None | Horsefeed | Poor |
| Near Town | Oakley | Firewood | Limited |

Get out the topographical map and your compass. There is a trail in some places, but for the most part you will depend on your cross-country travel skills. Start this hike at the end of the Gardner's Fork jeep road, which begins at the road that passes by Holiday Park. Don't look for a trailhead or a sign, because there isn't any. Just start bush-whacking. The mileage is listed at 5.8 miles, but due to some obscure trail, allow yourself ample time for some additional side-stepping and back tracking.

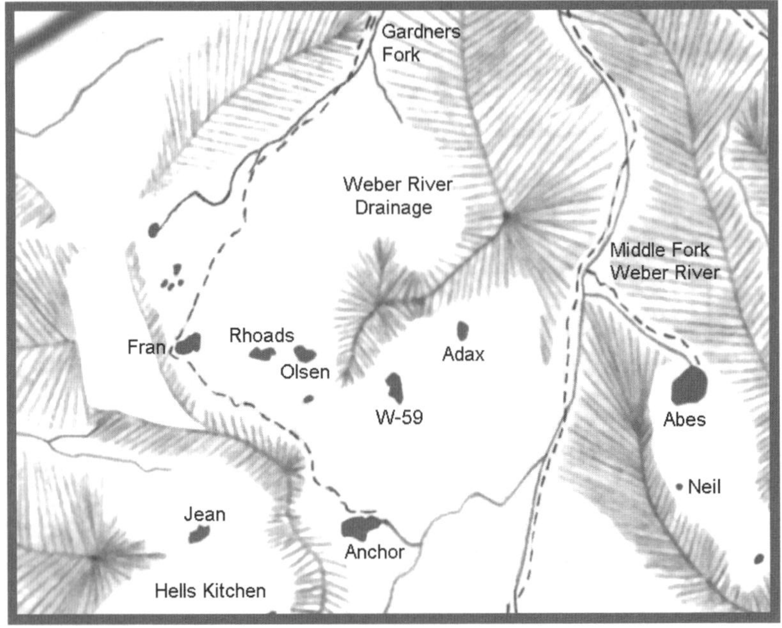

***Anchor Lake***

As you might of quessed, this area doesn't receive a lot of attention. Here is a great spot for solitude seekers. You could stay here a week, and probably not see anybody else. Fishermen will love it too. Anchor lake is loaded with pan-sized brook trout, and there is plenty of room for fly or spin casting. Try the outlet stream below Anchor Lake as well. It is full of brookies too. The stream drops rapidly for a couple hundred yards below the outlet, but then levels out for some fine spin fishing.

There are other angling opportunities in the area, but you'll have to hike a mile or two to take advantage of them. Adax Lake sits two miles to the northeast, and yields a lot of smallish brookies. And don't overlook W-59. This small lake can be red hot for chunky brook trout, if you hit it during the right time. W-59 can be tricky to locate, as it sits between two ridges. If you're not on top of either of these two ridges, you'll probably walk right by. You better have your topo map on hand again.

The Anchor Lake area offers a combination that is very rare in the High Uintas: solitude, great fishing, and low mileage. Let's hope we haven't spoiled a good thing by writing about it. It is a wonderful wilderness adventure.

# Abes Lake

| Trip Planner: | | | |
|---|---|---|---|
| Miles | 3.5 | Usage | Light |
| Elevation | 9,820 | Campsites | Fair |
| Elev. Gain | 950 | Springwater | Yes |
| Drainage | Weber | Fishing | Good |
| Trailhead | Holiday Park | Horsefeed | Poor |
| Near Town | Oakley | Firewood | Good |

***Abes Lake***

Abes Lake sits all alone, and you will likely be too if you take this short steep hike from Holiday Park. This lake can be a little tricky to locate, because you have to watch for a side trail that branches away from the main canyon about 2.5 miles up the trail. If you miss the cutoff, you will keep going up the Middle Fork of the Weber River until the trail peters out. The last mile to Abes Lake is the steep section, and you should be heading southeast.

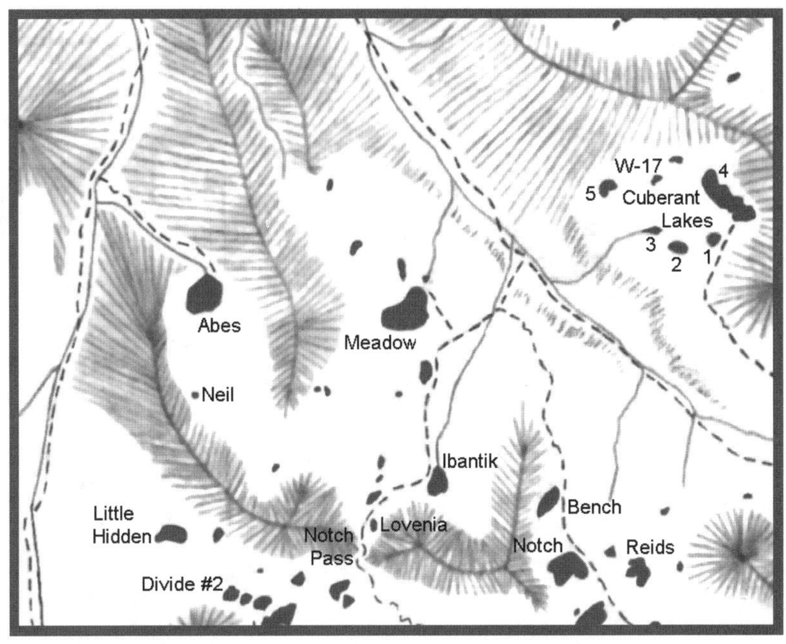


Camping at Abes Lake is limited. The terrain is rocky and uneven. Only small camps exists, with perhaps the best one being on the east side of the lake. But it's quiet here, and seldom used, so it can provide a wilderness experience with lots of firewood at your disposal. There is a small inlet on the south end. This is a good spot to refill water containers, but purifying is still recommended. The inlet is also a good place to find fish.

Cutthroat trout dominate these waters. They reach about 15 inches, but can be quite a challenge to catch. As with most larger fish, they are particular about the time of day and the offering. If you don't hit it just right, you may come away empty handed. There are good numbers of trout here, so just keep trying and you will eventually fill the frying pan.

There are not many other angling opportunities nearby. Tiny Neil Lake is half a mile south of Abes Lake, and may be good for small brookies.

These lakes are best reached by the trail from Holiday Park, but can also be found by heading west from Lovenia Lake over a rugged saddle, then descending 600 feet. Having done this route, we don't recommend it. It is not as easy as it looks on paper, and is certainly not an option by horseback.

# Fish Lake

| Trip Planner: | | | |
|---|---|---|---|
| Miles | 4.5 | Usage | Heavy |
| Elevation | 10,180 | Campsites | Fair |
| Elev. Gain | 2,200 | Springwater | No |
| Drainage | Weber River | Fishing | Good |
| Trailhead | Dry Fork | Horsefeed | Fair |
| Near Town | Kamas | Firewood | Limited |

***Fish Lake (Weber River Drainage)***

Despite the elevation gain, many enthusiastic people find the Dry fork loop trail a rewarding day hike. Backpackers with heavy loads usually avoid this steep rugged trail. But experienced horseback riders discover this trek isn't so difficult after all.

The main starting point is located on the east side of Holiday Park at the Dry Fork trailhead. The other connecting trail begins 1/2 mile south of the Dry Fork trailhead, but is hard to locate unless you've made this trip before. From the Dry Fork trailhead, follow a well marked trail two miles east to a shallow river crossing. At this point the trail twists another 1.5 miles southeast up a 1,300 foot incline to Round Lake. A large outlet releases a good supply of water that provides a wanna-be waterfall that crosses the trail just before arrival. This small lake has good campsites all around it, but it's heavily used and degraded by refuse.

Following the loop trail 1/2 mile east to Sand Lake, you'll obtain the privilege of being hosted by righteous scenery composed of beautiful timbered mountains and distant peaks. Sand has only a couple of good campsites and no spring water, but fishing is fast and furious for small grayling.

Arctic grayling inhabit Fish Lake too. This lake sits another 1/2 mile south on the loop trail from Sand. Fish Lake is surrounded by alpine mountains and pretty talus slopes that abut the water from the west. Running water is plentiful at three different outlets, but camping areas are limited due to rocky terrain. Angling is only fair but could be better in an inflatable raft.

Leaving Fish Lake, the loop trail proceeds west and up across a steep incline to the top of a scenic ridge. From here a hit-n-miss trail gradually declines down the ridge top for about 3 miles. A well defined trail then drops off the south side of the ridge and down a steep incline, intersecting with a logging road that winds down to the Dry Fork trailhead. Total distance around the loop is 9 miles.

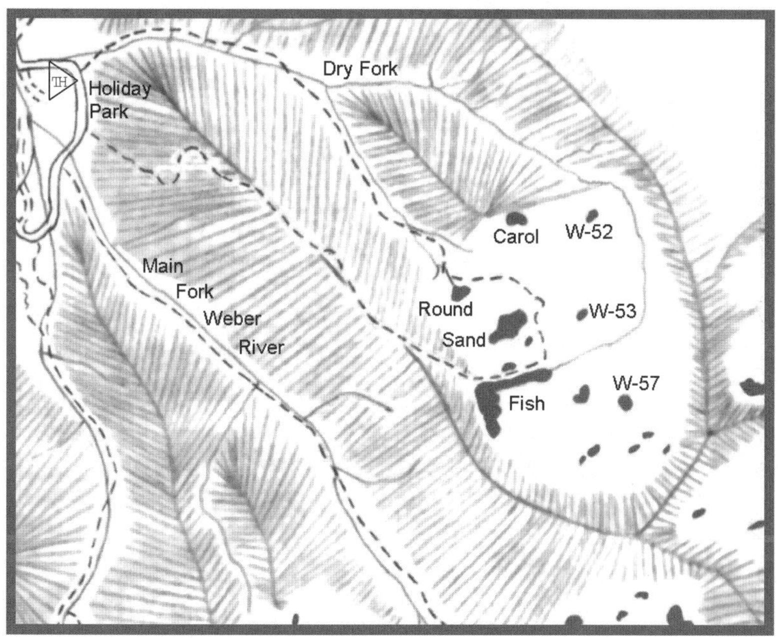

# Notch Lake

| Trip Planner: | | | |
|---|---|---|---|
| Miles | 2.3 | Usage | Heavy |
| Elevation | 10,300 | Campsites | Good |
| Elev. Gain | -500 | Springwater | Yes |
| Drainage | Weber | Fishing | Fair |
| Trailhead | Bald Mtn. | Horsefeed | Fair |
| Near Town | Kamas | Firewood | Limited |

Going down anyone? Boy, you sure don't find many hikes like this one in the High Uintas. You actually get to hike downhill on the hike in. A fast hiker should be able to cover the entire distance in an hour. But coming back out may be a bit slower as you'll have to make up 500 feet of elevation.

Notch Lake lies at the east base of Notch Mountain, and is visible from the trail. It is actually a reservoir that fluctuates quite a bit as the summer gets longer. Notch usually drops over twenty feet, and loses about half of its surface size. Campsites are abundant and spacious, so don't worry about a place to stay, although you might have some company. Spring water flows just west of the lake.

Notch is stocked with brook trout, but heavy pressure is to blame for only fair fishing. Bait fishermen can expect to have some luck here, as well as fly fishermen. Many high country lakes offer poor fishing for bait anglers, but Notch is one of the exceptions.

There are a couple of other lakes nearby. Give them a try if Notch doesn't fill your needs. Bench Lake is just half a mile north, and Dean Lake is half a mile south of Notch Lake. Bench lake often winterkills, but receives far less camping pressure. This scenic alpine lake is a great place for a small party to camp if you don't care if you catch fish.

If you don't want to hike back up to the trailhead, then park another vehicle at the Crystal Lake Trailhead near Trial Lake. From Notch Lake, follow the trail north a couple of miles around the mountain, then south over Notch Pass (gorgeous), and then down to the Crystal Lake Trailhead. The entire loop, from Bald Mountain Trailhead to Crystal Lake Trailhead, makes an easy and scenic day hike. After all, it's downhill almost all the way.

***Bench Lake***

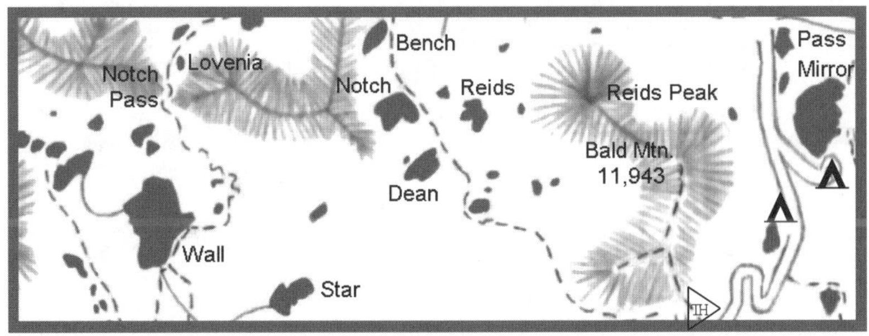

Bench
Lovenia
Notch
Pass
Notch
Reids
Reids Peak
Pass
Mirror
Bald Mtn.
11,943
Dean
Wall
Star
TH

# Ibantik Lake

| Trip Planner: | | | |
|---|---|---|---|
| Miles | 3.3 | Usage | Heavy |
| Elevation | 10,100 | Campsites | Good |
| Elev. Gain | 80 | Springwater | No |
| Drainage | Weber | Fishing | Fair |
| Trailhead | Crystal Lake | Horsefeed | Poor |
| Near Town | Kamas | Firewood | Scarce |

The trail goes right over Notch Pass. Even if you don't visit Ibantik Lake, you ought to hike to the top of Notch Pass and gaze into the deep turquoise depths of Lovenia Lake directly below. Absolutely gorgeous! Words cannot describe its beauty. Pictures cannot depict its depth, nor the feeling you get at the top of a cliff looking down. The view is a must for hikers searching for awesome alpine scenery. Campsites exist at Lovenia Lake, but there are better ones and fewer people at Ibantik.

There is more room for the crowds to disperse once you reach Ibantik Lake. It is well suited for a half-a-day hike, or a quick overnighter. Some backpackers can't get to the trailhead until the evening. Ibantik might be ideal for someone getting a late start, as it is easily reached within two hours of Crystal Lake Trailhead.

Day fisherman frequently try their luck in this area. Lovenia, Ibantik, and Meadow Lake to the north all receive frequent plants of brook and cutthroat trout. The fishing may be good or poor, depending on the time of year, the time of day, or your own fishing skill. Keep in mind that these lakes get heavy pressure, so don't be surprised if many of the fish are wary or already caught.

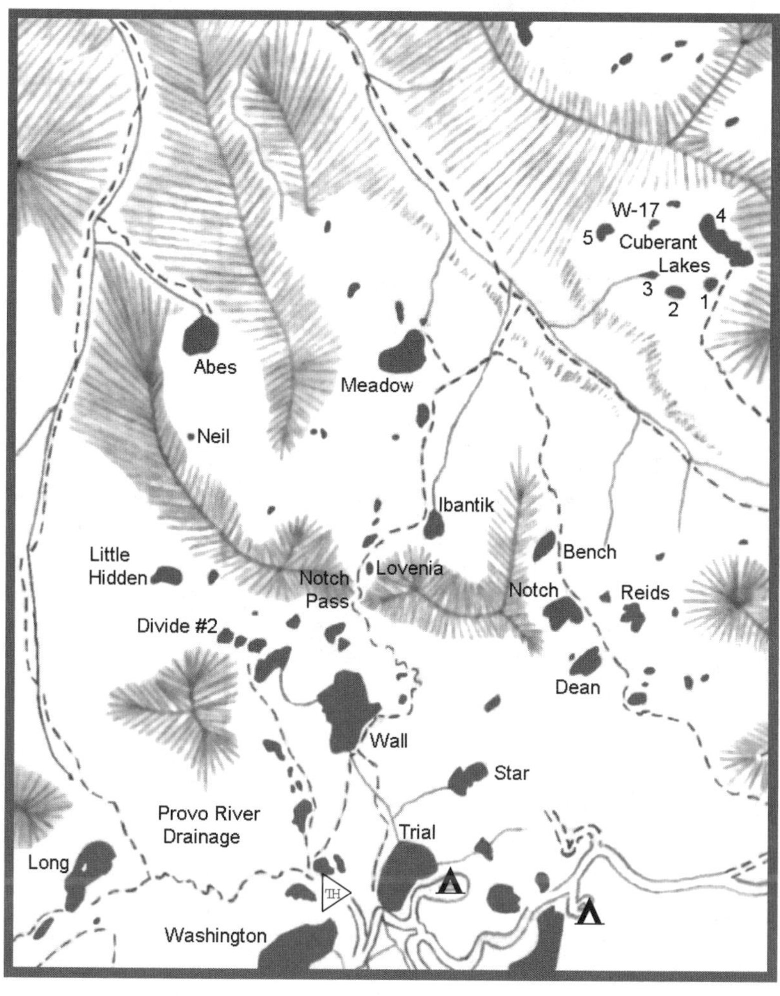

# Cuberant Lakes

| Trip Planner: | | | |
|---|---|---|---|
| Miles | 2.5 | Usage | Moderate |
| Elevation | 10,420 | Campsites | Very Good |
| Elev. Gain | 320 | Springwater | No |
| Drainage | Weber | Fishing | Good |
| Trailhead | Pass Lake | Horsefeed | Good |
| Near Town | Kamas | Firewood | Good |

The statistics above are for Cuberant Lake #2, which is the best place to camp among the five Cuberant Lakes. However, you may want to camp at #3. It is the only lake around with possible spring water. These lakes are all a little different from one another, and whether you are on a day hike or an overnighter, it is rewarding to experience each one and enjoy what each has to offer. Most of the lakes are nestled in the pines, except for #4 which sits against a talus slope in a "picture book" setting. Lake #4 is by far the largest and deepest of the Cuberant Lakes.

This is a relatively short and easy hike for these mountains. Park at the Pass Lake Trailhead, just across the road from Pass Lake. Or park at Pass Lake and catch the trail behind the guard rail

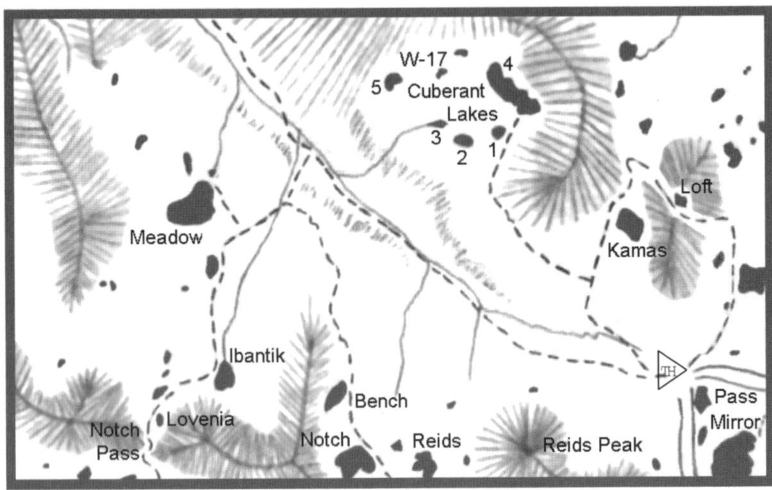

***Cuberant Lake #4***

where the road makes a 90 degree turn. Watch the trail signs closely, because before long you'll be branching off of the main trail (north) towards Kamas Lake, and then after another 1/2 mile take another fork northwest leading to Cuberant Lakes. If all goes according to plan, you will arrive at Cuberant Lake #1 first.

Fishing is generally good at these lakes for mostly pan-sized cutthroat and brook trout, although a few large fish can occasionally be fooled. All of the lakes, except #5, are stocked regularly. A fly and bubble combination is effective around here. The fish like tiny flies, but there isn't much space for traditional fly casting. The conifers surrounding these lake are notorious for gobbling up ill-presented flies. But the pines offer camouflage that can be used to your advantage when stalking wary trout in these small lakes.

If you like the calm, shade, quiet, and of lots of pine trees, then you will enjoy the Cuberant Basin. It's a great place to catch a nap and a few trout. Bring along the mosquito repellent, because there won't be much wind to help keep the bugs at bay.

# Ruth Lake

| Trip Planner: | | | |
|---|---|---|---|
| Miles | .8 | Usage | Heavy |
| Elevation | 10,340 | Campsites | Good |
| Elev. Gain | 200 | Springwater | Yes |
| Drainage | Bear River | Fishing | Good |
| Trailhead | Ruth Lake | Horsefeed | Fair |
| Near Town | Evanston | Firewood | Limited |

When you get to Ruth Lake, don't forget to look behind you. Hayden Peak looms larger than life just across the canyon to the west. The view from Ruth Lake is a must for shutter-bugs looking for some real photo trophies. You'll want to hang this one on your wall.

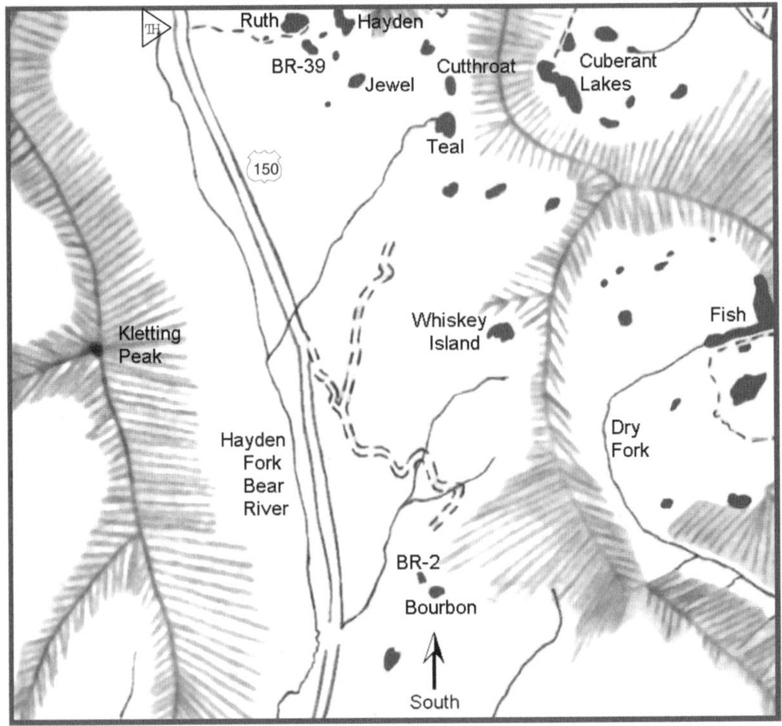

***Ruth Lake and Hayden Peak***

The hike to Ruth Lake begins at the Ruth Lake Trailhead, which is nothing more than a roadside pull-off with a sign pointing to Ruth Lake. There is only room for a few cars to park here. This is a short easy hike that even kids enjoy. The trail is well maintained, and there is a variety of natural sights along the way. Everything from miniature meadows and waterfalls to playful chipmunks are scattered along this hike that covers only 3/4 of a mile each way. Of course you can go further if you like. There are several other small lakes in the area. You can spend just a couple of hours, or a couple of days exploring this basin. The trail dissolves at Ruth Lake though, so have your map and compass handy if you're continuing on.

Camping and fishing pressure is heavy at Ruth Lake, but the crowds fan out past this point. The fish in these parts see mostly day use anglers. If you are one of them, try to be fishing during the most productive times - early morning or late evening. The hike in/out is short enough that you should have no problem managing your hike around prime fishing hours. If it's fish you're after, don't stop at Ruth Lake very long. You will probably have better success at nearby lakes such as Hayden, Cutthroat, Jewel, and Teal.

As with any popular area, litter can be a problem. But this area seems to be well preserved. Let's keep it that way. Pack out what you pack in, and avoid building any new fire rings.

# Whiskey Island

| Trip Planner: | | | |
|---|---|---|---|
| Miles | 1.3 | Usage | Light |
| Elevation | 10,340 | Campsites | Fair |
| Elev. Gain | 350 | Springwater | No |
| Drainage | Bear River | Fishing | Poor |
| Trailhead | N/A | Horsefeed | Poor |
| Near Town | Evanston | Firewood | Limited |

Alright, who names these lakes anyway? With Bourbon Lake and Whiskey Springs close by, someone must have been on an all-nighter when it came time to naming these. Solitude seekers will enjoy Whiskey Island. Few visit this rugged basin, but those who do will say it's easily worth the trip - for the aesthetics. If you're looking for a short interesting hike, where you can really get away from everyone, then this is a good bet. It's quiet. You can meditate. Maybe you'll catch a glimpse of an eagle riding the up-draft by the steep talus ridge. Most certainly you could tan (or burn) yourself, just laying back next to the turquiose waters.

Whiskey Island can be real tough to reach. If you choose the most direct route, you'll run right into several tricky boulder fields and deadfall timber. Instead, stay close to the mountain, and you should be able to skirt around all the trouble. There is no trail, so keep your map and compass handy. But you really can't miss this glacial cirque, if you just follow the bottom of the ridge.

As for fishing, who knows what to expect. The old Utah state record for grayling was caught here, but when we visited there were no signs of fish. The lake does have a history of winterkill. There are no other fishing opportunities in the immediate area, unless you go all the way back to where you started hiking, and drop into Bourbon Lake.

Those into mountaineering should enjoy this trek. Immediately to the northwest of Whiskey Island is a "chute" that will allow a steep climb to the ridge top. From the top you can see down the other side into the Dry Fork arm of the Weber River Drainage. That's Fish Lake in the distance. Looking back towards towards Whiskey Island is another incredible view. Notice the boulder fields that you hopefully avoided on your way in.

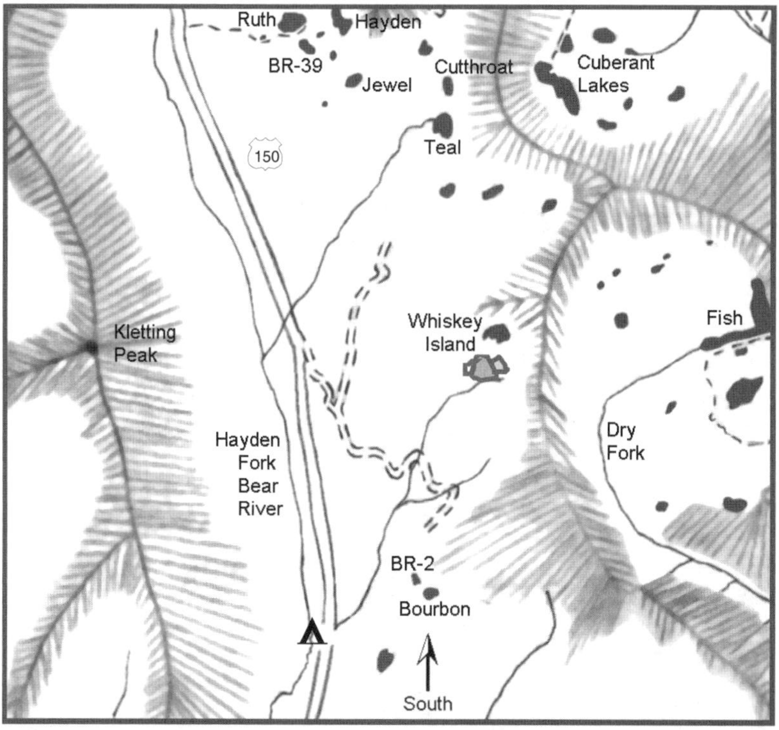

***Whiskey Island Lake***

# Hell Hole Lake

| Trip Planner: | | | |
|---|---|---|---|
| Miles | 5.0 | Usage | Moderate |
| Elevation | 10,340 | Campsites | Excellent |
| Elev. Gain | 1550 | Springwater | Yes |
| Drainage | Bear River | Fishing | Good |
| Trail | Main Fork | Horsefeed | Excellent |
| Near Town | Evanston | Firewood | Good |

*Hell Hole Lake*

Hell Hole is a gamble if you're a fisherman. Some years it's hot, and some years it's not. It all depends on the planting schedules, winter survival, and catch and release rates. It is a relatively small lake (8.5 acres), and could be fished out if people keep more than they eat for dinner. Most of the lake is shallow, which makes for good morning and evening fishing for healthy cutthroat trout. During midday the only feasible spot to fish is the deeper northeast corner of the lake. A small rubber raft may be worthwhile here. Maybe there are deeper holes out in the middle that the fish retreat to during the day. No other fishing opportunities exist nearby if Hell Hole doesn't produce.

But Hell Hole does have a lot to offer, especially if you are looking for a short weekend trip. Excellent campsites are available for backpackers and horsemen. The latter would probably prefer the east side of the lake for horsefeed, while backpackers should like the west side and its pine-sheltered camps. A good spring flows into the northeast corner of the lake.

The unmarked trail starts just off Highway 150. Look right across the road from the Gold Hill turnoff. It is a five mile hike, but you can cut that to about four if you have a four-wheel drive vehicle, and you are willing to brave a very muddy stream crossing. We opted for the extra hiking rather than risk getting stuck. Even if it looks favorable for crossing, remember you will have to cross it again coming out. Should a storm move in, things could turn awfully boggy in a hurry.

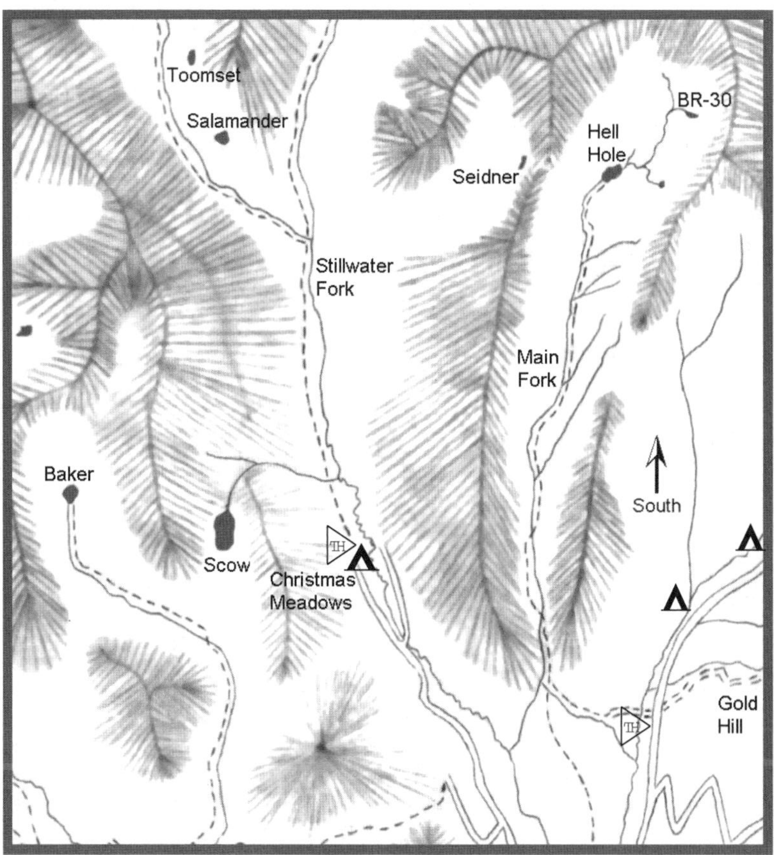

# Ryder & McPheters Lakes

| Trip Planner: | | | |
|---|---|---|---|
| Miles | 8.5 | Usage | Moderate |
| Elevation | 10,620 | Campsites | Good |
| Elev. Gain | 1,920 | Springwater | Yes |
| Drainage | Bear River | Fishing | Good |
| Trailhead | Christmas Meadows | Horsefeed | Good |
| Near Town | Evanston | Firewood | Limited |

As elaborate as it may seem, the Stillwater Trail is a little deceiving as far as the difficulty of this hike is concerned. It's not the elevation gain that will discourage the soul, but lots of rocks and many mudholes may dampen spirits. The trail does pick up some altitude. However, it is an effortless climb until the Ryder - Kermsuh junction. Then the trail proceeds up, up and up.

Ryder and McPheters occupy Middle Basin, and Mt. Agassiz, Spread Eagle, and Hayden are the dominate surrounding peaks. Ryder sits at the foot of three connecting ridges characterized by wind and steep rocky ledges. Beautiful meadows intersperse the

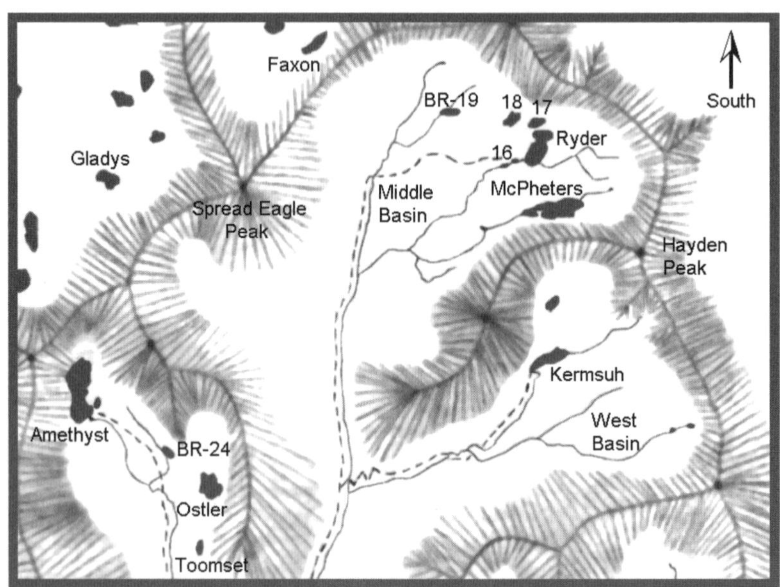

***Ryder Lake***

pines, while trickles of water cascade off the cliffs, adding to the artistic value.

Access begins at the south end of Christmas Meadows Campground. An excellent trail parallels the Stillwater River all the way to Middle Basin. The last 1.5 miles of the trail departs from the river and is hard to follow, but rock cairns clearly mark the way.

Other lakes in the vicinity are BR-17 & 18. These lakes are located on the south side of Ryder where you'll find good campsites and an abundant supply of springwater. BR-17 & 18 also contain good populations of brook trout, and only receive half the angling pressure of Ryder.

Another popular fishing hole is McPheters. This lake is located 1/2 mile north of Ryder on some bedrock shelves next to a talus slope. Campsites are not present in the immediate vicinity but can be found nearby. Due to open terrain, firewood is extremely sparse, but can be gathered near the camping areas to the south. Plenty of spring water endows McPheters, along with pan-sized cutthroat trout.

If solitude is what your lookin' for, Meadow Lake (BR-19) is a good one to visit. Meadow sits 1/2 mile east of BR-18 in rocky timbered country. This lake plays host to good camping areas and excellent spring water. Deep water channels circulate through the middle of this shallow lake, which may produce fairly good fishing.

# Kermsuh Lake

| Trip Planner: | | | |
|---|---|---|---|
| Miles | 6.8 | Usage | Light |
| Elevation | 10,300 | Campsites | Poor |
| Elev. Gain | 1,600 | Springwater | Yes |
| Drainage | Bear River | Fishing | Fair |
| Trailhead | Christmas Meadows | Horsefeed | Good |
| Near Town | Evanston | Firewood | Good |

***Kermsuh Lake and Hayden Peak***

Do ya wanna get lost? No, were not talking about losing your destination or drinking too much hooch. But we are contemplating losing the vast majority of crowds that trample the Stillwater Trail. Kermsuh is a gorgeous isolated lake situated in rocky timbered country just inside the wilderness area. Upon arrival you'll be greeted by several high peaks including Hayden, Kletting and A-1. These major peaks have connecting ridges that almost completely enclose the West Basin. This feature, and the fact that Kermsuh is the only lake in the basin, makes the area a remote and peaceful place.

From Christmas Meadows follow the Stillwater Fork trail 4.5 miles to a posted sign at the Kermsuh/Ryder junction. The Kermsuh Lake trail heads southwest to and across a narrow footbridge that scaffolds over the Stillwater Fork River. After the river crossing, several steep switchbacks are encountered, and startling scenes of a deep river gorge can be spotted at the ends of every other cut-back. The trail then gradually climbs to a marshy meadow where rock cairns, tree blazes, and short segments of trail mark the rest of the way.

Kermsuh is mostly visited by day hikers. This trek may be questionable for a day hike, but we think it is right on the border line of what is and what isn't. Allow yourself at least eight hours for a single day excursion, including half an hour for a shoreline lunch and a couple of fifteen minute breaks. A healthy hiker can make the round trip in eight hours, but allow yourself extra time for fishing or whatever.

Angling pressure is usually very light for native cutthroats in the 12 inch class. Fishing is unpredictable, but has been known to be good in the early summer months. Due to the rocky terrain that surrounds this lake, no decent campsites exist. Running water is no problem here, and horse feed can be found at a small meadow to the south.

This one is for the solitude seeker or the explorer. Go seek!

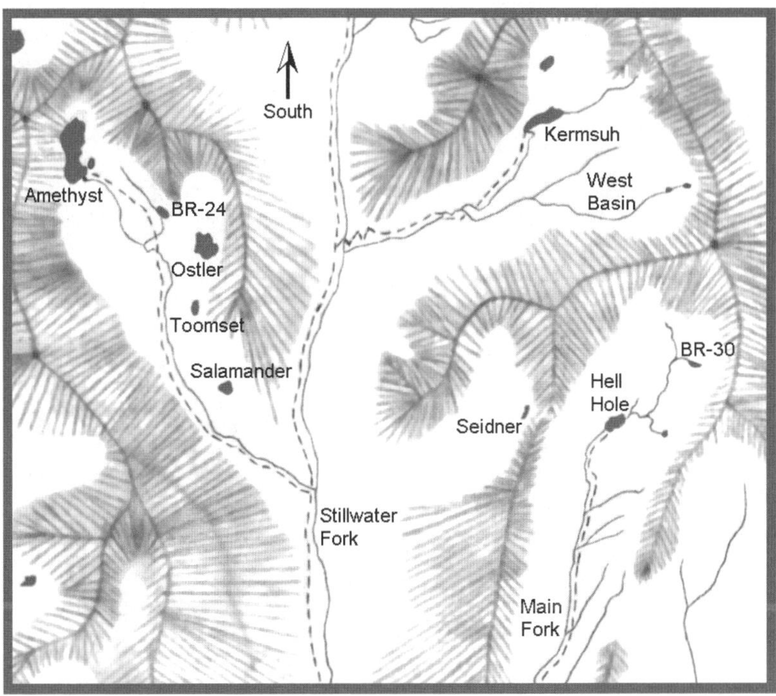

# Amethyst Lake

| Trip Planner: | | | |
|---|---|---|---|
| Miles | 5.8 | Usage | Moderate |
| Elevation | 10,750 | Campsites | Fair |
| Elev. Gain | 2,050 | Springwater | Yes |
| Drainage | Bear River | Fishing | Excellent |
| Trailhead | Christmas Meadows | Horsefeed | Fair |
| Near Town | Evanston | Firewood | Poor |

Set in the top of a glacial cirque, this is one of the prettiest alpine lakes. A few small pines dot its shores, and the massive cliffs and talus slopes add grandeur to the emerald green waters. This large lake (42.5 acres) attracts moderate crowds because of its scenery and frequently fast fishing. The hike in is only 5.8 miles, but seems longer. Two thousand feet of elevation is a lot to gain in such a short

***Amethyst Lake***

distance. The trail starts at beautiful Christmas Meadows, and is maintained well for the entire hike. It parallels the Stillwater Fork of the Bear River most of the way, which presents many tempting fishing holes. There's a lot to see along the route, so take your time and enjoy the hike.

Brook trout are active all around Amethyst Lake, but the best spots seem to be on the east side or the deeper southwest corner. Small flies draw attention on about every other cast, and even more regularly during the evening. During midday, try small spinners in the deeper sections. You'll have no trouble filling the frying pan here, but this is not the best place to setup your kitchen.

Excellent campsites are available at BR-24 about a mile below Amethyst Lake. This tiny lake is also emerald in color due to glacial turbidity. Several springs emerge here, and horse pasture is close by in the lower meadows. There is a small population of cutthroats, but don't plan on them for dinner. They are extremely wary. Firewood is limited, unless you care to walk west into the woods a few hundred yards.

Ostler Lake, 1/2 mile to the northwest of BR-24, should have fewer people if you are looking to be alone. It has a few rough campgrounds and several springs. Cutthroats and brookies grow larger at Ostler, so don't be surprised if you hook into one well over a pound. However, fishing is kind of slow, especially when compared to Amethyst Lake.

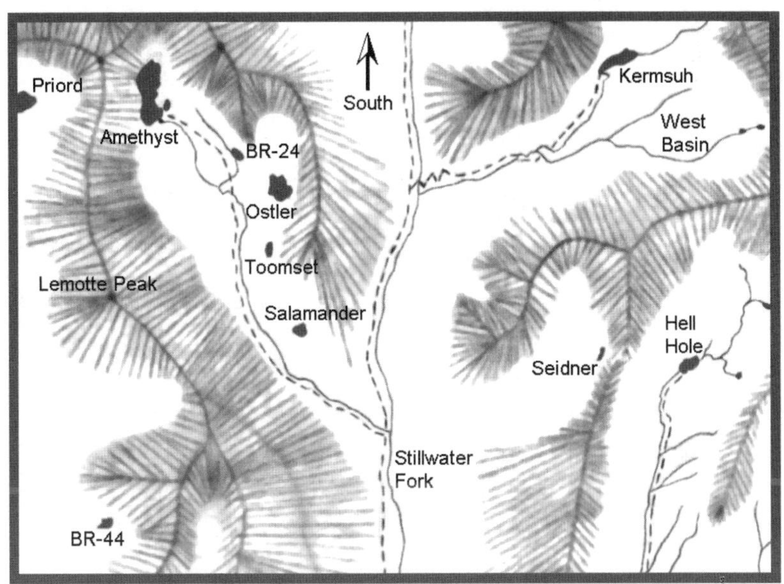

# Lake BR-24

| Trip Planner: | | | |
|---|---|---|---|
| Miles | 5.3 | Usage | Moderate |
| Elevation | 10,460 | Campsites | Excellent |
| Elev. Gain | 1,750 | Springwater | Yes |
| Drainage | Bear River | Fishing | Good |
| Trailhead | Christmas Meadows | Horsefeed | Good |
| Near Town | Evanston | Firewood | Fair |

In honor of all the great nameless lakes in the High Uintas, we just had to spotlight one of the best. Some of the lakes without names are the least visited, and so they have become some of the real jewels of the High Uintas. If solitude and a chance for some unspoiled fishing rank high on your list, then try the lakes with no names, especially the ones with no trails.

Well, we've just told you what to look for in a nameless lake, and BR-24 doesn't seem to fit the stereotype. It receives its share of visitors, its few fish are wary, and the main trail passes right by it. But

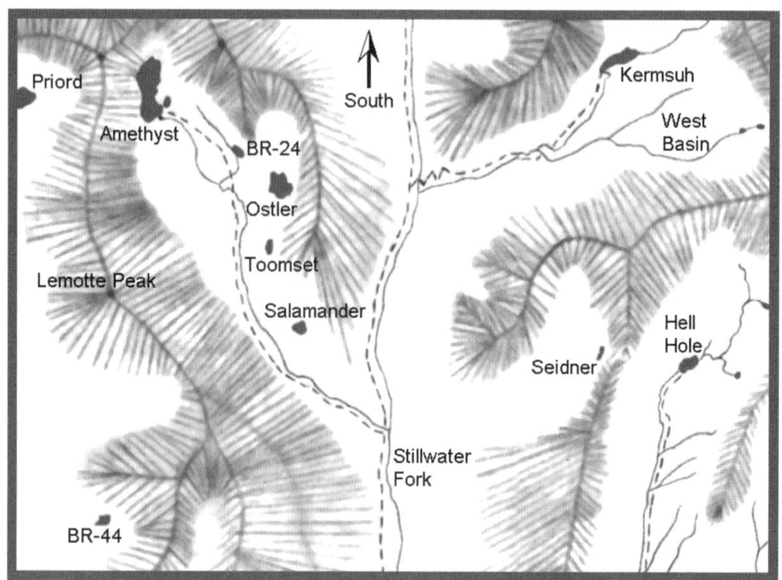

***BR-24 in Amethyst Basin***

it is still a gem! Its excellent campsites are the best in Amethyst Basin, with spring water at the lake, and horse feed nearby. BR-24 is a great place to camp if you are going to visit Amethyst Lake. Campsites at Amethyst Lake are above timberline, and offer little shelter, firewood, spring water, or horse feed. By staying at BR-24 you'll have all the commoditites you need. It's only a brisk 20 minute walk from BR-24 to Amethyst Lake for some grand sight-seeing and fast fishing for lots of pan-sized brook trout.

Fishing at BR-24 is unpredictable. A few large cutthroat trout patrol these sparkling waters, and they didn't get big by being stupid. You will have to be extremely lucky or tricky to hook one of these spooky lunkers. But you might fool a smaller trout or two. If you would like some trout larger than what Amethyst offers, then try Ostler Lake. It is less than half a mile northwest of BR-24, and frequently yields cutthroats in the one-pound class.

Like Amethyst Lake, BR-24 is emerald green in color due to glacial turbidity. It is fairly shallow, and therefore casts its own unique shade of turquoise. It is a great place to sit back and just enjoy the placid scenery while a pan of trout sizzle on the fire. Catch the fish at Amethyst, then retire to BR-24 for the evening.

# Scow Lake

| Trip Planner: | | | |
|---|---|---|---|
| Drainage | 3.3 | Usage | Moderate |
| Trailhead | 10,100 | Campsites | Good |
| Near Town | 1,400 | Springwater | Yes |
| Miles | Bear River | Fishing | Fair |
| Elevation | East Fork Bear River | Horsefeed | Fair |
| Elev. Gain | Evanston | Firewood | Limited |

***Scow Lake***

Scow Lake can be reached from either the Boundary Creek trail at the East Fork Bear River Drainage, or the Wolverine Trailhead, located by the Bear River Stillwater Road. Both trails connect near the Boundary Creek trailhead, but the East Fork access is about 1.5 miles shorter. Follow the Boundary Creek trail 2.5 miles south to a small meadow. Then depart from the trail continuing south three quarters of a mile, through heavy timber to the lake.

This meadow lake sits on a ridge between the Stillwater and Boundary Creek drainages. Heavy timber surrounds the lake, along with a few spring-fed meadows. Campsites and horse goodies are numerous in the area, but spring water is usually only available in the early summer months. Due to the shallow depth of this lake, it often winterkills. However, brook trout are stocked on a rotational basis. This lake also sustains lots of bugs and mosquitoes, so remember the repellent.

If Scow doesn't fit your fancy, we suggest you try Baker Lake at the end of the Boundary Creek trail. The last three quarters of a mile are hard to follow, which makes Baker Lake difficult to find. Baker is characterized by a large meadow with a gradual timbered slope located on the south end. Good camping areas and plenty of horse feed exist, and spring water can be found one quarter mile north of the outlet. Fishing is considered unpredictable. Hear-say warns that brook trout are most often wary.

Day hikers looking for solitude will like this area. On weekdays, expect to have the whole place to yourself - unless a herd of elk happen to be passing through.

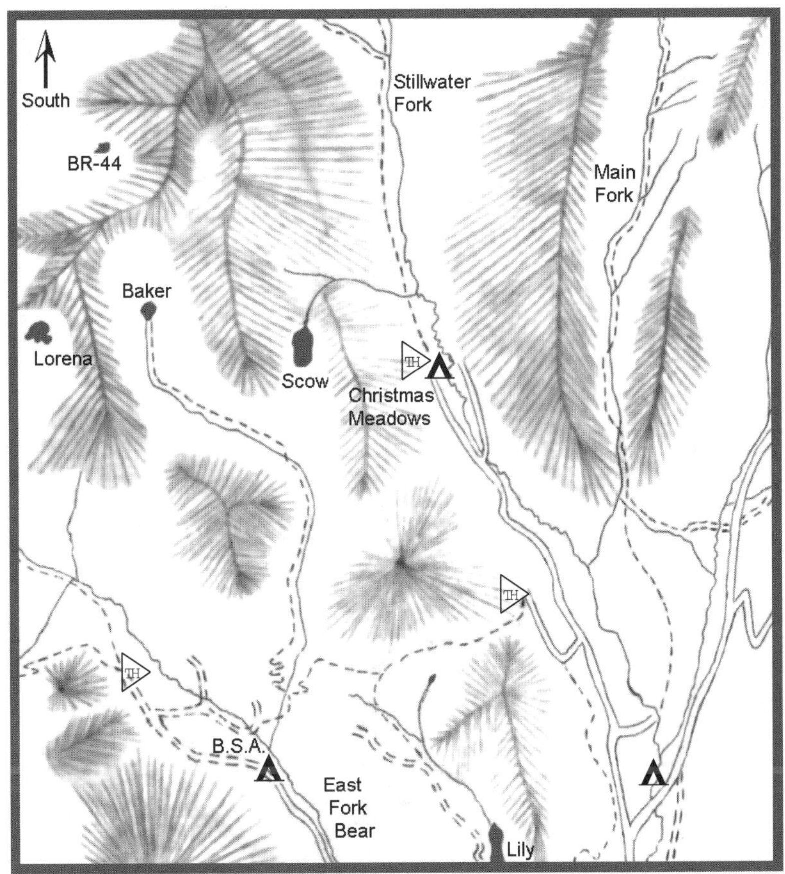

# Priord and Norice Lakes

| Trip Planner: | | | |
|---|---|---|---|
| Miles | 8.3 | Usage | Moderate |
| Elevation | 10,470 | Campsites | Good |
| Elev. Gain | 1,500 | Springwater | Yes |
| Drainage | Bear River | Fishing | Good |
| Trailhead | East Fork Bear | Horsefeed | Good |
| Near Town | Evanston | Firewood | Limited |

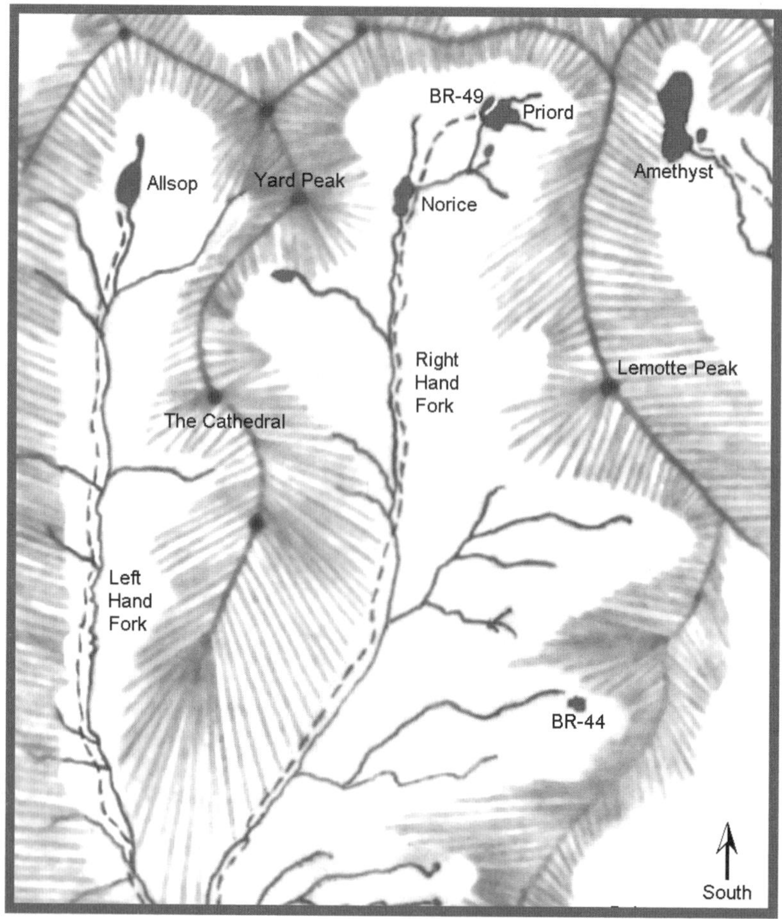

***LeMotte Peak***

Start your journey on the East Fork Bear River trail, 1/2 mile southeast of the B.S.A. turnoff. Follow the East Fork trail 4 miles southeast to the Right Hand - Left Hand Fork trail junction. Then go south on the Right Hand Fork trail. The trail deteriorates when traveling through bogs and dead fall. When this occurs, follow the stream and it will take you to Norice Lake. From Norice, the trail becomes difficult to locate. Just head south for a half mile, then west a quarter mile and you'll find Priord Lake.

Priord sits at the head of the Right Hand Fork drainage. This timberline lake is encircled by a rugged cirque basin, and the lake itself is a pretty emerald green. Camping areas exist east of the lake, and spring water is present. However, horse feed and firewood are limited. Windy conditions may hinder fly-casting, but the fish should be cooperative since Priord Lake only receives light fishing use for cutthroat trout.

Norice is shallow, but despite the depth of this lake it contains an excellent population of cutthroat trout. Norice is a meadow lake that is quite boggy in spots. This means one thing. It is a perfect breeding ground for bugs and mosquitos. Don't forget your repellent!

The East Fork Bear River Drainage receives moderate to heavy usage from Boy Scouts and camera-clickers alike. A B.S.A. camp is located 1/2 mile north of the main trailhead. So, don't be alarmed if you see a bunch of tiny khaki-green men congregated at any one spot. It's just the Boy Scouts of America.

# Allsop Lake

| Trip Planner: | | | |
|---|---|---|---|
| Miles | 8.5 | Usage | Moderate |
| Elevation | 10,580 | Campsites | Good |
| Elev. Gain | 1,400 | Springwater | Yes |
| Drainage | East Fork Bear River | Fishing | Fair |
| Trailhead | East Fork Bear River | Horsefeed | Good |
| Near Town | Evanston | Firewood | Scarce |

***Allsop Basin***

What a pretty hike. The East Fork Bear River trail caresses a wide flowing river while steering leisurely by ruins of old log cabins, lush green meadows, and sky-reaching pines. Possible camping areas exist all along the river and all the way to the Allsop / Priord junction. After the junction, the Left Hand Fork trail ascends high along the side of a steep ravine. Here you'll find a stunning overlook of consecutive waterfalls gushing down a shear rock canyon.

Moving on, the Allsop Lake trail slowly gains altitude as exotic mountain peaks appear through the tops of gangling conifers. Once progress is made out of these tall strands of trees, a tantalizing view of

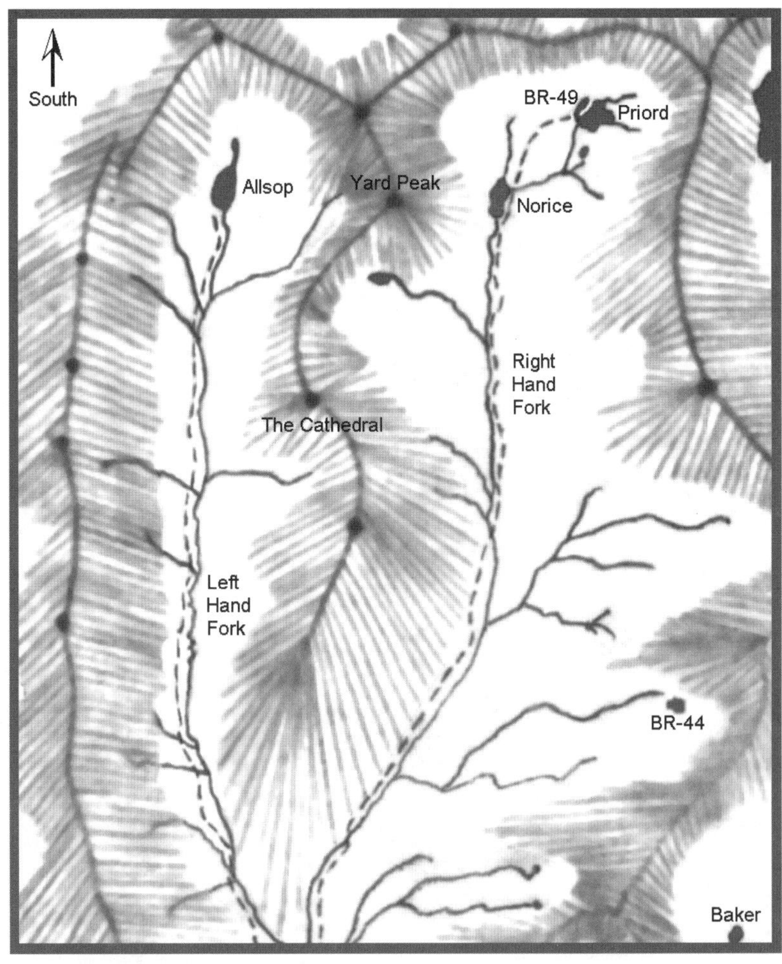


The Cathedral and Allsop Basin is sighted just beyond a long stretch of meadows.

Allsop is a beautiful bluish-green lake nestled within a spectacular talus and timbered sloped basin. Excellent campsites with superb spring water sources are plentiful at the lake, while horse feed can be found nearby or downstream. Fishing for cutthroat trout is often consistent around these parts, and open shorelines make fly casting quite easy. However, sudden stiff winds may ravage a long distance cast. It's probably a wise decision to pack some spinners or bait for those unexpected gusts. Other angling prospects can be found in the Left Hand or East Fork of the Bear River. Tasty trout populate these deluxe fishin' holes as well.

# Buck Pasture

| Trip Planner: | | | |
|---|---|---|---|
| Miles | 1 - 4 | Usage | Moderate |
| Elevation | 9,600 - 9,800 | Campsites | Good |
| Elev. Gain | 50 - 200 | Springwater | Scattered |
| Drainage | Blacks Fork | Fishing | Very Good |
| Trailhead | West Fork | Horsefeed | Excellent |
| Near Town | Evanston | Firewood | Excellent |

Some people would rather fish or camp by a stream than at a lake. There are many benefits to stream camping, especially if you can seclude your camp away from the trail. Any hikers you bump into will just be passing through, the fishing pressure is light, and there is plenty of firewood available. It sounds kind of like a well kept secret to me, doesn't it? If you would like to try the stream camping experience, there's no better place than Buck Pasture.

Buck Pasture is a long beautiful meadow spanning a good portion of the hike to Dead Horse Lake. The West Fork of the Blacks Fork River runs right through the middle of it. This river houses many small trout, and maybe even a few old smart ones. They are bound to be a little wary, since they live in a small stream in an open meadow. Cutthroats and brooks thrive in this ice-cold water, so don't feel guilty about keeping enough for lunch.

Several marginal campsites are noticeable from the trail, but it would be better to leave the trail and explore around a bit. Move back into the trees to find a camp away from the wet meadow, otherwise you may have more mosquitoes than you bargained for. Sheep are a smelly problem at times, and may be another reason to camp away from the meadows. Horses will have no trouble finding feed in this lush meadow, but they can easily wander....better hobble them.

Stream water is plentiful of course. It looks crystal clear, but you would be wise to purify it. There is lots of livestock above, and the dreaded giardia bug is probably lurking about. Springs may be in the area, depending on where you stake out your claim. Maybe you'll be lucky enough to find a spring, but don't count on it.

To the west of Buck Pasture lie several small no-name lakes that receive very few visitors. Mostly, they are stocked with brook trout.

They may provide fast fishing, or they might be duds. Who knows? Get your compass, check your map, and find G-78. This is probably your easiest access into the area, then several of the lakes can be reached by going north or south along the same ridge line.

Upon returning to camp, we think you'll particularly enjoy having the river sing you to sleep at night. That's just one of the perks of camping by a river. The others you will have to discover for yourself.

***West Fork of Blacks Fork River***

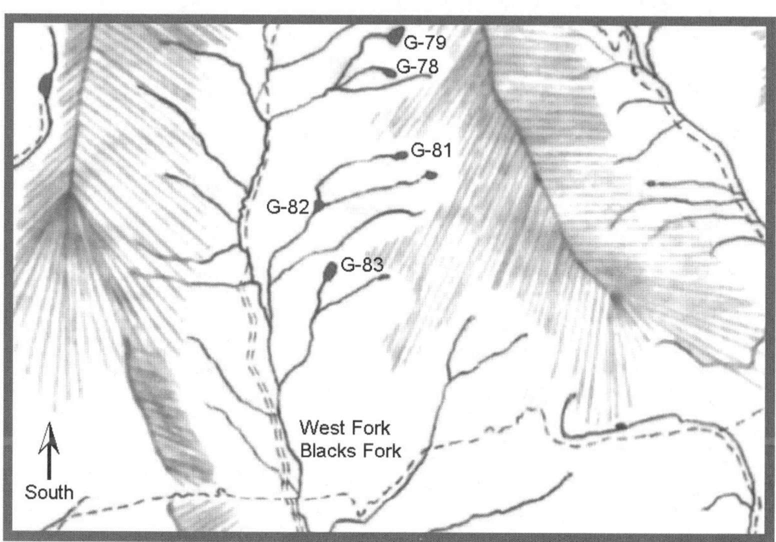

# Dead Horse Lake

| Trip Planner: | | | |
|---|---|---|---|
| Miles | 8 | Usage | Moderate |
| Elevation | 10,878 | Campsites | Fair |
| Elev. Gain | 1,280 | Springwater | No |
| Drainage | Blacks Fork | Fishing | Fair |
| Trailhead | West Fork | Horsefeed | Good |
| Near Town | Evanston | Firewood | Limited |

*Dead Horse Lake from Dead Horse Pass*

Follow one of the prettiest trails to one of the prettiest lakes. The West Fork Blacks Fork Trail parallels a river by the same name almost all the way to Dead Horse Lake. It's pure torture to take an avid stream fisherman on this hike. He will constantly be tempted to cast into the many pools that beckon for someone to try their luck. If you have the time, do it. It may be the best fishing you'll find on this hike.

Dead Horse Lake sits at the base of the mountain, right at the edge of timberline. Its turquoise waters present a picture-book setting if sheep don't happen to be grazing in the area at the time. Immediately south of the lake is Dead Horse Pass. The trail is not easily visible from across the lake, but it is there. Some years it may be late July before you will be able to cross this pass. We haven't figured out if Dead Horse Pass is named after Dead Horse Lake or vice-versa. The pass looks like it could be lethal for horses, while on the other hand the lake looks much like a horse head when viewed from the pass. But then, who cares about such trivia when you are surrounded by such magnificent alpine terrain.

Campsites are plentiful on the north side of Dead Horse Lake. Firewood and spring water are not so plentiful. Plan on purifying all of your drinking water, and searching deep into the timber for fuel wood.

Fishing is not very good at Dead Horse Lake (too many fishermen). If you're looking for some faster finny action, trek over to Ejod Lake just 1/4 mile northwest of Dead Horse Lake. Expect to catch enough pan-sized cutthroats for dinner. If Ejod doesn't pan out, don't forget the great looking stream you passed on your hike in to Dead Horse Lake.

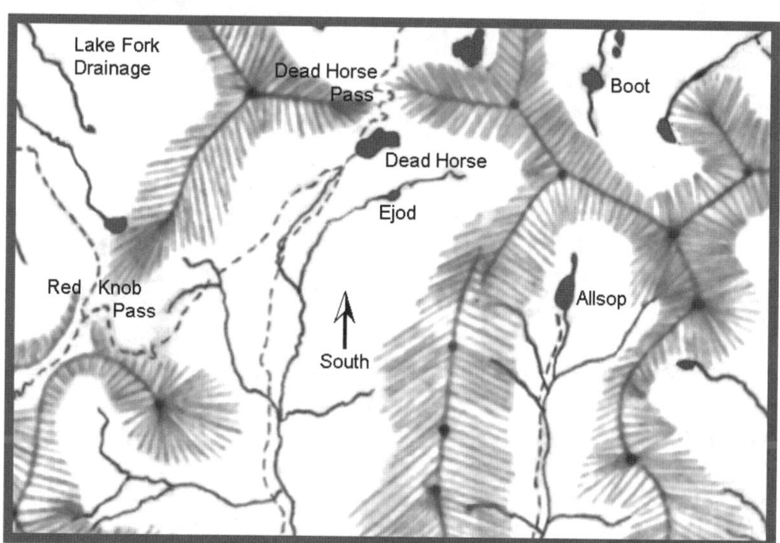

# East Fork Blacks Fork

| Trip Planner: | | | |
|---|---|---|---|
| Miles | 10 | Usage | Light |
| Elevation | 12,200 | Campsites | Fair |
| Elev. Gain | 2,900 | Springwater | Yes |
| Drainage | East Fork Blacks Fork | Fishing | Poor |
| Trailhead | East Fork Blacks Fork | Horsefeed | Good |
| Near Town | Evanston | Firewood | Good |

***Upper region of East Fork Blacks Fork***

It just goes to show, some high mountain passes are inaccessible much of the summer. Red Knob is no exception. After a long hard winter, the northeast side of Red Knob Pass is plagued with snow drifts until the middle of August. You may try your luck during late July, but it could be a rugged trip. Snow drifts are difficult to cross when hoisting a heavy pack, and so is the East Fork river when the glaciers melt and fill its banks to capacity. Even when these mountains experience a light winter, Red Knob should not be attempted from the East Fork trail until mid-July.

East Fork has no lakes what so ever. The main purpose of this drainage is a route for hikers making the 50 mile trek from the

Highline Trailhead, or the 26 mile loop trail that ventures around Mount Lovenia, the upper Lake Fork Drainage, and then back through Little East Fork. The loop trail begins at the foot bridge northeast of the East Fork Campground. From the bridge, follow a well used trail 1 mile south to another foot bridge that crosses over the Little East Fork river. Just beyond the bridge the trail forks to the right and to the left. Both trails take off to the south, then connect again in the upper portion of the Lake Fork drainage. From the fork it is 10 miles to either Squaw or Red Knob Pass. Take your pick!

Scenery in the East Fork Blacks Fork is spectacular. Mount Lovenia and other high peaks surround the narrow ridged canyons, which sometimes stay snow capped year round. Beautiful lodgepole pines cover the valley floor, while prolonged rivers ease through the misty meadows. Scenic campsites can be found along the trail, and firewood is plentiful for the overnight camper.

Occasionally, a large herd of moose can be spotted grazing in the open meadows. It is a good idea to keep your distance from these animals. Moose are sometimes intrepid, and may attack.

The Little East Fork trail serves as the main sheep thoroughfare for the upper portions of the Lake Fork Drainage. If either route is taken after mid-July, be prepared to encounter herds of sheep. Take precautions where drinking water is concerned.

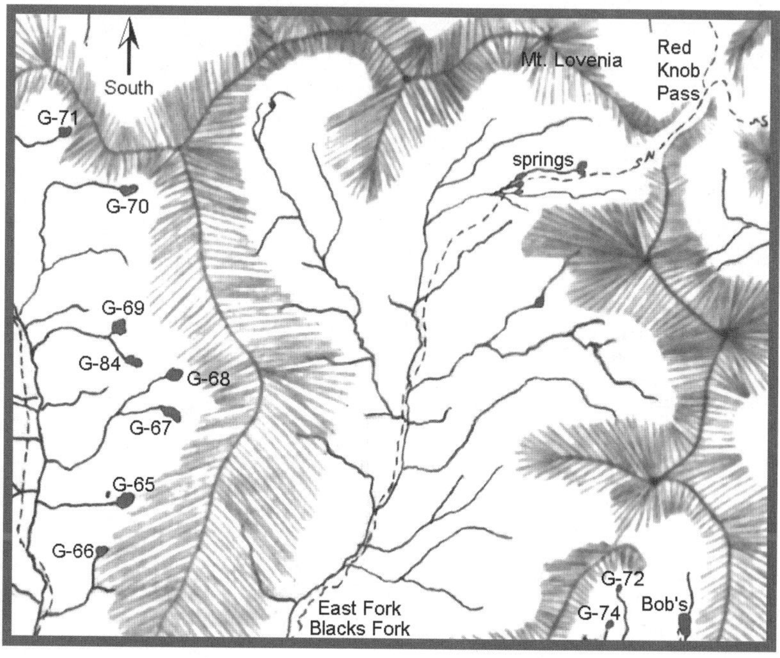

# Little East Fork

| Trip Planner: | | | |
|---|---|---|---|
| Miles | 6 - 10 | Usage | Light |
| Elevation | up to 11,527 | Campsites | Fair |
| Elev. Gain | up to 2,200 | Springwater | Yes |
| Drainage | East ForkBlacks Fork | Fishing | Good |
| Trailhead | East ForkBlacks Fork | Horsefeed | Poor |
| Near Town | Evanston | Firewood | Fair |

Open windswept tundra dotted with alpine lakes characterize this remote hike. The Little East Fork Blacks Forks Drainage has several tiny high lakes that almost nobody visits. Camping opportunities are few, firewood is scarce, spring water is hard to find, horsefeed is scant, and there are no trails to the lakes. All of these factors add up to no visitors. But if you're looking for solitude and a chance to discover some unknown fishing waters, here it is. You've got to have a sense of adventure, but you'll know you've been to some of the least traveled country these mountains have to offer.

G-66 is the most logical choice to establish a base camp. There are several campsites, and spring water can be found. It is also the first lake you will encounter. You will need a topographical map and

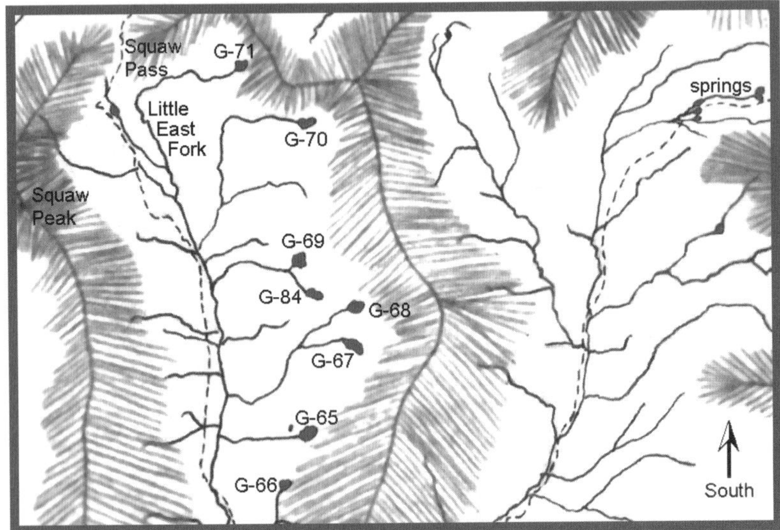

***Little East Fork Blacks Fork as seen from Squaw Pass***

a compass to find G-66, or any of these lakes.

Fishing opportunities may be great, or they may be lousy. Stocking schedules are irregular, and winterkill could take its toll, but the fishing may still be excellent at times. Who knows? You'll just have to take your chances. There are several of these small lakes within a few miles of each other. Try several. A good horse can make its way around up here, but there isn't much feed. You may want to camp by the lower meadows if you have a horse.

# Bald Lake

| Trip Planner: | | | |
|---|---|---|---|
| Miles | 5 | Usage | Light |
| Elevation | 11,030 | Campsites | Good |
| Elev. Gain | 1,400 | Springwater | No |
| Drainage | Smiths Fork | Fishing | Good |
| Trailhead | Mansfield Meadow | Horsefeed | Poor |
| Near Town | Mountain View | Firewood | Good |

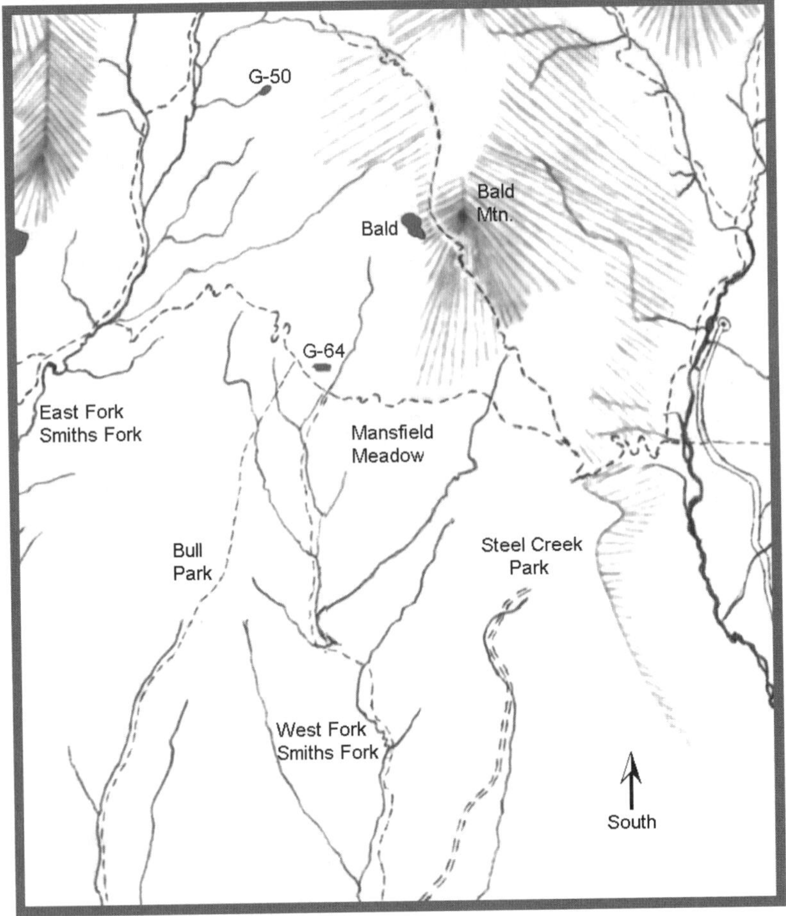

***Bald Lake***

Bald Lake is probably the only lake in the Smiths Fork Drainage containing campsites that still only receives light fishing and camping use. This natural cirque lake harbors a large population of native brook trout. Stocking has been discontinued since natural reproduction has met its quota over-n-over. You should have no problem filling your skillet here.

Bald Lake sits near a glacial talus slope with a snowy ice pack that is the main source of water for this alpine lake. Small stunted pines dot the north and east shorelines where a few sheltered campsites are found. Just south of the lake, a spectacular panorama of the upper Smiths Fork Drainage awaits your viewing.

The hike begins from either East Fork Blacks Fork or the Mansfield Meadows Road. The latter is the easiest. From the Mansfield Meadows Road follow the West Fork Smiths Fork Trail 3.5 miles south to the Mansfield Meadows trail junction. At this point, follow the stream southwest another 1.5 miles to Bald Lake.

No other lakes exist in the vicinity; Bald Lake is all alone. You will be too if you choose this hike. Here's a great place to spend the weekend <u>and</u> beat the crowds. Relax, breathe deep, and enjoy it.

# Red Castle Lakes

| Trip Planner: | | | |
|---|---|---|---|
| Miles | 11 | Usage | Moderate |
| Elevation | 11,295 | Campsites | Poor |
| Elev. Gain | 1,900 | Springwater | No |
| Drainage | Smiths Fork | Fishing | Good |
| Trailhead | China Meadows | Horsefeed | Poor |
| Near Town | Mountain View | Firewood | Scarce |

Red Castle Lake is one of the largest and deepest lakes in the High Uintas. It is offset by a beautiful steep walled basin including a reddish colored mountain shaped somewhat like a castle.

Campsites are nonexistent near the lake, but can be found along with running water at the timbered area to the north. Angling and camping usage is excessively heavy on weekends, and fishing is considered only fair for pan-sized cutthroats. Because of the size, depth, and popularity of this lake, an inflatable raft may increase the number and size of fish in your creel. If inflatables are used, use extreme caution. Red Castle is subject to sudden high winds and rapid weather changes. Life jackets are essential!

Lower Red Castle is a popular scenic lake resting in a large alpine meadow. Camping and fishing pressure are extremely heavy here too, but good campsites are available. If there has been a heavy snow pack, you should be able to rustle up some spring water, but firewood is scarce due to over-usage.

Upper Red Castle is in a rugged cirque basin, just 1/8 mile south of Red Castle. This lake is known as a poor fishery, but occasionally a large cutthroat trout is netted. No camping areas exist in this windy basin, but spring water is abundant.

East Red Castle is in a steep walled basin at the east base of Red Castle Peak. Ice-cold spring water can be acquired from several different sources, but campsites, firewood, and horse feed are not readily available. However, there are several good camping areas in the timbered areas to the northeast, along with a generous supply of horse feed. You can easily reach East Red Castle from the inlet of Lower Red Castle Lake by picking your way up a steep hill to the east, then around the mountain.

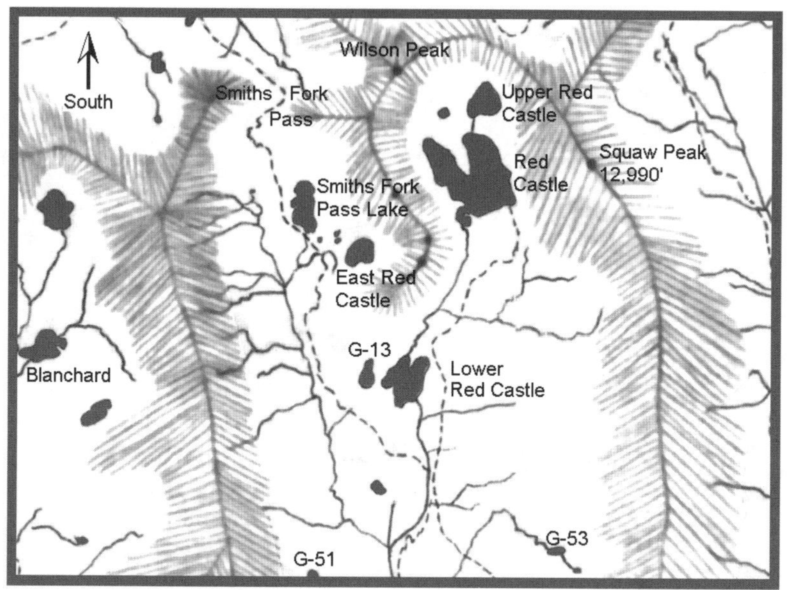


This Lake receives moderate fishing pressure for large but wary cutthroat trout. Try a #16 red or black ant at sundown. If the weather is foul, which happens a lot up here, tie on a small silver spinner. It's okay to fish in the rain if you can stay dry, but if the lightning starts, head for shelter.

Smiths Fork Pass Lake is projected to have better angling. This lake is noted for its open terrain and irregular shorelines that make fly casting a pleasure. Due to the nature of this country, prospects for campsites and firewood are poor. Good camping areas and shelter are located in the wooded areas to the north, and spring water is present around the lake. This lake is next to the trail in a large cirque basin, 11 miles from either China Meadows or the East Fork Blacks Fork Campground.

Compared to most trails in the High Uintas, the East Fork Smiths Fork Trail is like a freeway. Not only is it well groomed, superb bridges are built over every major river crossing. But don't let these statements fool you. After a hard rain, horses and cows riddle the trail with tracks of slippery slimy mudholes.

From China Meadows the trail gradually picks up altitude for the first seven miles. Then shortly after passing Broadbent Meadow, several steep switchbacks are encountered. The trail levels off while passing Lower Red Castle Lake, but sharply gains elevation the last mile.

See photos on next page.

Red Castle Mountain

*East Red Castle Lake*

*Lower Red Castle Lake*

# Hessie Lake

| Trip Planner: | | | |
|---|---|---|---|
| Miles | 5.8 | Usage | Heavy |
| Elevation | 10,620 | Campsites | Good |
| Elev. Gain | 1,200 | Springwater | Yes |
| Drainage | Smiths Fork | Fishing | Fair |
| Trailhead | China Meadows | Horsefeed | Good |
| Near Town | Mountain View | Firewood | Limited |

Hessie Lake

This heavily timbered lake lies at the base of a rocky point in the East Fork of Smiths Fork Drainage. Access starts at the south side of China Meadows Campground. Take the East Fork trail 3.5 miles south to the Henrys Fork Trail junction. Then head east toward Henrys Fork 2 miles to the Hessie Lake turnoff. Travel another 1/4 mile west and you'll be at Hessie Lake.

Expect heavy weekend pressure at this popular lake. Several well used camping areas are found along the east and south sides of the lake. However, firewood is limited. Heavily timbered shorelines make fly casting difficult, and for some reason cutthroat trout are quite skeptical. But by late evening, the fish become a little hungry and not so particular.

A couple of other lakes that are in the proximity of Hessie are G-60 & G-61. These lakes are easily located by following their outlet stream that crosses the trail just east of the Hessie Lake turnoff. G-60 is the first lake you'll run into. This small meadow lake is situated at the base of a timbered ridge. Excellent campsites can be found near the lake, and plenty of horse feed and spring water is available. Light to moderate fishing pressure is sustained by stocked brook trout.

Find G-61 by following the inlet of G-60 up a steep timbered ridge 1/8 mile to the south. This shallow lake sits in partially timbered terrain at the base of Flat Top Mountain. Camping areas are present, and lots of horse feed can be found in the large park to the west and north. Spring water is limited, especially in the late summer months. G-61 is subject to winterkill, but it has been experimentally stocked with brook trout anyway. You might want to give it a try. This lake receives little angling use, which means it could produce a big thrill.

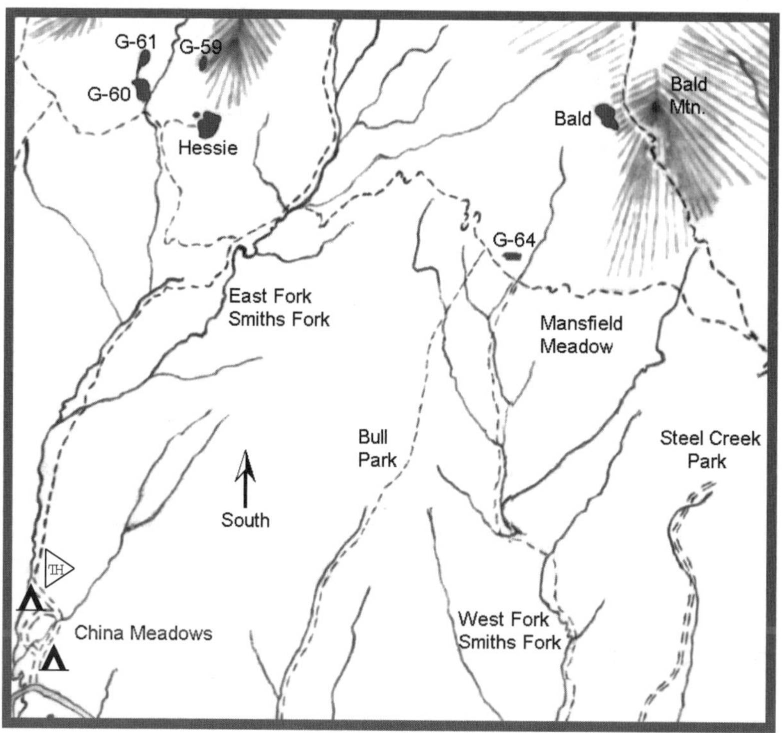

# Alligator Lake

| Trip Planner: | | | |
|---|---|---|---|
| Miles | 2.7 | Usage | Heavy |
| Elevation | 10,033 | Campsites | Good |
| Elev. Gain | 1,200 | Springwater | No |
| Drainage | Henrys Fork | Fishing | Fair |
| Trailhead | Henrys Fork | Horsefeed | Good |
| Near Town | Mountain View | Firewood | Fair |

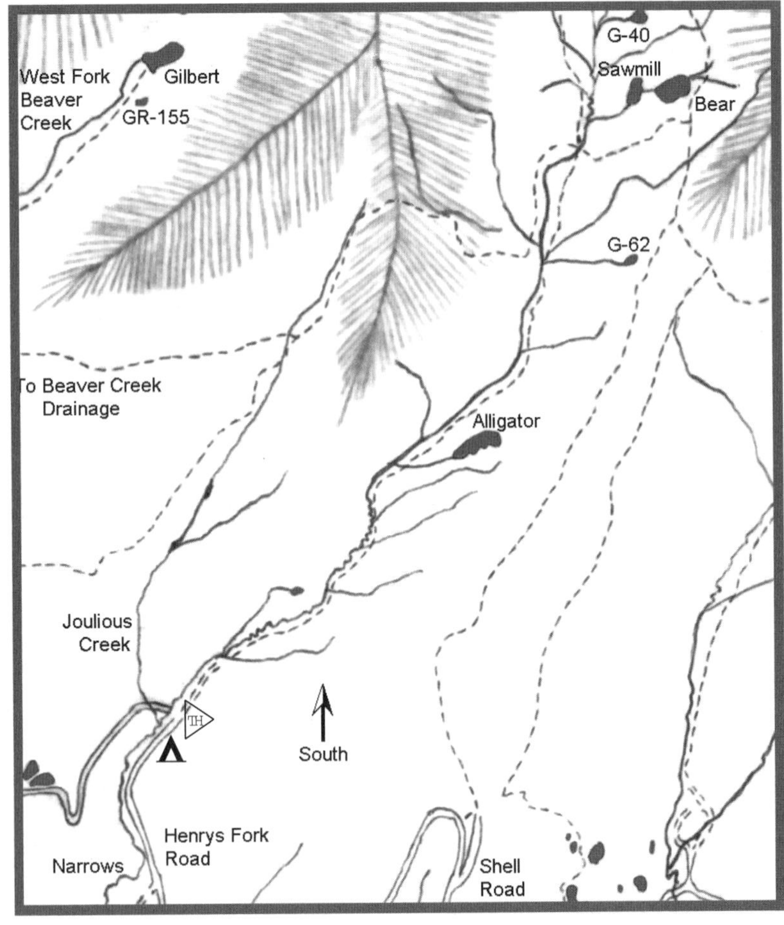

No, this lake is not a swamp where alligators or snakes feed. In fact, it's rather uncommon to encounter any reptile above 9,000 feet in the High Uintas. However, Alligator Lake can be exploited by human creatures. Dominate pressure persists on weekends, but during the weekdays you should experience a solemn piece of solitude.

Alligator Lake can be found by following the Henrys Fork trail 2 miles to a spur trail that parallels the outlet. Good to excellent camping areas exist all around the lake, while angling is considered decent for pan-sized brookies. The best fishing should take place along the north side. The south side is relatively shallow for some distance out.

About 4 or 5 campsites with tables, toilets and fireplaces accommodate the trailhead. Plenty of parking is found for hikers and equestrians, and a good road will ease you into location. Alligator Lake would make a nice day excursion for kids, while the old folks can just lay back and enjoy a nap.

***Alligator Lake***

# Bear Lake

| Trip Planner: | | | |
|---|---|---|---|
| Miles | 6.5 | Usage | Moderate |
| Elevation | 10,767 | Campsites | Good |
| Elev. Gain | 1,350 | Springwater | No |
| Drainage | Henrys Fork | Fishing | Fair |
| Trailhead | Henrys Fork | Horsefeed | Poor |
| Near Town | Mountain View | Firewood | Good |

Bear Lake

Surrounded by mature pines, Bear Lake offers a quiet picture-book setting for the weary traveler. Its deep placid waters seem to beckon, "Rest here, rest here." And a lot of hikers do. Bear Lakes receives its share of backpackers that come to visit the popular

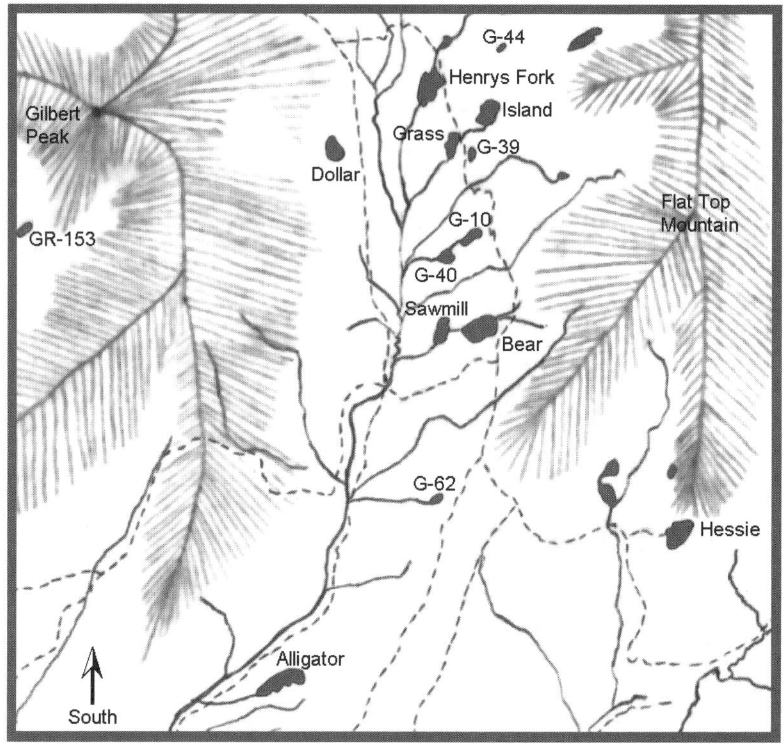


Henrys Fork Drainage. You might have some company here, but there are plenty of nice campsites, and the thick pines will serve as privacy barriers.

To reach Bear Lake, simply follow the Henrys Fork Trail about five miles to Elkhorn Crossing. There a sign will direct you west. Just stick with the trail. It passes right next to Bear Lake.

Bring some means of water purification, as there are no springs in the immediate area. If you need spring water, head east a quarter of a mile to Sawmill Lake. Horses won't find a lot to eat around these parts, so if you have pack animals, keep going up the trail.

There are numerous existing campsites at Bear Lake. Please don't build any more. As with any heavily used area, use low impact camping techniques, and lend a hand gathering any left-over litter.

Bear Lake and Sawmill Lake have good populations of brook trout that provide fast fishing at times. These deep lakes can be fished successfully with either fly or spinner. Just keep your offerings small and work them slowly. You'll catch fish. For a change of pace, try the little creek connecting the two lakes. But practice your stealth. If these wild trout see or hear you, you won't see them.

# Henrys Fork Lake

| Trip Planner: | | | |
|---|---|---|---|
| Miles | 7.5 | Usage | Heavy |
| Elevation | 10,830 | Campsites | Good |
| Elev. Gain | 1,420 | Springwater | Yes |
| Drainage | Henrys Fork | Fishing | Good |
| Trailhead | Henrys Fork | Horsefeed | Good |
| Near Town | Mountain View | Firewood | Fair |

Henrys Fork is a beautiful alpine mountain basin. Winding streams flow through misty meadows, and tall pines hiss in the wind while caressing big boulder formations. Campsites are plentiful below timberline, and fishing for brook and cutthroat trout is exciting at most lakes and rivers.

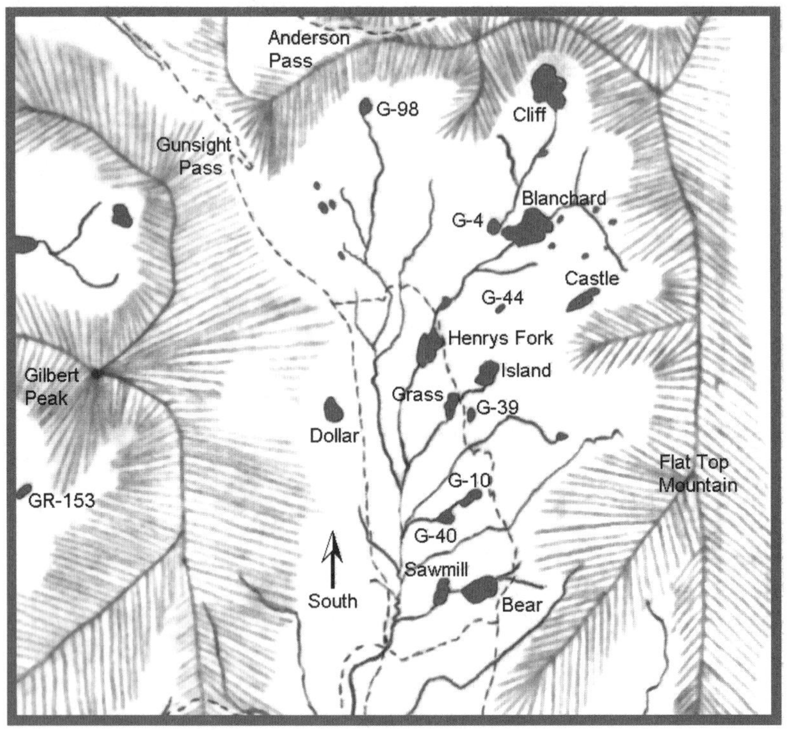

*Henrys Fork Lake and inlet pond (foreground)*

Well there, we said enough. It's a great place to visit. In addition to these attractions, Henrys Fork features an excellent Forest Service trail that has a gradual climb. However, this trail is not too scenic and seems long until you arrive at Elk Horn Crossing. From the crossing, a frail trail heads south across the river and through the basin. Watch for cairns to mark the way. These rock piles are spaced along the trail to Gunsight Pass, and beyond. Kings Peak is located on the other side of the pass, and is the highest point in Utah (elevation 13,528 feet).

Henrys Fork Lake offers the best accommodations for a base camp. It has several excellent campsites along the east shore, and ample running water flowing into and out of the lake. With the exception of Cliff, Castle and Blanchard, all other lakes in this basin contain good camping areas and shelter.

Fishing can be unpredictable at most lakes and streams. If there is no action at one lake, move to another. There are many to choose from. The best angling might happen at Cliff Lake. For access, follow the inlet of Henrys Fork 1 mile south to Blanchard Lake, then follow the inlet of Blanchard another mile south to Cliff. After passing Blanchard, the terrain is composed of rocky shelves and small waterfalls.

Castle Lake probably receives the least amount of attention in Henrys Fork Basin. Nobody really knows too much about it. We've heard conflicting stories. It may be a good prospect for anglers, or it may just be a stagnant hole.

# Kings Peak

| Trip Planner: | | | |
|---|---|---|---|
| Miles | 15 | Usage | Moderate |
| Elevation | 13,528 | Campsites | None |
| Elev. Gain | 4,120 | Springwater | No |
| Drainage | Uinta/Yellowstone | Fishing | None |
| Trailhead | Henrys Fork | Horsefeed | Poor |
| Near Town | Mountain View | Firewood | None |

Kings Peak, the highest point in the state of Utah, is the most popular destination of "peak baggers" in the High Uintas. It can even be reached by novice mountaineers with no special equipment. However, it is a long steep hike to the top, and good health and conditioning are a must. We have not written much about other peaks, but we feel Kings Peak deserves some special attention - partly because it gets a lot of attention.

There are three primary routes to Kings Peak. The one that appears to be the most direct is the trail that goes up the Uinta River

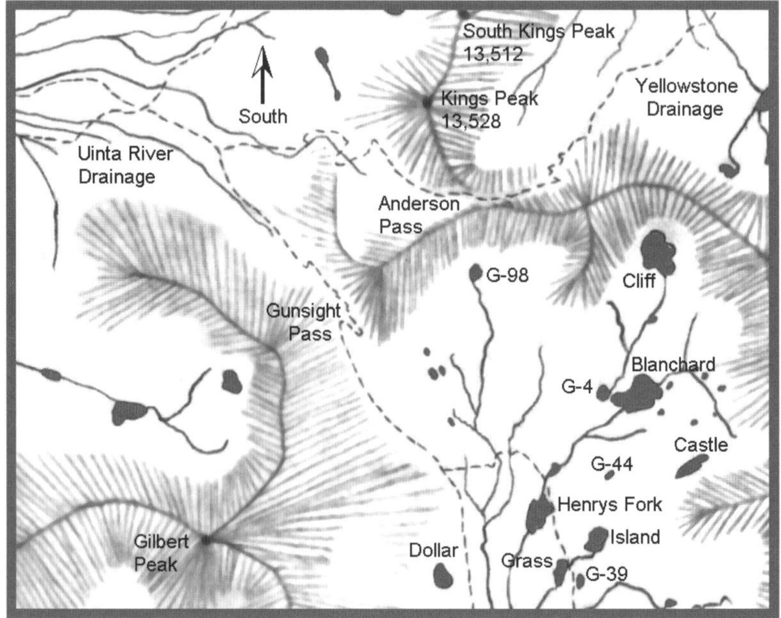

***Kings Peak from Trail Rider Pass***

Drainage past Atwood Basin. Others will travel up the Swift Creek Drainage, then cross over Bluebell Pass to the Yellowstone Drainage. But the easiest and shortest route starts at the Henrys Fork Trailhead and goes past Henrys Fork Lake, and over Gunsight Pass. This is the most popular trail. Regardless of the route you choose, you'll want to end up at Anderson Pass. From there, Kings Peak can be safely approached from its north slope. This is big country, and a horse that could get you near Anderson Pass would be a prized commodity.

Camping opportunities in the immediate vicinity are extremely rough. Most hikers establish a base camp at Henrys Fork Lake or Lake Atwood. Kings Peak is best attempted on a day hike carrying only day packs. From your base camp, start out early in the day (thunderstorms are common in the afternoon). Plan on a fair amount of boulder hopping and cliff traversing, especially between Anderson Pass and Kings Peak.

Allow plenty of time to complete your trip. You wouldn't want to have to hurry through this terrain. Not only would that be unsafe, but you might miss some extraordinary views.

# Gilbert Lake

| Trip Planner: | | | |
|---|---|---|---|
| Miles | 8 | Usage | Moderate |
| Elevation | 10,905 | Campsites | Good |
| Elev. Gain | 1,500 | Springwater | Yes |
| Drainage | Beaver Creek | Fishing | Very Good |
| Trailhead | West Fork Beaver | Horsefeed | Excellent |
| Near Town | Mountain View | Firewood | Good |

If fly fishing is your thing, then Gilbert Lake might be your idea of heaven. Plenty of open shoreline and lots of eager trout make this a good fly fishing lake. This lake is a must for fly fishermen seeking fast action for brookies and cutthroat trout. Make sure your casting arm is in good shape. It will give out long before the fish do.

Horsemen are attracted to this area too. Horse feed is plentiful around the lush meadows, and flowing water is everywhere. Campsites are well suited to horse travelers who want to set up a large base camp. The best camping is found on the south side of Gilbert Lake, or in the trees just north of GR-151. Because of the

***Gilbert Lake***

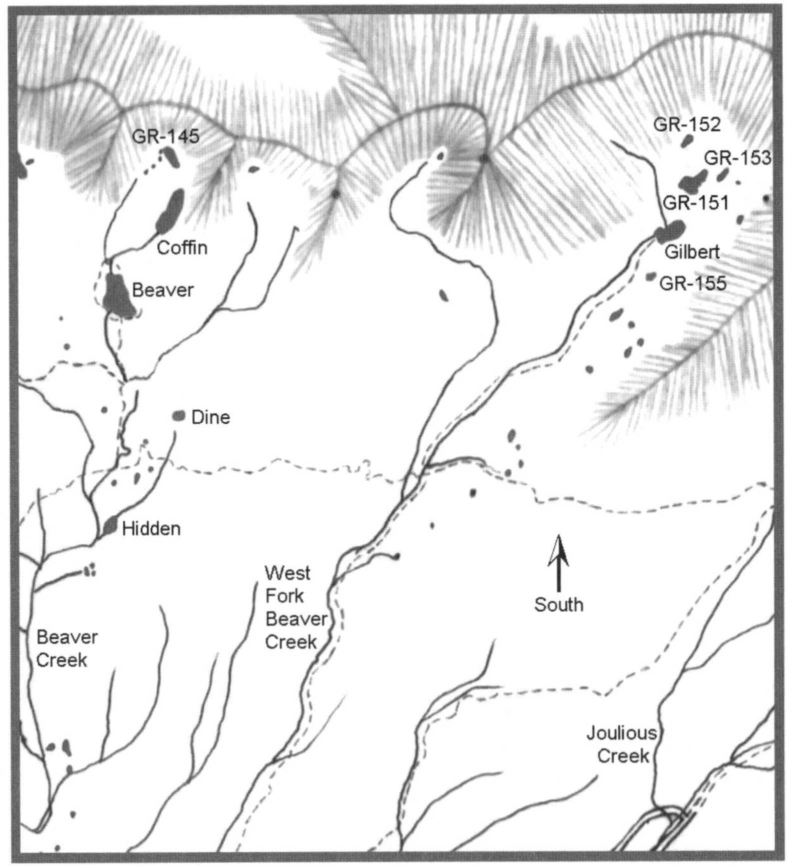


moist nature of the area, mosquitoes are often a problem. Plan your trip late in the summer, and always bring along sufficient quantities of bug dope.

Now lets get back to the fishing. Although Gilbert Lake can offer fine fishing, check out some of the other lakes nearby. They are probably just as good, and maybe even better. South of Gilbert Lake lie GR-151, GR-152, and GR-153. These lakes and their connecting steams are stuffed with fish that seldom see an artificial lure. As with most High Uinta lakes, great fishing is never guaranteed. If the lakes are not producing, then check out the streams. They can be hot when the lakes are not.

The trail to Gilbert Lake is sometimes "hit and miss", so check your map and compass often. There are several wet areas along the route, and a good riding horse or waterproof boots can serve you well to keep your feet dry.

# Beaver Lake

| Trip Planner: | | | |
|---|---|---|---|
| Miles | 6.8 | Usage | Heavy |
| Elevation | 10,505 | Campsites | Excellent |
| Elev. Gain | 1300 | Springwater | Yes |
| Drainage | Beaver Creek | Fishing | Fair |
| Trailhead | Georges Park | Horsefeed | Good |
| Near Town | Mountain View | Firewood | Limited |

***Coffin Lake***

Beaver Lake is located in the Middle Fork of Beaver Creek Drainage. Begin your trek from either Hoop Lake or the Georges Park Trailhead. The trail from Hoop Lake is the more popular start, because of the rough road to Georges Park and the fact that the Beaver Creek trail is more rugged than the trail from Hoop Lake. However, it is at least 2 miles shorter.

Beaver Lake is characterized by timbered shorelines with shallow water prevailing on the east side of the lake. Excellent campsites are in a large park to the west, and several sources of spring water and horse feed are in nearby meadows. Brook trout and a few cutthroats inhabit this lake. Stocking has been discontinued due to the success of natural reproduction.

Just southwest of Beaver lies Coffin Lake. Coffin gets its name from its oblong shape and small shelves surrounding the water. No trail exists to the lake, but you can find it by following the inlet of Beaver 3/4 mile south then west to the base of some steep talus slopes. Rough and rocky describes the wilderness around this lake. Horse travel is quite difficult, and camping areas are a poor prospect. On the bright side, spring water is present, and angling usage is light for unsophisticated cutthroat trout.

Other lakes that you might happen upon in the Beaver Lake Basin are Hidden and Dine. Hidden Lake lies 1/2 mile north of Long Meadow. There is no trail, but access is not difficult. This lake is often passed up by anglers and backpackers alike. There is no spring water here, but there are several good camping areas near the inlet.

Discover Dine Lake by following the inlet of Hidden Lake 1 mile southwest, or 1/2 mile west of Long Meadow. This lake is surrounded by rocky timbered terrain and has a talus slope bordering the water on the southwest. Due to the rugged nature of this country, only mediocre campsites are available. Horse feed is not present in the vicinity, but plenty of spring water is. Although this lake has been stocked throughout the years, Dine will sometimes winterkill during harsh winters.

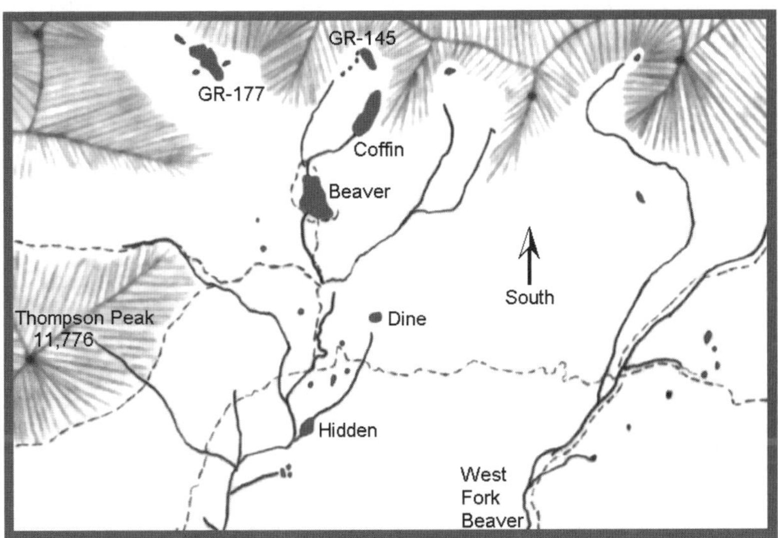

# Kabell Lake

| Trip Planner: | | | |
|---|---|---|---|
| Miles | 5.2 | Usage | Moderate |
| Elevation | 10,348 | Campsites | Fair |
| Elev. Gain | 1,150 | Springwater | Yes |
| Drainage | Burnt Fork | Fishing | Fair |
| Trailhead | Hoop Lake | Horsefeed | Good |
| Near Town | Mountain View | Firewood | Fair |

Even though Kabell is a popular lake, campsites are scarce and heavy timber surrounds the shoreline. You may ask, "Why then is this lake so popular?" Probably because Kabell is the only lake within a day's hiking distance (round trip) that can be reached from the ever popular Hoop Lake.

To get to Kabell Lake, follow the trail from Hoop Lake to Kabell Meadows. At the upper portion of the meadows, the trail forks to the south and southwest. From here, take the trail south up Kabell Ridge a couple hundred yards. A side trail then takes off to the southwest ending at Kabell Lake.

Dense timber surrounds the lake hindering all but the best fly casters. A good spinning outfit will solve that problem. Fisherman usage is moderate for pan-sized cutthroat trout. No decent camping areas can be found in the lake vicinity, but a few wanna-be's with horse feed exist along the outlet in the meadows to the north. There is spring water on the south side of the lake.

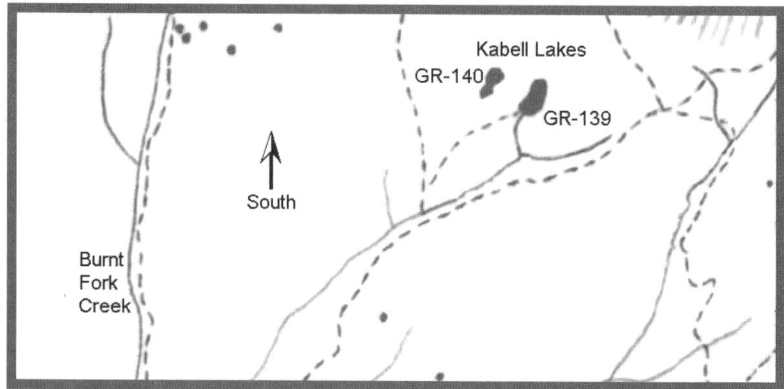

This is far from the ultimate wilderness experience, but it could be a welcome retreat if you are camping among the masses at Hoop Lake. We suggest that you try out Kabell Lake as a hearty day hike. You could see a lot of great country, eat lunch at the lake, fish a little, and be back at the campground before dark.

***Winter comes early in the high country.***

# Island Lake

| Trip Planner: | | | |
|---|---|---|---|
| Miles | 7.8 | Usage | Heavy |
| Elevation | 10,777 | Campsites | Excellent |
| Elev. Gain | 1,580 | Springwater | Yes |
| Drainage | Burnt Fork | Fishing | Good |
| Trailhead | Hoop Lake | Horsefeed | Fair |
| Near Town | Mountain View | Firewood | Limited |

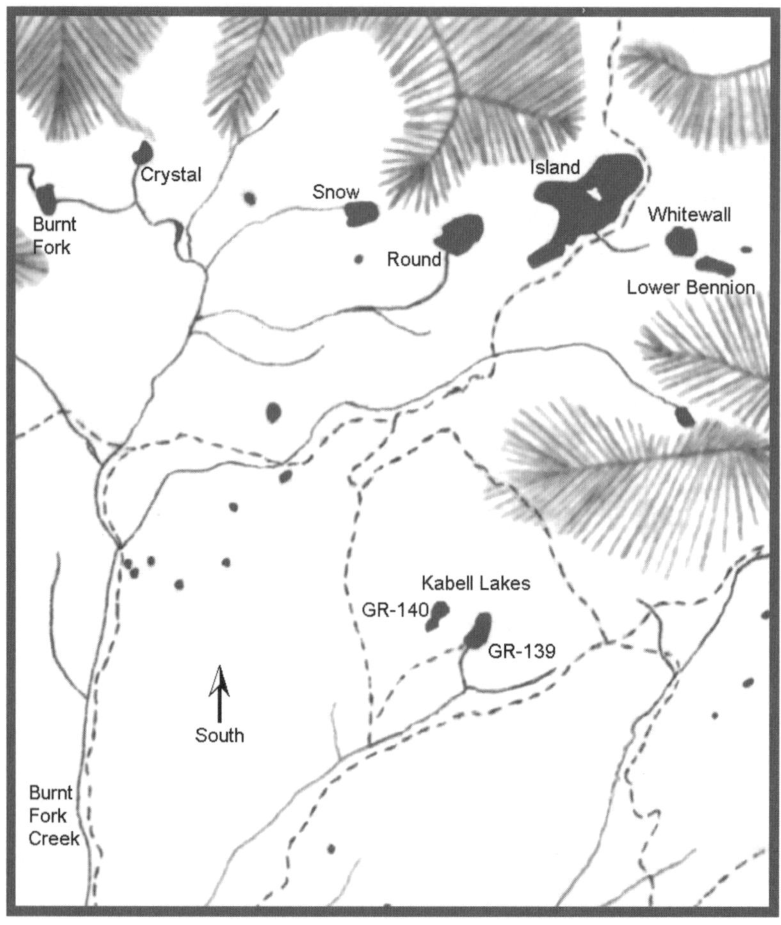

Many lakes in the High Uintas claim the name of Island. However, this lake is the king of all the Island lakes - mainly because it's the biggest. Island Lake is reached from either Hoop Lake or Spirit Lake. The Spirit Lake trail is about a mile longer, but the elevation gain is 1,000 feet less.

Island is a large alpine lake located in the southwest corner of the Burnt Fork Drainage. It receives fairly heavy usage from scouts and backpackers alike. Excellent campsites exist around the lake, while spring water is located along the south shore. Angling is often good for brook and cutthroat trout using small flies or spinners. Throughout the summer, Island Lake experiences a gradual draw-down as irrigation water is needed downstream.

*Island Lake*

The further you get away from Island Lake, the better the solitude. For instance, Round Lake receives only moderate pressure, yet features excellent campsites, horse feed, and spring water.

Snow Lake is impossible for horse travel, which makes fishing pressure for cutthroat trout all the lighter. This lake comes with an excellent source of spring water, but camping areas are nonexistent.

Whitewall and the Bennion Lakes can prove to be worth a visit. They receive light angling use for brook and cutthroat trout. Several springs and campsites with plenty of horse feed can be found on the west side of Whitewall Lake. Access from Island is west through a large meadow, then up a timbered slope. Get your map and compass out. The best fishing should take place at Lower Bennion. Whitewall and Upper Bennion are shallow and often winterkill.

# Tamarack Lake

| Trip Planner: | | | |
|---|---|---|---|
| Miles | 1.4 | Usage | Heavy |
| Elevation | 10,429 | Campsites | Good |
| Elev. Gain | 230 | Springwater | Yes |
| Drainage | Sheep Creek | Fishing | Good |
| Trailhead | Spirit Lake | Horsefeed | Good |
| Near Town | Manila | Firewood | Limited |

*Tamarack Lake*

If your looking for a nice excursion for the entire family, then Tamarack Lake is a good choice. A well-maintained Forest Service trail takes off from the southwest side of Spirit Lake Campground. From here, it is only 1.4 miles south then west on the Middle Fork trail. The trail splits about 1 mile from the trailhead, but both trails reunite near the east side of Tamarack Lake. The left-hand trail is a little bit longer, but passes by Jessen Lake, while the right-hand trail heads straight to Tamarack Lake.

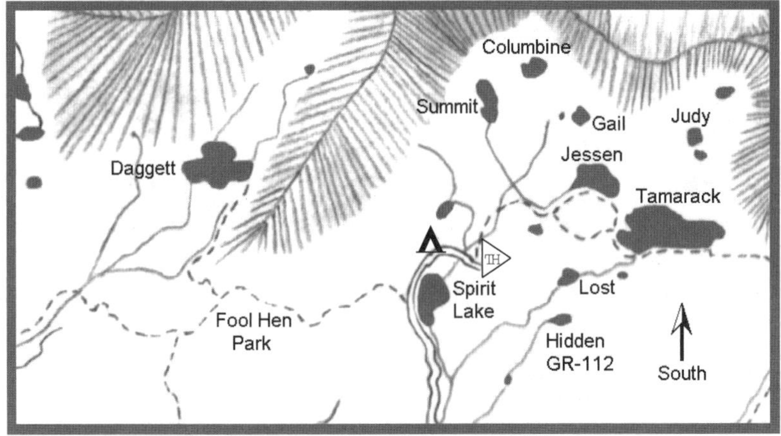


Tamarack is the biggest body of water in the Sheep Creek Drainage. Although it receives heavy usage, brook and a few cutthroat trout are maintained by stocking and natural reproduction. The best campsites are on the east side. In fact, perhaps the best campsite can be found just a hundred yards south down the trail where it splits off and heads south toward the lake. This site can accommodate a large group. Spring water seeps up along the south shoreline, and horse feed is present to the east.

Just southeast of Tamarack, lies Jessen Lake. Both are about the same type of lake, except Jessen is half the size and has no real campsites. It sits right next to the trail in rocky timbered country.

If these lakes contain too many people for your taste, try Lost Lake. Get there by following the outlet of Tamarack Lake 1/2 mile northeast. Lost Lake has several campsites to choose from, and angling usage remains relatively light. Fill your canteen before coming here, because there's no spring water in the vicinity. Lost Lake is more or less a shallow pond, but good water exchange enables cutthroat trout to survive the winter.

Nearby Hidden Lake is an another great place to escape. There are no campsites or spring water, but it could produce fast fishing for brookies. It is only 1/4 mile north of Lost Lake, but many hikers don't make the extra effort to see what Hidden Lake offers.

Judy Lake is perched upon a rocky and timbered bench within a scenic alpine basin, and can provide fantastic brook trout angling. Follow a steep ridge up the southeast side of Tamarack, then head southwest. Gail Lake may also produce good opportunities. It receives little attention, and is deep enough to support a fair supply of cutthroat trout.

# Daggett Lake

| Trip Planner: | | | |
|---|---|---|---|
| Miles | 2.8 | Usage | Heavy |
| Elevation | 10,462 | Campsites | Good |
| Elev. Gain | 260 | Springwater | Sometimes |
| Drainage | Sheep Creek | Fishing | Good |
| Trailhead | Spirit Lake | Horsefeed | Fair |
| Near Town | Manila | Firewood | Limited |

We've heard a lot of discouraging stories about Daggett Lake. Some say angling is desperately poor, and others tell of the hordes of mosquitoes that can suck you dry. Perhaps these people are mis-informed, or maybe they just want to keep a few secrets for themselves. Whatever the reason, we found Daggett to be one of

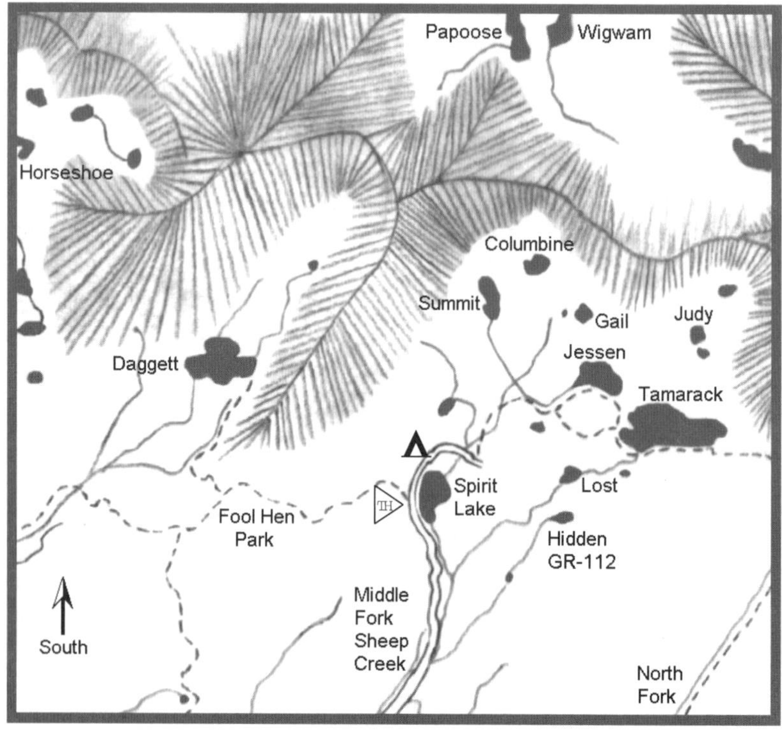

***Daggett Lake***

the better Rainbow fisheries in the High Uintas. In the short time we spent here, we managed to hook several hefty trout. A small orange fly seemed to get their attention, and bait anglers using green sparkled PowerBait pulled 'em in just as fast.

The mosquito population can be a nasty problem. The trail winds around swampy water holes, and a large meadow sits just south of the lake. This presents no difficulty in reaching your destination, but it is prime habitat for a large assortment of bugs and mosquitoes. To avoid these pesky critters, plan your trip after mid August. By this time, hail storms and other elements have diminished their numbers.

Access to Daggett begins on the east side of Spirit Lake. Follow a well groomed trail 1 mile east up a steep slope. Then head across Fool Hen Park to a posted sign at the Daggett Lake trail junction. From here, the trail drops 400 feet down rocky switchbacks and to one of the outlets of Daggett Lake. Proceed along the outlet another 3/4 mile through a couple of boggy meadows and up a bouldered ravine.

Daggett Lake plays host to a number of campsites along the northwest shore. Horse feed is in a meadow to the north, but spring water is hard to come by. This pretty lake receives moderate to heavy usage. Please help keep it clean.

# Summit Lake

| Trip Planner: | | | |
|---|---|---|---|
| Miles | 1 | Usage | Very Light |
| Elevation | 10,460 | Campsites | Good |
| Elev. Gain | 260 | Springwater | No |
| Drainage | Sheep Creek | Fishing | Poor |
| Trailhead | Spirit Lake | Horsefeed | Good |
| Near Town | Manila | Firewood | Good |

Summit Lake is also known as Sasquina. Years ago a legend was told about its trailhead, (Spirit Lake). According to the story, Sasquina was a beautiful Indian maiden. One day while picking berries, a strong handsome Indian chief named Walkara peered through the trees. As he gazed into her eyes of beauty, they became one. However, being from different tribes, they where forbidden to marry. Then one day in the valley of Hickerson Park, tribal Indians performed a special wedding ceremony. They then went on there honeymoon to Spirit Lake. This is where Chief Walkara placed a necklace made out of sacred elk bones around her neck.

A few days after their honeymoon, Chief Walkara went in search for food. When he returned, Sasquina was no where to be found. He looked at all the places where they had spent time together, but Sasquina had disappeared. Then he went to the lake they both loved. He yelled out her name "Sasquina; Sasquina." Out of the lake, swam a herd of elk. Sasquina then arose from the lake, wearing the sacred necklace of bones. Legend has it, if you are at Spirit Lake just before dawn, you'll see the spirit of Sasquina rise from the waters.

To find Summit or Sasquina Lake, follow the Tamarack trail 1/4 mile to an open meadow. Take a spur trail south to the base of a rocky ravine. At the top of the ravine lies Summit Lake. There are no fish in this lake, but it is a great place to be alone.

If you want to see some lakes that no one ever really visits, then put on your rock-hoppin' boots, and get ready for some rugged trekking. The lakes we are speaking of are Columbine, Gail and Judy. These lakes sit in the upper portion of the Middle Fork of Sheep Creek Drainage.

***Summit Lake***

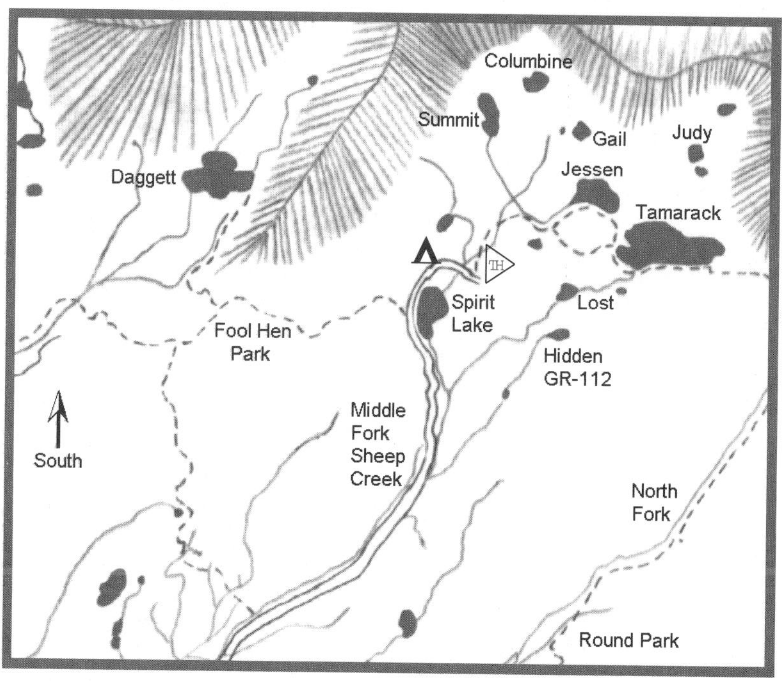
Columbine
Summit
Gail
Judy
Daggett
Jessen
Tamarack
TH
Spirit
Lake
Lost
Fool Hen
Park
Hidden
GR-112
Middle
Fork
Sheep
Creek
South
North
Fork
Round Park

# Anson & Weyman Lakes

| Trip Planner: | | | |
|---|---|---|---|
| Miles | 6.5 | Usage | Moderate |
| Elevation | 10,575 | Campsites | Fair |
| Elev. Gain | 375 | Springwater | Yes |
| Drainage | Sheep Creek | Fishing | Good |
| Trailhead | Spirit Lake | Horsefeed | Fair |
| Near Town | Manila | Firewood | Limited |

There are a number of lakes in the High Uintas that some people feel are misnamed. According to old-timers, the D.W.R. booklets are somewhat misconstrued. This is a real possibility, but to avoid confusion we'll stick with the D.W.R. names. If you are interested in unclarified names of lakes in this vicinity, they are: Clear Lake was once called Horseshoe, Hidden as Clear, and GR-13 is remembered as Hidden. If this doesn't confuse you, try telling a friend.

The first lake you'll arrive at is Lower Anson. Upper Anson Lake is just a little further. Follow a scant trail 1/4 mile south, as it parallels the east side of the inlet to Lower Anson. Both lakes are in rugged and rocky terrain. There is one small camp on the south end of Lower Anson, but the best campsite is located a couple of hundred yards above Lower Anson Lake near the creek.

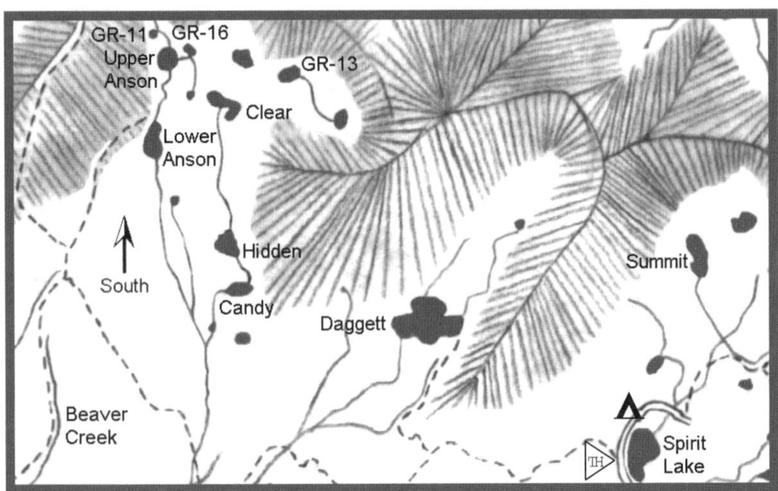

***Fishing might be better with a pole.***

Fishing should be pretty good if the water is clear. Anson Lakes can get murky during rainy years. Natural reproduction keeps the brook trout population up. In fact, sometimes there are too many trout and they become stunted.

Leave your horses behind at Anson Lakes when traveling into the Weyman Lakes area. Treacherous terrain makes horses impractical. Expect the best fishing at either Clear or Hidden Lake, although Hidden will likely be murky if Anson Lakes are. Clear Lake is always clear, and has some fat cutts. Candy Lake offers some of the biggest and tastiest trout that will ever tickle your tonsils. Angling is rather slow, but their meat will fulfill your most savory cravings.

# Lamb Lakes

| Trip Planner: | | | |
|---|---|---|---|
| Miles | 6.5 | Usage | Light |
| Elevation | 10,350 | Campsites | Fair |
| Elev. Gain | 1,750 | Springwater | No |
| Drainage | Carter Creek | Fishing | Good |
| Trailhead | Browne Lake | Horsefeed | Fair |
| Near Town | Manila | Firewood | Good |

Just before arrival you might say, "What a bummer." That's because the last mile is extremely rocky and impossible for horse travel. The trail begins on Road 96, just before arriving at Browne Lake. Follow the West Fork trail 5.5 miles south, then drop over the ridge 1 mile west to Bummer Lake.

Lamb Lakes can provide prime angling. However, fishing is unpredictable. Although these lakes receive little pressure, most have a history of winterkill during long hard winters. In the summer months, an excellent elk population expresses its existence here. Signs of elk are everywhere. To experience the appearance of

***Un-named lake near Potter Lakes***

these animals can be quite difficult. One sniff, sound, or sight of a human, and all that will be detected is the sound of scampering hooves pouncing through the trees.

Several lakes occupy Lamb Lakes Basin. They are Bummer, Mutton, Lamb, Ram, Ewe, GR-20 & GR-21. All of these lakes are in rough and rocky timbered country, and campsites are few and far between. Except for the Bummer Lake area, spring water can be found at all of the lakes.

Discover Mutton Lake by following the inlet of Bummer Lake 1/2 mile south. This lake plays host to the best camping areas in Lamb Lakes Basin. Fishing pressure is considered light for stocked brook trout.

Lamb Lake is next to a steep rocky slope 1 mile west of Bummer. There is no trail and the going gets rough when crossing over rocks and dead timber. This lake may also experience winterkill during harsh winters. For better angling possibilities, try Ram Lake. It is a little deeper, and is fed by a fresh supply of spring water. Ram Lake is just 1 mile southwest of Bummer Lake.

Ewe Lake is a fishless pond sitting at the base of a talus slope 1 mile west of Bummer. The hike is over rough terrain. Ewe can also be reached by dropping over the ridge from the Beaver Creek Trail. No campsites or fish exist, but spring water can be found around the lake. GR-20 & GR-21 receive very light angling pressure. However, fishing is quite slow due to shallow water. Get out and see this remote wilderness. Few people do.

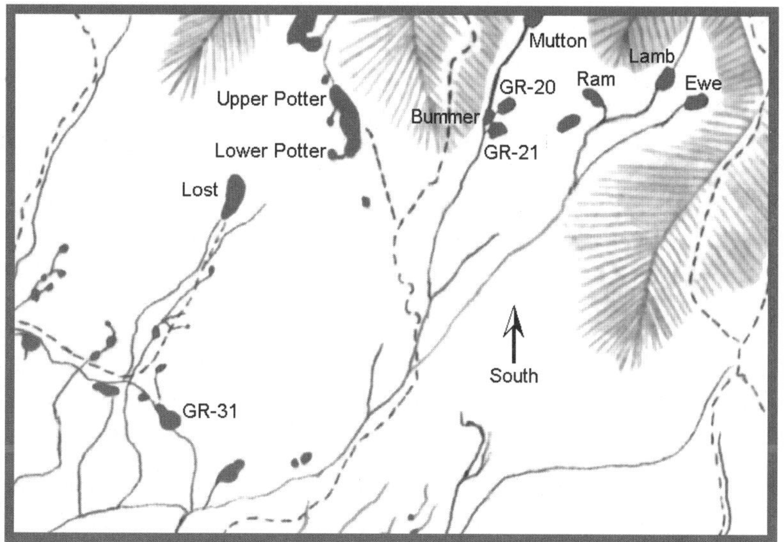

# Teepee Lakes

| Trip Planner: | | | |
|---|---|---|---|
| Miles | 3.5 | Usage | Heavy |
| Elevation | 9,410 | Campsites | Good |
| Elev. Gain | 1,010 | Springwater | Yes |
| Drainage | Carter Creek | Fishing | Very Good |
| Trailhead | Browne Lake | Horsefeed | Good |
| Near Town | Manila | Firewood | Good |

While an elevation of 1,000 Ft. in 3.5 miles doesn't sound like much, not much elevation is picked up until the last mile. For the first couple of miles, the trail topples over several rolling hills. After the second bridge crossing, the trail then proceeds up a steady incline. At times this excursion feels like a constant uphill battle. On the other hand, it becomes rather relaxing on the way out.

Teepee Lakes attract a vast variety of visitors. Boy Scout groups congregate near Brownie Lake, while many others use this recreation area as well. Good campsites and spring water are near the west side of the trail of Lower Teepee, and angling is usually good for pan-sized brookies. Upper Teepee Lake is somewhat slow for fishing. During hard cold winters, it often winterkills.

Other good fishing holes that can be found in the Middle or East Fork drainage are Red, Lost, and One Fish. Red Lake is at the end of a rugged trail, 2 miles south of Teepee Lakes. This pretty lake lies beneath Leidy Peak, and angling pressure remains light for stocked brook trout. Lost Lake (also known as Mystery Lake) is a beautiful body of water nestled within a secluded pocket formed by two ridges. Find Lost Lake by following a skimpy trail, which is marked with a posted sign. In other words, this would be a good time to break out the map.

One Fish Lake, just might be that. You may catch one fish or you could net a bundle. This lake is surround by heavy timber. Angling techniques don't match up with those of a fly-fisherman, as troublesome tree branches will constantly tangle your tackle. Campsites are not found in the immediate vicinity. However, camping areas, spring water and horse feed are 1/8 mile southeast in a large meadow.

***Lower Teepee Lake***

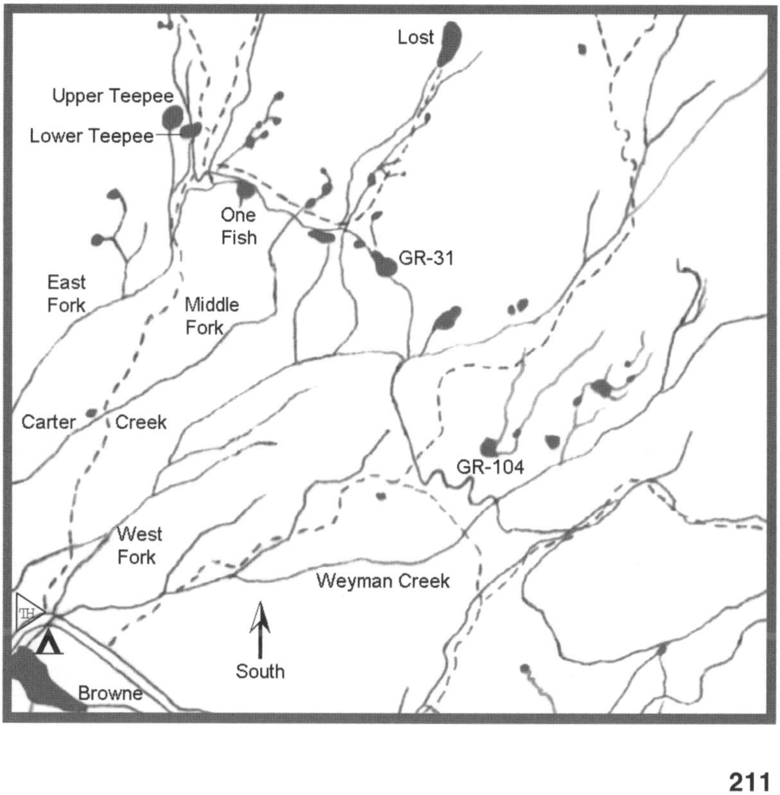

Lost
Upper Teepee
Lower Teepee
One Fish
GR-31
East Fork
Middle Fork
Carter Creek
GR-104
West Fork
Weyman Creek
TH
South
Browne

# The Highline Trail

| Trip Planner: | | | |
|---|---|---|---|
| Miles | 83 | Usage | Moderate |
| Elevation | up to 12,600 | Campsites | Good |
| Elev. Gain | 600 | Springwater | Yes |
| Drainages | South Slope | Fishing | Good |
| Trailhead | Highline | Horsefeed | Good |
| Near Town | Kamas | Firewood | Limited |

There's a certain breed of backpackers that practically live on the trail. These are the long-haulers. It takes a lot of stamina and will power to take on a long hike lasting many days or even weeks. If you are strong enough, crazy enough, and have lots of time, then maybe you can join the elite long-haulers on the Highline Trail.

The trail begins at either the Highline Trailhead (west end) or at the Leidy Peak Trailhead on the eastern end of the High Uinta Mountains. The Leidy Peak trail starts about 600 feet higher, but that factor will have little effect on the total wear-n-tear of this lengthy trek. The Highline Trail takes you up and down seven mountain passes. They are (west to east): Rocky Sea, Dead Horse, Red Knob, Porcupine, Tungsten, Anderson, and Gabbro Pass. It is these passes that make this journey something special. From atop the backbone of the High Uintas, you'll witness one spectacular vista after another.

Almost all of the Highline experience happens on the south slope of the Uintas. The only exception is where the trail takes a brief detour over Dead Horse Pass into the West Fork Blacks Fork Drainage. After less than 4 miles, the trail winds its way back to the south slope over Red Knob Pass.

Because much of the Highline Trail is above timberline, plan carefully where to spend your nights. Choose camps with pines for shelter from wind and rain. Low stands of pines are also the safest place to be when lightning is flashing. Speaking of bad weather, allow yourself at least a couple of extra days to complete this hike. You might get holed-up for awhile waiting for the skies to settle down.

It should go without saying that excellent physical conditioning is a prerequisite to this alpine adventure. The steep rocky miles will tear at your muscles, and the high altitude will take your breath away. But then, so will the scenery.

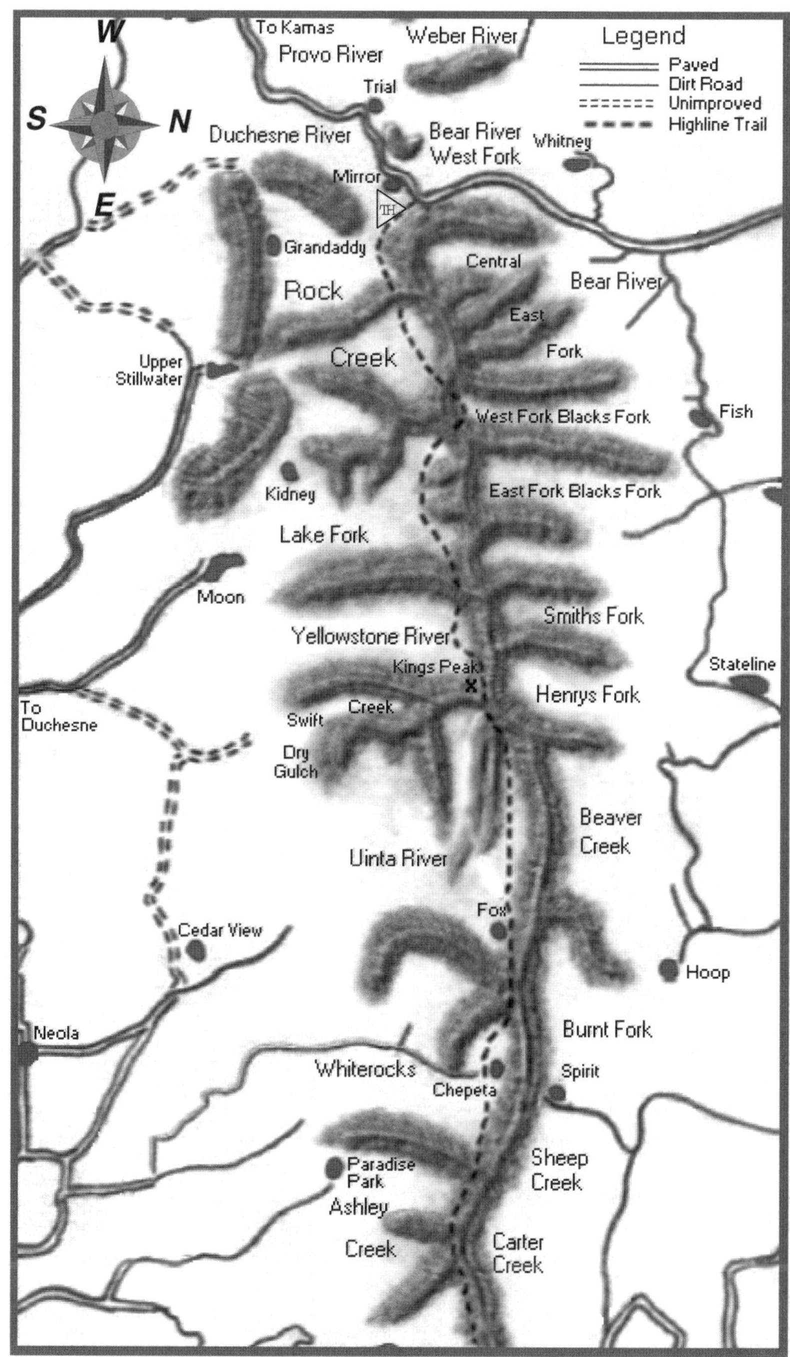


See next page for photos.

Rocky Sea Pass

Red Knob Pass

Deadhorse Pass

I love to think of nature as an unlimited broadcasting station, through which God speaks to us every hour, if we only will tune in.

-- *George Washington Carver*

# Maps & Stats

***Legend:***

| Fish | Use (Usage) | Cmp (Campsites) | Spr (Spring water) | Fd (Horse Feed) |
|---|---|---|---|---|
| B=Brook | VH=Very Heavy | E=Excellent | Y=Yes | E=Excellent |
| C=Cutthroat | H=Heavy | VG=Very Good | N=No | G=Good |
| G=Grayling | M=Moderate | G=Good | | F=Fair |
| Go=Golden | L=Light | F=Fair | | P=Poor |
| R=Rainbow | VL=Very Light | P=Poor | | |

Λ Campground  Trailhead

# Provo River Drainage

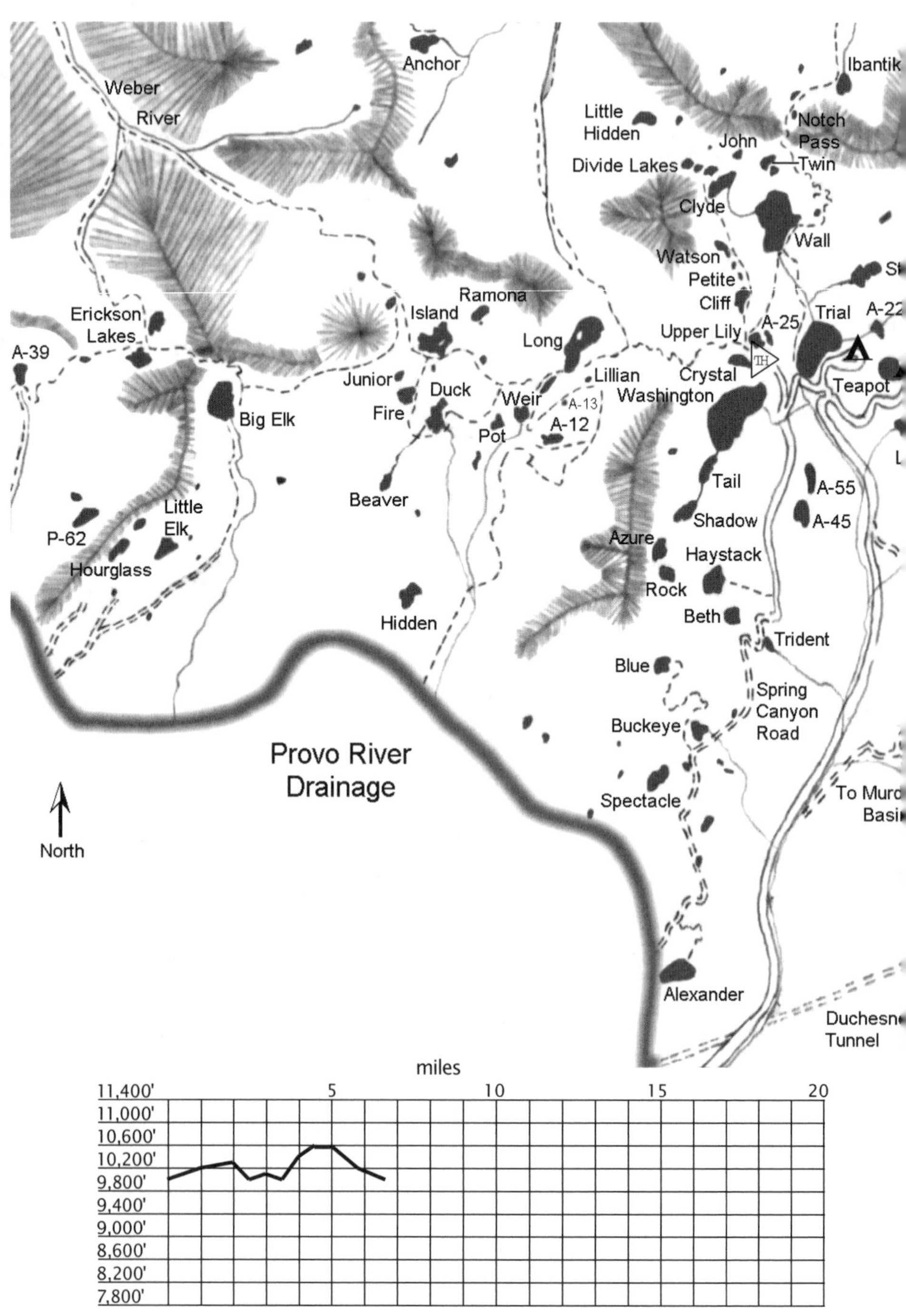


***Crystal Lake Trailhead to Big Elk Lake***

# Provo River Drainage

| Lake | Ref # | Elev. | Miles | Acres | Deep | Fish | Use | Cmp | Spr | Fd |
|---|---|---|---|---|---|---|---|---|---|---|
| Alexander | A-1 | 9,360 | 0.3 | 23 | 28 | B | H | G | N | F |
| Azure (alias Lock) | A-11 | 10,140 | 0.5 | 9 | 23 | C | M | P | N | P |
| Beaver | A-17 | 9,900 | 3.8 | 3.5 | 15 | B | L | F | N | F |
| Beth | A-6 | 9,780 | 0 | 5.4 | 10 | B | H | G | N | F |
| Big Elk | A-18 | 10,020 | 1.1 | 43 | 110 | B,C | H | G | N | P |
| Blue | A-5 | 9,680 | 0 | 8 | 26 | B,G | H | G | Y | F |
| Booker | A-35 | 10,460 | 2 | 4.1 | 8 | B | M | G | N | F |
| Brook | A-20 | 9,720 | 4 | 1.1 | 6 | B | M | G | Y | F |
| Buckeye | A-3 | 9,660 | 0 | 5 | 8 | B | H | E | Y | G |
| Clegg | A-47 | 10,460 | 1.5 | 5.1 | 12 | B | M | G | N | F |
| Cliff | A-34 | 10,230 | 0.5 | 9 | 20 | C | H | G | Y | F |
| Clyde | A-28 | 10,420 | 1.5 | 16 | 21 | B | H | P | N | F |
| Crystal | A-51 | 10,020 | 0.1 | 9.8 | 10 | B | H | G | Y | G |
| Cutthroat (alias Clint) | A-40 | 9,940 | 3 | 3 | 10 | B | L | E | Y | G |
| Diamond | A-22 | 9,900 | 0.5 | 3 | 7 | B | M | F | Y | G |
| Divide #1 | A-36 | 10,460 | 2.5 | 3.5 | 5 | B | M | G | Y | F |
| Duck | A-7 | 9,780 | 3.3 | 32.6 | 31 | B,C | M | G | N | F |
| Fire | A-14 | 10,200 | 4 | 12.4 | 65 | C | M | P | N | P |
| Haystack | A-9 | 9,940 | 0 | 17 | 29 | B,C | H | G | N | F |
| Hidden | A-15 | 9,760 | 5 | 8.2 | 25 | B | M | F | N | P |
| Hourglass | A-48 | 9,980 | 0.3 | 5.7 | 20 | B,C | H | F | N | P |
| Island | A-57 | 10,140 | 3.5 | 30.5 | 42 | B,C | M | G | Y | F |
| Jacks | A-13 | 9,980 | 2.7 | 1.2 | 23 | B | L | F | N | P |
| James | A-31 | 10,500 | 2.3 | 2.1 | 8 | B | M | F | Y | F |
| John | A-30 | 10,500 | 1.7 | 4 | 10 | B | M | F | N | F |
| Junior | A-56 | 10,220 | 3.8 | 2.8 | 11 | C | L | G | N | G |
| Lambert | A-2 | 9,630 | 0.1 | 2 | 8 | B | H | F | N | F |
| Lillian | A-43 | 10,100 | 2 | 2 | 8 | B | L | E | Y | G |
| Lilly | A-58 | 9,910 | 0 | 5.1 | 12 | R,B | VH | E | Y | F |

***Continued***

# Provo River Drainage (continued)

| Lake | Ref # | Elev. | Miles | Acres | Deep | Fish | Use | Cmp | Spr | Fd |
|---|---|---|---|---|---|---|---|---|---|---|
| Lily, Lower | A-25 | 10,030 | 0.1 | 3.2 | 16 | B | H | G | N | F |
| Lily, Upper | A-24 | 10,020 | 0.1 | 3.2 | 12 | N | M | G | N | F |
| Little Elk | A-19 | 9,780 | 0.5 | 13.2 | 31 | N | H | G | N | F |
| Long Pond | A-62 | 10,100 | 2 | 2 | 5 | B,C | M | G | N | F |
| Long | A-37 | 10,100 | 2 | 55 | 37 | B,C | H | E | N | G |
| Lost | A-59 | 9,890 | 0 | 64.3 | 28 | R | VH | E | Y | P |
| Marjorie | A-12 | 9,980 | 2.8 | 27 | 26 | G | M | G | N | P |
| Norway Flats | P-8 | 9,900 | 0.5 | 3 | 16 | N | L | F | N | P |
| Petite | A-26 | 10,300 | 0.8 | 2 | 3 | B | L | F | N | F |
| Pot | A-8 | 9,940 | 2.8 | 4 | 28 | B | M | F | N | F |
| Ramona | A-38 | 10,340 | 3.8 | 4.7 | 21 | B | L | F | N | P |
| Rock | A-10 | 10,140 | 0.5 | 8 | 14 | B | M | G | Y | F |
| Shadow | A-52 | 10,060 | 0.5 | 14 | 20 | B | H | F | Y | F |
| Shingle Creek, East | A-39 | 9,700 | 1.5 | 7 | 44 | B | H | G | Y | F |
| Shingle Creek, Lower | P-62 | 9,620 | 1.5 | 4 | 14 | B | L | G | Y | P |
| Shingle Creek, West | P-60 | 9,940 | 1.8 | 4 | 17 | B | L | G | Y | F |
| Spectacle | A-44 | 9,740 | 0.3 | 9.3 | 17 | B | L | F | N | F |
| Star | A-42 | 9,980 | 0.5 | 18.5 | 41 | B,C | M | F | N | F |
| Tail | A-53 | 9,980 | 0.5 | 9.8 | 13 | B,R | H | G | N | F |
| Teapot | A-60 | 9,930 | 0 | 14.4 | 48 | B,R | VH | F | N | F |
| Trial | A-61 | 9,820 | 0 | 69.3 | 68 | B,R,C | VH | E | Y | P |
| Trident | A-41 | 9,400 | 0 | 4 | 5 | B | H | E | N | F |
| Twin, Lower | A-33 | 10,410 | 2.3 | 3 | 14 | B,C | M | F | N | P |
| Twin, Upper | A-32 | 10,420 | 2.4 | 9 | 13 | B | M | G | Y | F |
| Wall | A-29 | 10,140 | 1 | 85 | 122 | C | H | F | N | F |
| Washington | A-23 | 9,980 | 0 | 100.2 | 72 | B,C | VH | E | N | P |
| Watson | A-27 | 10,420 | 1 | 6 | 10 | B | M | G | Y | F |
| Weir | A-50 | 9,940 | 2.5 | 14 | 21 | C,G | M | G | Y | P |

# Notes:

# Naturalist Basin

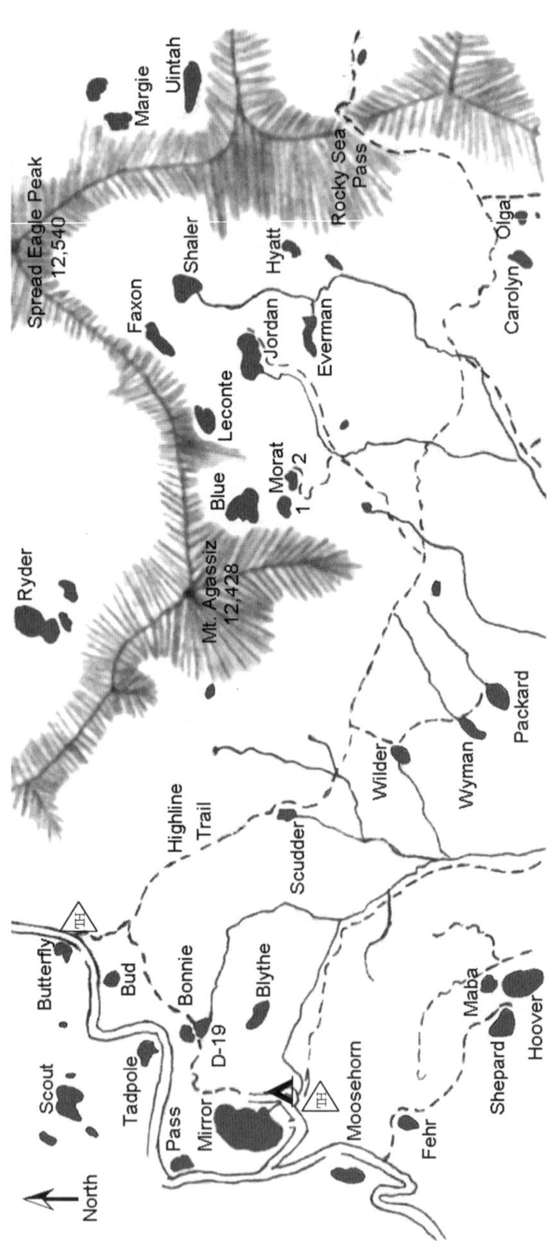

# Naturalist Basin

| Lake | Ref # | Elev. | Miles | Acres | Deep | Fish | Use | Cmp | Spr | Fd |
|---|---|---|---|---|---|---|---|---|---|---|
| Blue | Z-32 | 10,940 | 6 | 19 | 36 | B | M | P | Y | P |
| Blythe | Z-20 | 9,900 | 0.5 | 5 | 16 | B | M | G | Y | F |
| Bonnie | Z-6 | 10,100 | 0.2 | 3.6 | 7 | B | H | G | N | F |
| Bud | Z-2 | 10,220 | 0.1 | 3.7 | 13 | B | H | G | N | F |
| Butterfly | Z-1 | 10,340 | 0 | 5.2 | 13 | R,B | VH | E | Y | P |
| Carolyn | Z-42 | 10,460 | 6.5 | 5 | 17 | G | M | G | Y | G |
| Castle | D-14 | 10,300 | 0.4 | 1 | 12 | C | M | G | Y | F |
| Everman | Z-36 | 10,520 | 5.5 | 7.8 | 7 | B | L | G | Y | G |
| Fehr | Z-7 | 10,260 | 0.3 | 5.7 | 27 | B | H | G | Y | G |
| Hoover | Z-10 | 9,900 | 0.1 | 18.6 | 28 | B | VH | E | Y | F |
| Hyatt | Z-37 | 10,740 | 6 | 2.4 | 10 | B | L | G | N | G |
| Jordan | Z-35 | 10,660 | 5.8 | 2.3 | 30 | B | H | G | Y | F |
| Leconte | Z-33 | 10,920 | 6.3 | 9.5 | 15 | C | L | P | N | F |
| Maba | Z-8 | 9,900 | 0.1 | 4.2 | 20 | B | M | F | N | F |
| Mirror | Z-3 | 10,020 | 0 | 53.4 | 36 | R,B | VH | E | Y | P |
| Moosehorn | Z-4 | 10,380 | 0 | 7.2 | 11 | R | VH | E | Y | P |
| Morat #1 | Z-31 | 10,740 | 5.5 | 5.4 | 15 | C | M | G | N | F |
| Morat #2 | Z-27 | 10,740 | 5.5 | 3.6 | 8 | C | M | G | Y | F |
| Packard | Z-15 | 9,980 | 3.5 | 9.2 | 52 | B | M | G | Y | F |
| Pass | Z-5 | 10,060 | 0 | 6.5 | 8 | R,B | VH | P | N | P |
| Scout | Z-12 | 10,380 | 0.5 | 19 | 17 | R | H | P | N | P |
| Scudder | Z-21 | 9,940 | 2 | 4.5 | 10 | N | H | G | N | P |
| Shaler | Z-34 | 10,920 | 6.5 | 13 | 7 | C | M | P | Y | P |
| Shepard | Z-9 | 9,980 | 0.2 | 14.2 | 32 | B,C | M | G | Y | P |
| Wilder | Z-13 | 9,900 | 2.8 | 3.7 | 14 | B | M | G | N | G |
| Wyman | Z-14 | 9,980 | 3.3 | 6.5 | 19 | B | M | G | N | E |
| | D-19 | 10,100 | 0.2 | 1.2 | 6 | B | M | F | N | G |

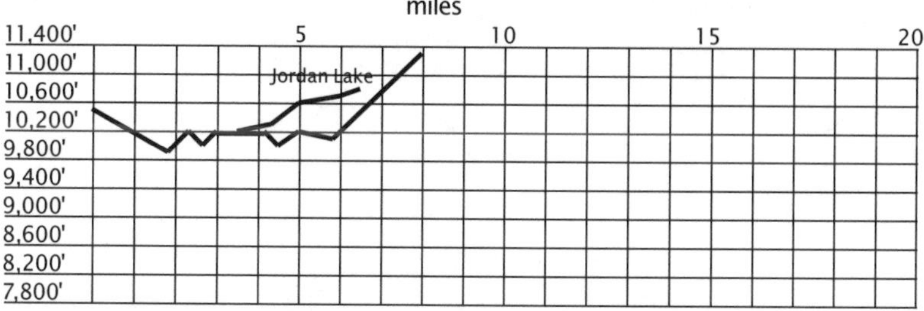

# Duchesne Drainage (Lower)

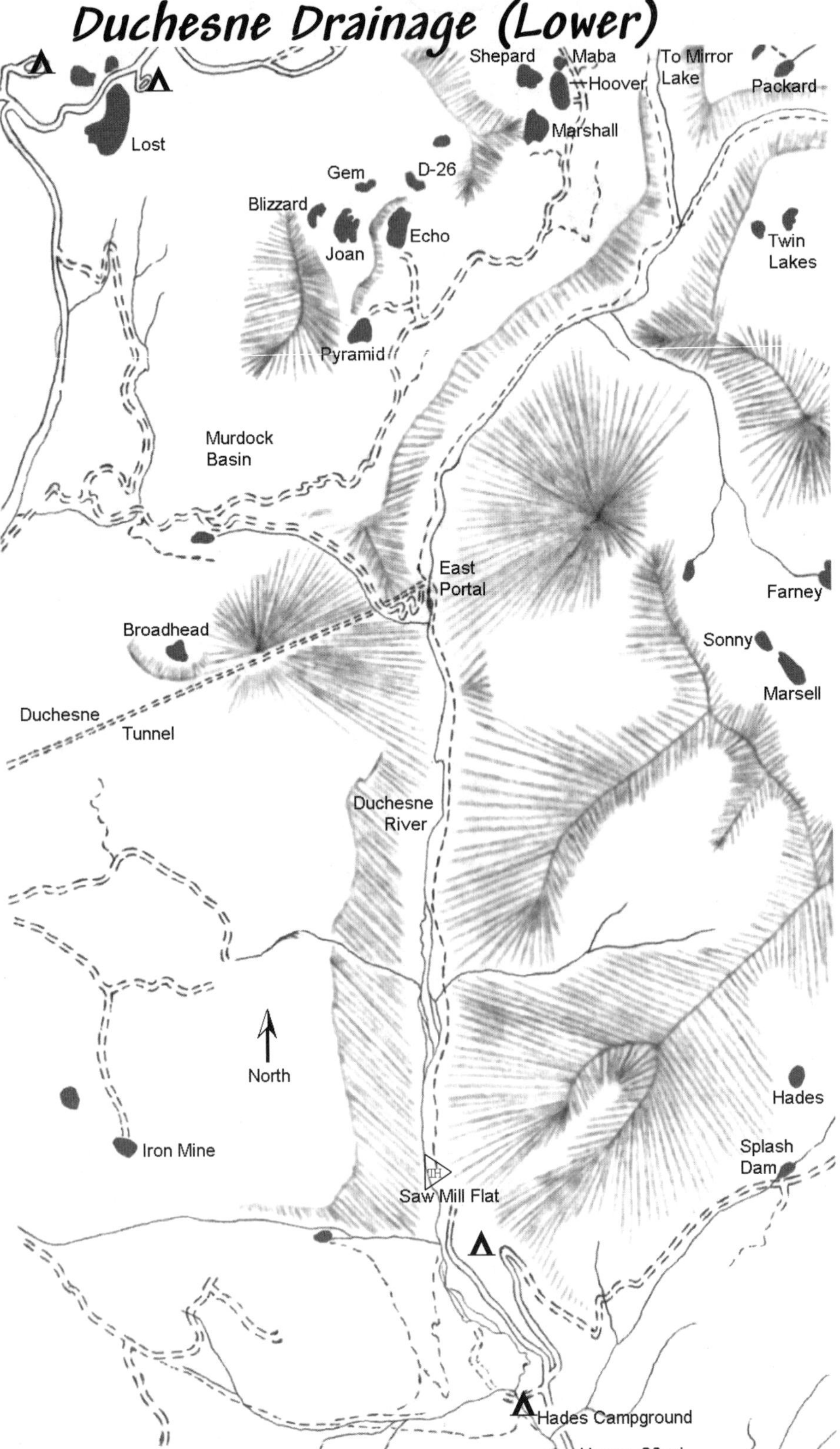

# Duchesne Drainage (Lower)

| Lake | Ref # | Elev. | Miles | Acres | Deep | Fish | Use | Cmp | Spr | Fd |
|---|---|---|---|---|---|---|---|---|---|---|
| Broadhead | D-40 | 9,960 | 0.8 | 8.8 | 16 | B | L | G | Y | F |
| Echo | Z-16 | 9,740 | 0 | 18 | 44 | B,Go | H | E | Y | F |
| Farney | X-14 | 10,430 | 5.5 | 12.6 | 14 | C | L | F | Y | F |
| Gem | Z-18 | 10,070 | 0.7 | 3.8 | 14 | B,C | L | G | Y | G |
| Hades | D-11 | 9,990 | 0.8 | 5.3 | 23 | B | M | F | N | F |
| Hoover | Z-10 | 9,900 | 0.1 | 18.6 | 28 | B | VH | E | Y | F |
| Iron Mine | D-33 | 9,580 | 0 | 7.3 | 21 | N | M | G | N | F |
| Joan | Z-19 | 10,050 | 0.3 | 15.2 | 20 | B,C | M | G | Y | G |
| Marsell | X-11 | 10,460 | 5 | 16.4 | 50 | C | L | G | Y | P |
| Marshall | Z-11 | 9,980 | 0.1 | 18 | 36 | B,C | H | G | N | F |
| Packard | Z-15 | 9,980 | 3.5 | 9.2 | 52 | B | M | G | Y | F |
| Pyramid | Z-17 | 9,700 | 0 | 15 | 36 | B | H | G | N | F |
| Shepard | Z-9 | 9,980 | 0.2 | 14.2 | 32 | B,C | M | G | Y | P |
| Sonny | X-12 | 10,450 | 5.1 | 5 | 14 | C | L | E | N | F |
|  | D-26 | 10,060 | 0.3 | 3 | 10 | B | L | G | Y | F |

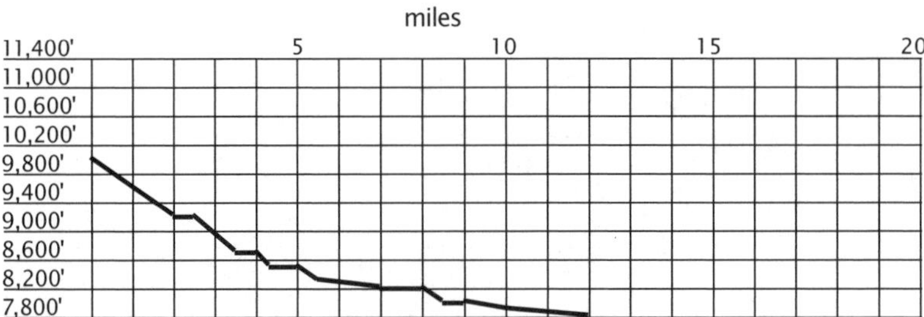


***Mirror Lake to Mill Flat***

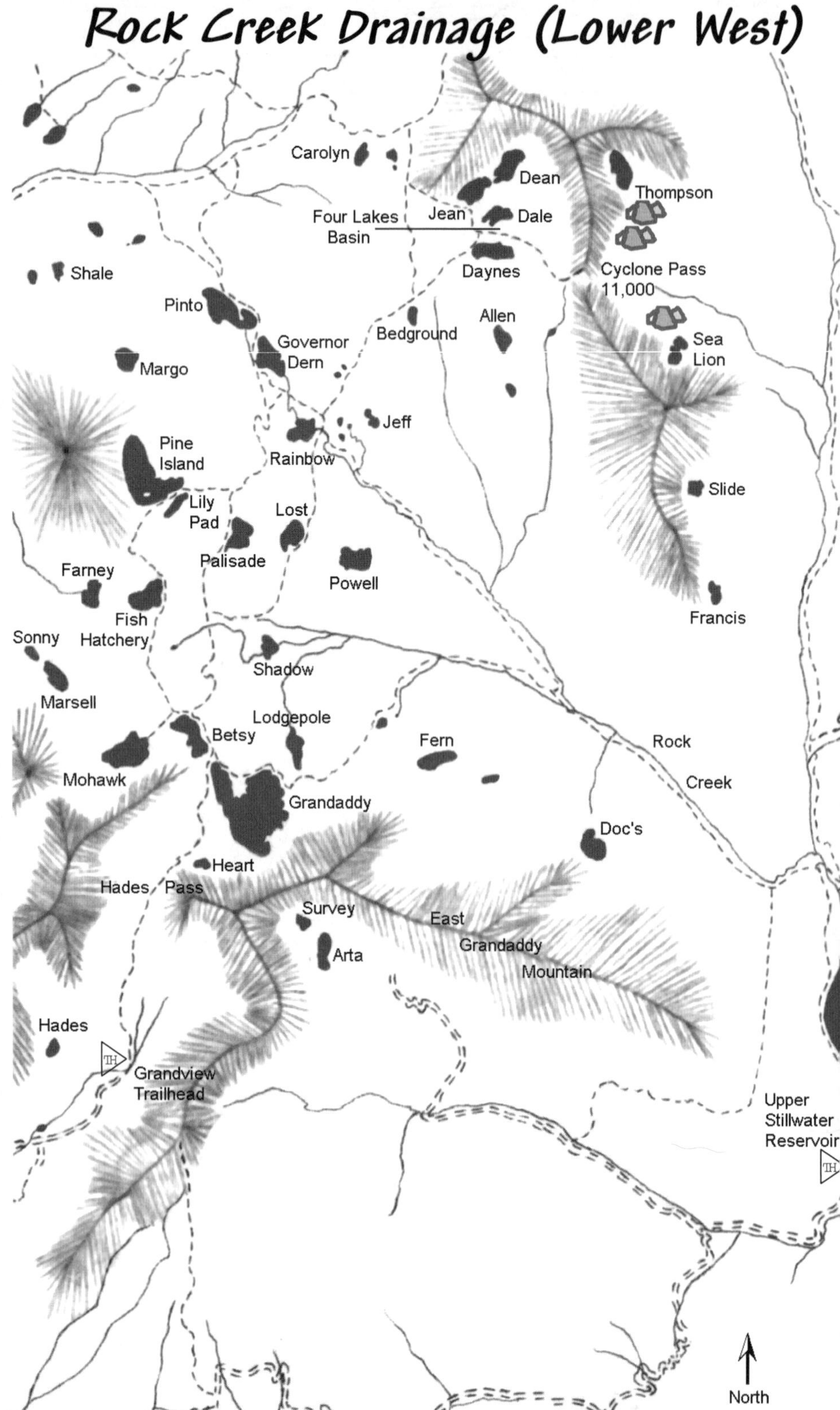
Rock Creek Drainage (Lower West)
Carolyn
Dean
Thompson
Four Lakes
Basin
Jean
Dale
Daynes
Cyclone Pass
11,000
Shale
Pinto
Allen
Bedground
Governor
Dern
Sea
Lion
Margo
Jeff
Pine
Island
Rainbow
Slide
Lily
Pad
Lost
Palisade
Powell
Farney
Francis
Fish
Hatchery
Sonny
Shadow
Marsell
Lodgepole
Betsy
Fern
Rock
Creek
Mohawk
Grandaddy
Doc's
Heart
Hades
Pass
Survey
East
Grandaddy
Mountain
Arta
Hades
TH
Grandview
Trailhead
Upper
Stillwater
Reservoir
TH
North

# Rock Creek Drainage (Lower West)

| Lake | Ref # | Elev. | Miles | Acres | Dee | Fish | Us | Cmp | Spr | Fd |
|---|---|---|---|---|---|---|---|---|---|---|
| Allen | Z-44 | 10,390 | 9 | 15.2 | 16 | G | L | VG | Y | E |
| Arta | RC-23 | 10,450 | 0.5 | 5.4 | 6 | C | L | G | N | P |
| Bedground | Z-46 | 10,500 | 8.5 | 2 | 15 | B | M | E | N | E |
| Betsy | X-7 | 10,350 | 3.5 | 33.8 | 44 | B,C | H | G | Y | G |
| Dale | Z-39 | 10,700 | 9 | 12.9 | 25 | B | H | G | Y | G |
| Daynes | Z-38 | 10,670 | 9 | 23.2 | 21 | B,G | H | G | Y | G |
| Dean | Z-40 | 10,755 | 9.2 | 24 | 44 | B,C | M | F | Y | F |
| Doc's | X-15 | 9,882 | 5 | 14.5 | 45 | B | L | F | N | P |
| Fern | X-5 | 9.890 | 5.7 | 19.3 | 19 | B | M | F | Y | F |
| Fish Hatchery | X-6 | 10,230 | 5.3 | 37.2 | 28 | B,C | H | G | Y | G |
| Gibby | RC-30 | 10,320 | 3.5 | 1.9 | 25 | B | M | F | N | F |
| Governor Dern | Z-24 | 9,990 | 9.1 | 32 | 9 | B,C | M | E | Y | G |
| Grandaddy | X-9 | 10,310 | 3.2 | 173 | 40 | B,C | H | G | Y | G |
| Heart | X-13 | 10,500 | 2.6 | 5.7 | 19 | C | H | F | Y | F |
| Jean | Z-41 | 10,753 | 8.5 | 23.2 | 23 | B,C | H | F | N | F |
| Lily Pad | X-2 | 10,270 | 6.1 | 9.5 | 14 | B | M | E | Y | E |
| Lodgepole | X-3 | 10,140 | 4.1 | 20.4 | 29 | B | M | G | Y | F |
| Lost | Z-29 | 10,030 | 5.8 | 14 | 15 | B | M | G | Y | G |
| Margo | Z-23 | 10,420 | 9.5 | 11.1 | 29 | C | L | G | Y | G |
| Mohawk | X-10 | 10,380 | 4.1 | 50.8 | 23 | B,C | H | E | Y | G |
| Palisade | Z-28 | 10,140 | 5.3 | 22.7 | 45 | B,C | H | G | Y | G |
| Pine Island | X-8 | 10,300 | 5.9 | 79.6 | 44 | B,C | H | G | N | F |
| Pinto | X-22 | 10,020 | 8.2 | 46.6 | 36 | B | H | E | Y | E |
| Powell | Z-30 | 9,980 | 6.3 | 22.4 | 15 | C | M | F | N | P |
| Rainbow | Z-25 | 9,930 | 7 | 17.9 | 15 | B,C | H | E | Y | E |
| Sea Lion | RC-11 | 10,385 | 10.7 | 7.9 | 11 | C | L | P | Y | P |
| Shadow | X-1 | 9,940 | 5.3 | 7.2 | 22 | B,C | M | F | N | G |
| Survey | RC-20 | 10,700 | 0.8 | 6 | 12 | B | L | G | N | G |
| Thompson | RC-8 | 10,690 | 11.2 | 21.2 | 26 | B | VL | P | N | P |

***See page 276 for Elevation Grid***

# Rock Creek Drainage (Main)

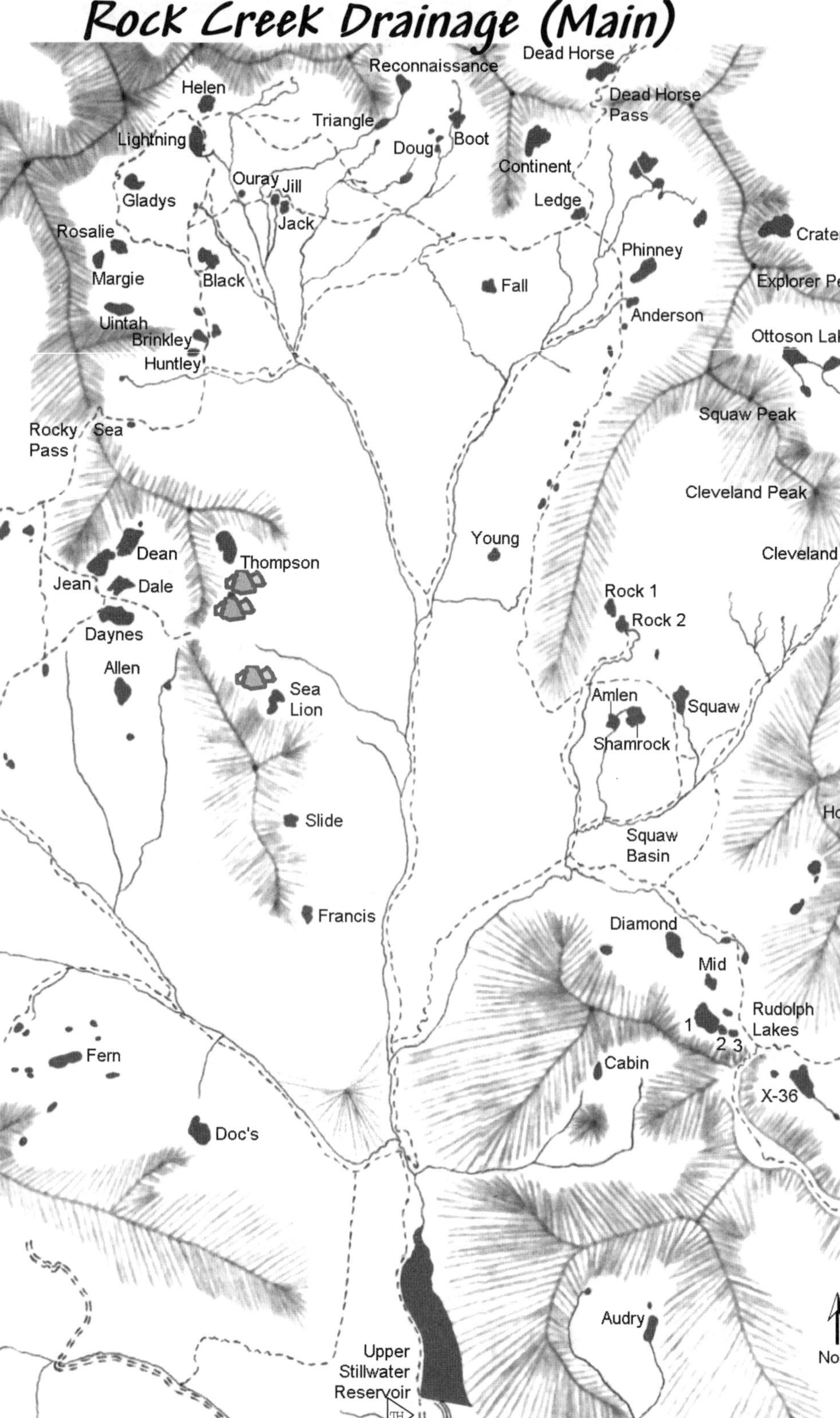

# Rock Creek Drainage (Main)

| Lake | Ref # | Elev. | Miles | Acres | Deep | Fish | Use | Cmp | Spr | Fd |
|---|---|---|---|---|---|---|---|---|---|---|
| Amlen | X-99 | 10,340 | 11 | 7.3 | 9 | B | M | VG | N | G |
| Anderson | X-117 | 10,590 | 15.6 | 5.8 | 12 | B | M | E | Y | G |
| Black | X-132 | 10,403 | 11 | 11.8 | 14 | B,C | H | G | Y | G |
| Boot | X-124 | 11,096 | 14.7 | 9.1 | 17 | C | M | P | Y | P |
| Brinkley | RC-4 | 10,460 | 10 | 4.2 | 18 | B | H | E | Y | E |
| Cabin | RC-42 | 10,450 | 11 | 4.3 | 16 | B | VL | F | N | P |
| Continent | X-121 | 11,285 | 15.6 | 27.4 | 23 | B,C | L | P | N | P |
| Diamond | X-43 | 10,230 | 9 | 13 | 45 | B,C | M | P | N | P |
| Doc's | X-15 | 9,882 | 5 | 14.5 | 45 | B | L | F | N | P |
| Doug | X-123 | 11,060 | 14.5 | 0.9 | 8 | C | L | P | N | P |
| Gladys | X-128 | 10,900 | 12.8 | 7.5 | 6 | B | M | P | Y | P |
| Helen | X-126 | 10,869 | 12.8 | 8.4 | 14 | B | M | F | Y | P |
| Jack | X-133 | 10,460 | 12.6 | 2.7 | 14 | B,C | M | F | Y | F |
| Jill | X-111 | 10,460 | 12.5 | 3.6 | 25 | C | M | G | Y | F |
| Ledge | X-113 | 10,845 | 14.4 | 3.1 | 13 | B | M | G | Y | G |
| Lightning | X-127 | 10,819 | 12.5 | 14.1 | 23 | B,C | M | F | Y | G |
| Margie | X-129 | 10,980 | 12.3 | 7.5 | 11 | B | L | F | N | F |
| Ouray | X-112 | 10,380 | 12.1 | 4 | 6 | B,C | M | E | Y | E |
| Phinney | X-119 | 10,625 | 13.6 | 13.6 | 30 | B,C | M | G | Y | G |
| Reconnaissance | X-125 | 11,145 | 15.4 | 8.8 | 30 | B,C | L | F | Y | G |
| Rock 1 | X-96 | 10,559 | 11.8 | 4.8 | 19 | B | L | G | N | G |
| Rock 2 | X-97 | 10,550 | 11.5 | 7.7 | 17 | B | L | G | N | G |
| Rudolph 1 | X-39 | 10,420 | 9.8 | 25.6 | 46 | B | M | F | Y | F |
| Rudolph 2 | X-40 | 10,470 | 9.8 | 2.9 | 9 | B | M | G | Y | G |
| Sea Lion | RC-11 | 10,385 | 10.7 | 7.9 | 11 | C | L | P | Y | P |
| Shamrock | X-98 | 10,365 | 11 | 18.2 | 33 | B | M | F | Y | G |
| Squaw | X-95 | 10,483 | 10.5 | 10.4 | 9 | B | H | G | Y | E |
| Thompson | RC-8 | 10,690 | 11.2 | 21.2 | 26 | B | VL | F | N | P |
| Uinta | X-131 | 10,840 | 12.5 | 8.4 | 14 | B | L | P | N | P |
| Young | X-100 | 10,310 | 10.5 | 4 | 19 | C | VL | F | N | P |

***See page 276 for Elevation Grid***

# Lake Fork Drainage

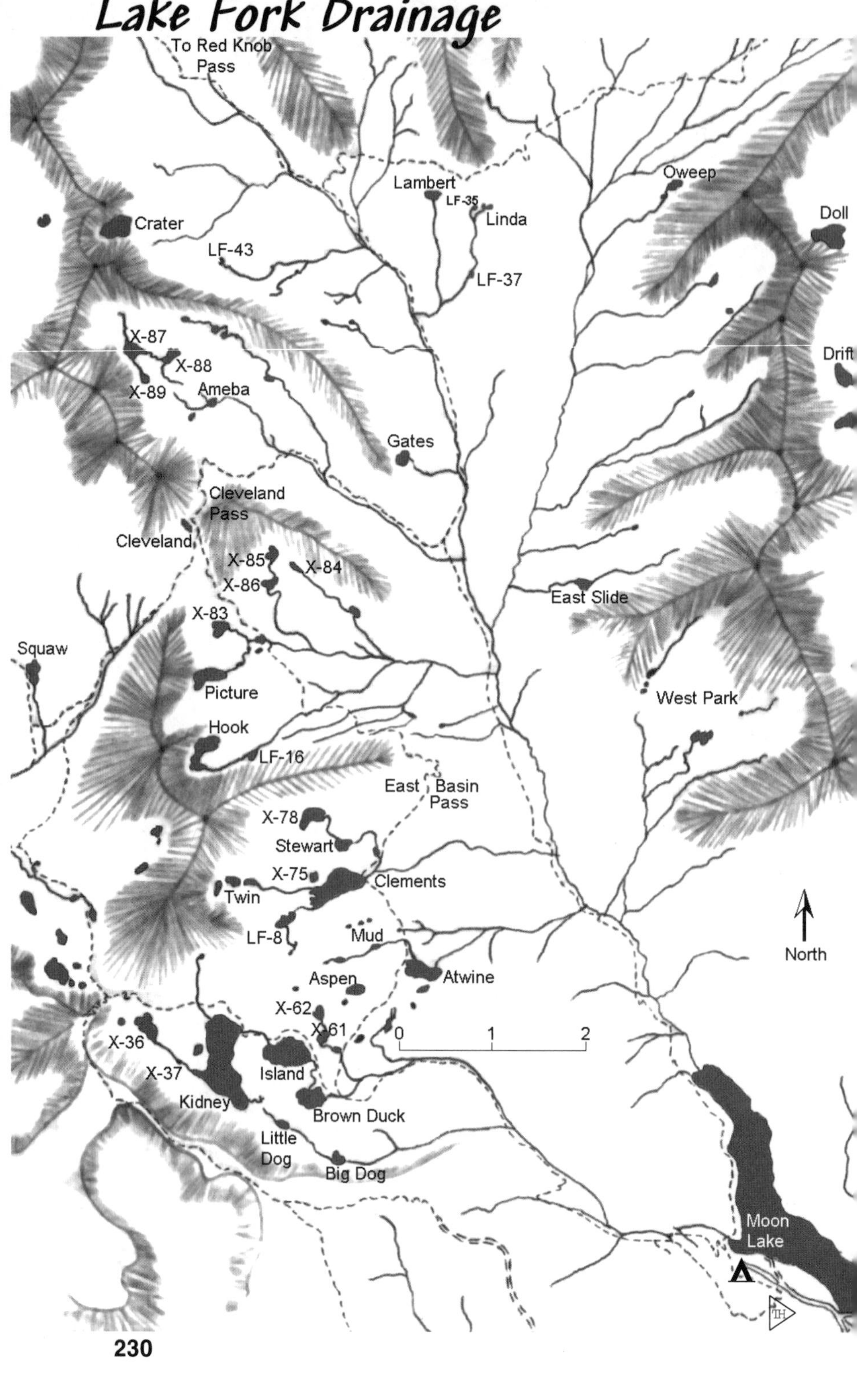

# Lake Fork Drainage

| Lake | Ref # | Elev. | Miles | Acres | Deep | Fish | Use | Cmp | Spr | Fd |
|---|---|---|---|---|---|---|---|---|---|---|
| Ameba | X-90 | 10,850 | 14 | 4.6 | 4 | C | L | G | N | G |
| Aspen | X-63 | 10,265 | 9 | 8 | 26 | B | M | P | N | P |
| Atwine | X-64 | 10,150 | 9 | 32 | 35 | B | H | G | Y | F |
| Big Dog | X-32 | 10,117 | 8 | 6 | 12 | G | L | F | N | F |
| Brown Duck | X-31 | 10,186 | 7 | 31 | 38 | C | H | G | N | P |
| Cleveland | LF-18 | 11,200 | 18.5 | | | N | L | P | N | P |
| Clements | X-74 | 10,444 | 10.4 | 70 | 50 | C | H | G | Y | F |
| Crater | X-94 | 11,268 | 17 | 28 | 147 | B | L | G | Y | F |
| East Slide | LF-44 | 10,314 | 9.5 | 6 | | B | VL | F | N | P |
| Gates | LF-34 | 10,450 | 12 | 5.4 | 20 | B | VL | F | N | P |
| Hook | X-81 | 10,722 | 18 | 21 | 19 | B | L | F | Y | F |
| Island | X-34 | 10,250 | 8 | 66 | 48 | B,C | H | E | Y | F |
| Kidney | X-35 | 10,267 | 9 | 190 | 112 | B,C | H | G | Y | G |
| Lambert | LF-21 | 10,990 | 16 | 6.6 | 15 | B | L | G | Y | G |
| Lilly Pad | X-37 | 10,275 | 9.5 | 1.4 | 8 | B,C | M | F | N | F |
| Linda | LF-36 | 10,940 | 17.3 | 3.8 | 5 | B | L | F | Y | E |
| Little Dog | X-33 | 10,230 | 7.5 | 4.5 | 17 | B | M | G | N | G |
| Mud | X-66 | 10,340 | 9.5 | 2.5 | 5 | B | L | P | N | G |
| Oweep | LF-30 | 10,865 | 21 | 6.4 | 16 | B | VL | F | Y | F |
| Ottoson, Lower | X-88 | 11,075 | 15.2 | 9 | 8 | C | L | F | N | F |
| Ottoson, Upper | X-87 | 11,099 | 15.5 | 12.4 | 30 | C | L | F | N | F |
| Picture | X-82 | 10,731 | 17 | 20 | 13 | R | M | F | Y | G |
| Porcupine | LF-22 | 11,301 | 25 | 12.8 | 14 | B | L | P | N | P |
| Stewart | X-79 | 10,530 | 11.5 | 9.2 | 22 | B | L | G | Y | P |
| Toquer | LF-25 | 10,470 | 3.2 | 11.1 | 32 | B,C | L | G | Y | G |
| Twin | X-77 | 10,594 | 12 | 12.9 | 15 | B | L | F | N | P |
| Tworoose | X-36 | 10,310 | 11 | 21.9 | 37 | C | L | G | Y | F |
| | LF-8 | 10,498 | 12.5 | 7 | 17 | C | L | P | N | G |
| | LF-16 | 10,550 | 17.5 | 3 | 6 | B | L | G | Y | E |

***Continued on next page....***

# Lake Fork Drainage (Continued)

| Lake | Ref # | Elev. | Miles | Acres | Deep | Fish | Use | Cmp | Spr | Fd |
|---|---|---|---|---|---|---|---|---|---|---|
| | LF-35 | 10,955 | 17.5 | 1 | | B | VL | F | Y | G |
| | LF-37 | 10,700 | 18.3 | 2 | 3 | B | VL | G | N | E |
| | LF-43 | 10,820 | 15.8 | 1.4 | 4 | B | VL | E | Y | E |
| | X-61 | 10,265 | 8.3 | 5.2 | | C | L | G | N | G |
| | X-62 | 10,300 | 8.5 | 6 | 10 | C | L | F | N | G |
| | X-75 | 10,450 | 11.2 | 4.4 | 6 | C | L | G | Y | G |
| | X-78 | 10,636 | 12 | 17 | 18 | C | L | F | N | P |
| | X-80 | 10,580 | 16 | 4.6 | 5 | B,C | M | E | Y | E |
| | X-84 | 10,815 | 17 | 4.6 | 18 | B | VL | F | N | F |
| | X-85 | 10,860 | 17 | 4.7 | 14 | B | VL | G | Y | F |
| | X-86 | 10,819 | 16.5 | 6.9 | 12 | B | L | F | N | F |
| | X-89 | 11,110 | 15.2 | 3.4 | | C | VL | P | N | P |

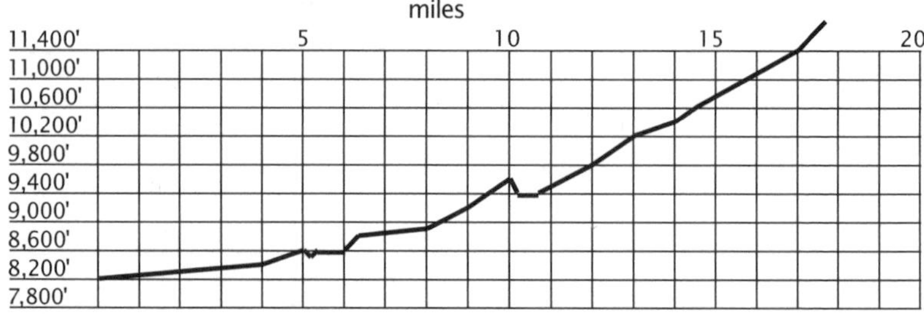


**Moon Lake to Red Knob Pass**

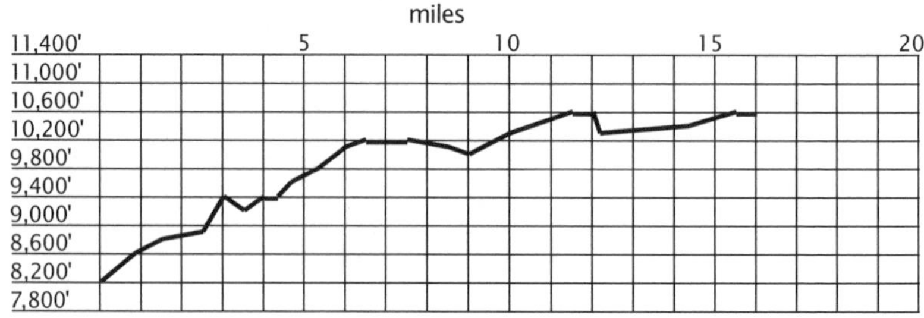


**Moon Lake to East Basin**

## Notes:

# Yellowstone Drainage

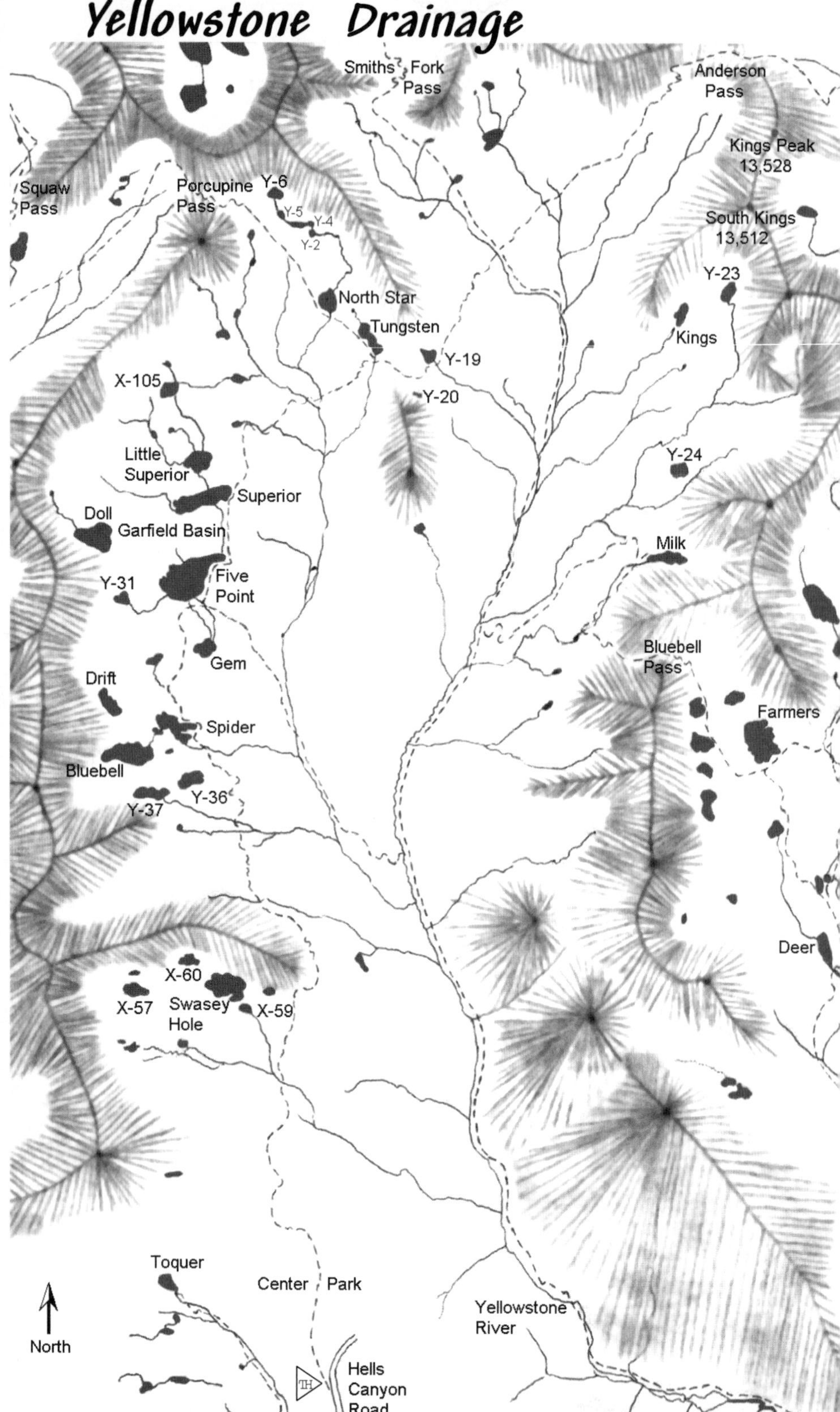

| Lake | Ref # | Elev. | Miles | Acres | Dee | Fish | Us | Cmp | Spr | Fd |
|---|---|---|---|---|---|---|---|---|---|---|
| Bluebell | X-110 | 10,894 | 8.1 | 38.3 | 32 | B,C | M | P | N | P |
| Doll | Y-16 | 11,352 | 13 | 42.5 | 47 | B | L | F | N | P |
| Drift Res. | Y-41 | 11,064 | 8.2 | 14.8 | | B | L | P | N | P |
| Five Point Res. | X-106 | 11,009 | 12 | 82 | 21 | B,C | H | VG | Y | F |
| Gem | Y-34 | 10,830 | 8.2 | 11.1 | 15 | B,C | M | G | N | P |
| Kings | Y-22 | 11,416 | 15 | 10 | | C | VL | P | N | P |
| Little Superior | X-104 | 11,208 | 13.3 | 13.9 | 24 | B | VL | P | N | F |
| Milk | Y-25 | 10,983 | 11 | 17.5 | 20 | B | L | F | N | F |
| North Star | X-108 | 11,395 | 15.5 | 14 | 15 | B | L | F | N | F |
| Spider | X-109 | 10,876 | 7.8 | 20 | 31 | B,C | H | E | Y | F |
| Superior | X-103 | 11,163 | 13 | 36 | 26 | B | M | F | N | F |
| Swasey | X-58 | 10,715 | 6 | 36 | 30 | B,C | H | G | Y | G |
| Tungsten | X-107 | 11,344 | 15.2 | 13 | 13 | B,C | M | P | N | F |
| | X-57 | 10,976 | 7 | 8.8 | 30 | B | L | P | N | P |
| | X-59 | 10,706 | 7 | 4.5 | 13 | C,R | M | F | N | F |
| | X-60 | 10,810 | 6.5 | 8 | 30 | B,C | L | P | N | F |
| | X-105 | 11,456 | 14.5 | 8.1 | 14 | C | L | P | N | F |
| | Y-2 | 11,670 | 16.5 | 1.8 | 20 | B | VL | P | N | P |
| | Y-4 | 11,679 | 16.7 | 5.8 | 12 | B | VL | P | N | P |
| | Y-5 | 11,685 | 17 | 1.8 | 6 | B | VL | P | N | P |
| | Y-19 | 11,268 | 17 | 6.2 | 15 | B | L | P | N | F |
| | Y-20 | 11,176 | 17.5 | 5 | 20 | C | L | P | N | P |
| | Y-31 | 11,082 | 12.5 | 4.6 | 7 | B | M | G | Y | G |
| | Y-36 | 10,820 | 8.3 | 14 | 15 | B | L | F | N | P |
| | Y-37 | 10,823 | 8.7 | 13 | 12 | B | L | G | N | F |

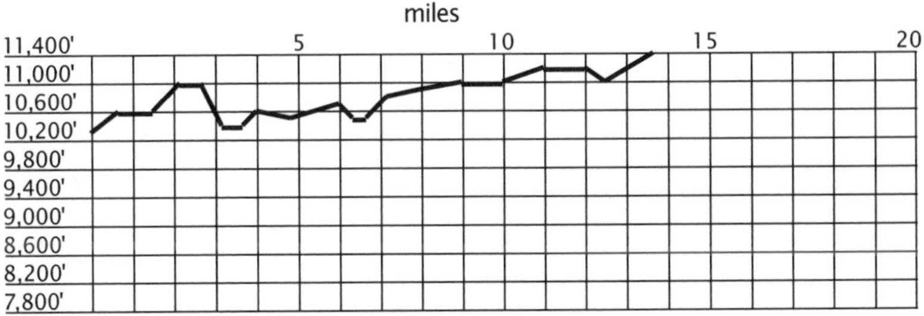


**Center Park to North Star Lake**

# Swift Creek Drainage

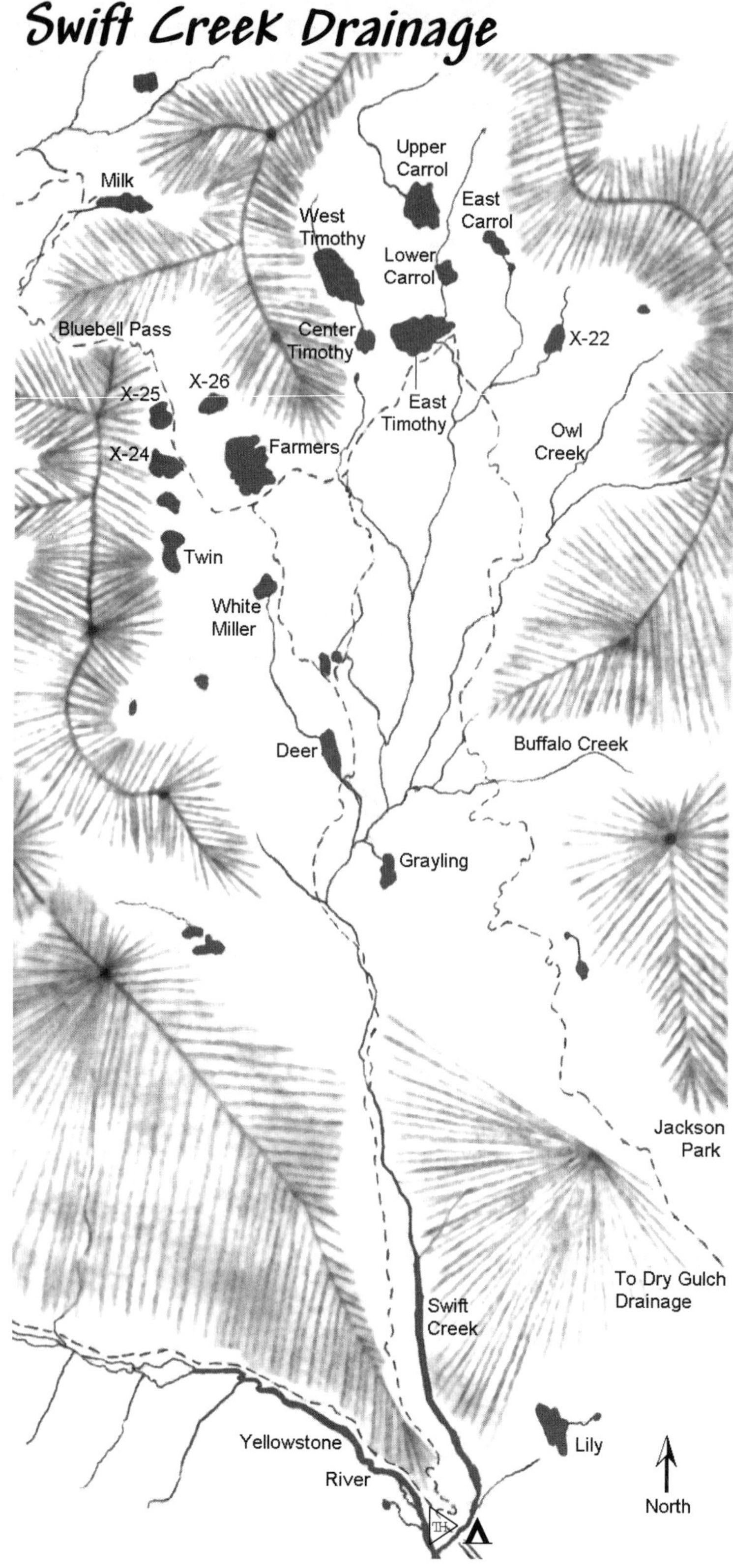

# Swift Creek Drainage

| Lake | Ref # | Elev. | Miles | Acres | Deep | Fish | Use | Cmp | Spr | Fd |
|---|---|---|---|---|---|---|---|---|---|---|
| Carrol, East | X-21 | 11,230 | 9.5 | 10 | 19 | C | L | P | N | F |
| Carrol, Lower | X-17 | 11,060 | 9 | 9 | 7 | B,C | M | F | Y | G |
| Carrol, Upper | X-18 | 11,140 | 9.5 | 35 | 48 | B | M | P | Y | F |
| Deer | X-55 | 10,240 | 5.4 | 12 | 47 | B,C | M | F | Y | F |
| Farmers | X-23 | 10,990 | 7.5 | 63 | 24 | B | M | G | Y | E |
| Grayling | X-56 | 9,980 | 5 | 8.5 | 33 | B,C | M | F | N | P |
| Lily | S-15 | 9,346 | 1 | 20 | 39 | B | M | F | N | P |
| Timothy, Center | X-20 | 11,030 | 8.7 | 10 | 18 | B,C | H | G | Y | G |
| Timothy, East | X-16 | 11,000 | 8.5 | 40 | 35 | B,C | H | G | N | G |
| Timothy, West | X-19 | 11,100 | 9.2 | 45 | 45 | B,C | M | P | N | P |
| Twin | X-49 | 10,816 | 8.1 | 13.7 | 15 | C | L | F | N | F |
| White Miller | X-54 | 10,670 | 6.7 | 11 | 18 | B | H | G | Y | E |
|  | X-22 | 11,060 | 9.5 | 9 | 8 | B,C | L | F | Y | G |
|  | X-24 | 10,919 | 8.2 | 21.4 | 30 | C | L | P | N | G |
|  | X-25 | 10,966 | 8.4 | 16.9 | 27 | C | L | F | Y | F |
|  | X-26 | 11,008 | 8.7 | 7.7 | 23 | B | L | P | N | P |

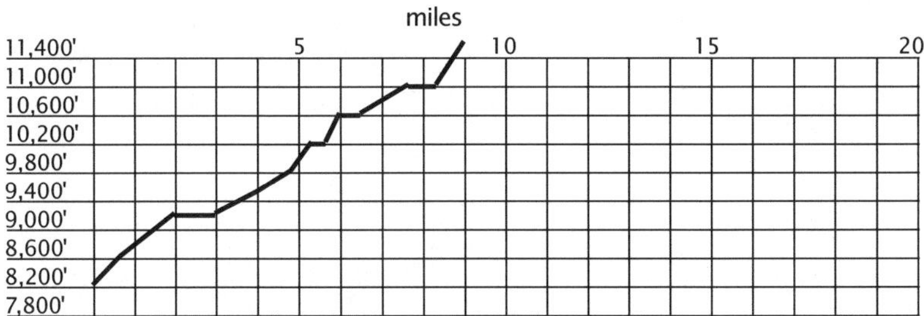


***Swift Creek Trailhead to Bluebell Pass***

# Dry Gulch Drainage

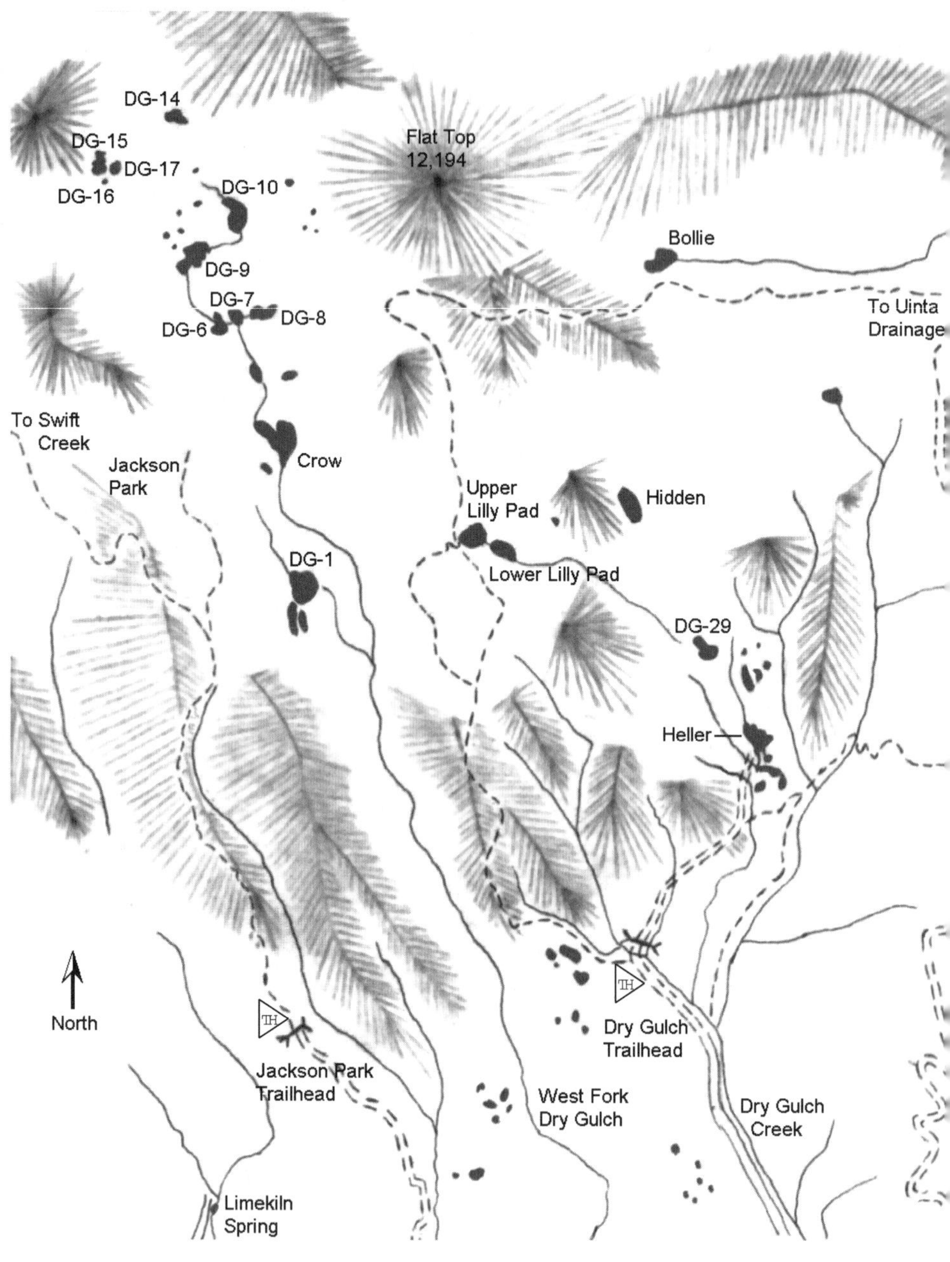

# Dry Gulch Drainage

| Lake | Ref # | Elev. | Miles | Acres | Deep | Fish | Use | Cmp | Spr | Fd |
|---|---|---|---|---|---|---|---|---|---|---|
| Crow | DG-3 | 10,320 | 3 | 18 | 26 | C | M | G | Y | G |
| Heller Res. | DG-28 | 9,520 | 2 | 10 | 39 | B,C | H | G | Y | P |
| Hidden | DG-27 | 10,108 | 4 | 12 | 37 | B | L | P | Y | P |
| Lilly Pad, Lower | DG-26 | 10,275 | 4.1 | 9 | 11 | B,C | L | G | N | F |
| Lilly Pad, Upper | DG-25 | 10,280 | 4 | 12 | 37 | B,C | H | E | N | G |
| | DG-6 | 10,550 | 2 | 3 | 5 | C | L | G | Y | G |
| | DG-7 | 10,550 | 2.1 | 6 | 4 | C | L | G | Y | G |
| | DG-8 | 10,550 | 2.3 | 7 | 8 | C | L | F | N | G |
| | DG-9 | 10,710 | 2.5 | 10 | 27 | C | L | F | Y | G |
| | DG-10 | 10,780 | 3 | 10 | 14 | C | L | F | N | G |
| | DG-14 | 11,070 | 3.8 | 2 | 12 | C | VL | P | Y | P |
| | DG-15 | 10,950 | 4 | 2 | 15 | C | VL | P | N | P |
| | DG-16 | 10,956 | 4 | 2 | 8 | C | VL | P | N | P |
| | DG-17 | 10,935 | 4 | 3.5 | 10 | C | VL | P | N | P |
| | DG-29 | 9,700 | 3 | 3 | 8 | B | VL | P | N | E |

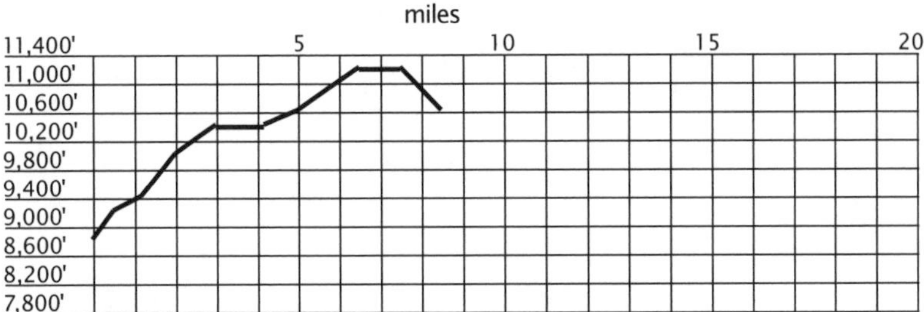


***Dry Gulch to Bollie Lake via Lily Lakes***

# Uinta Drainage

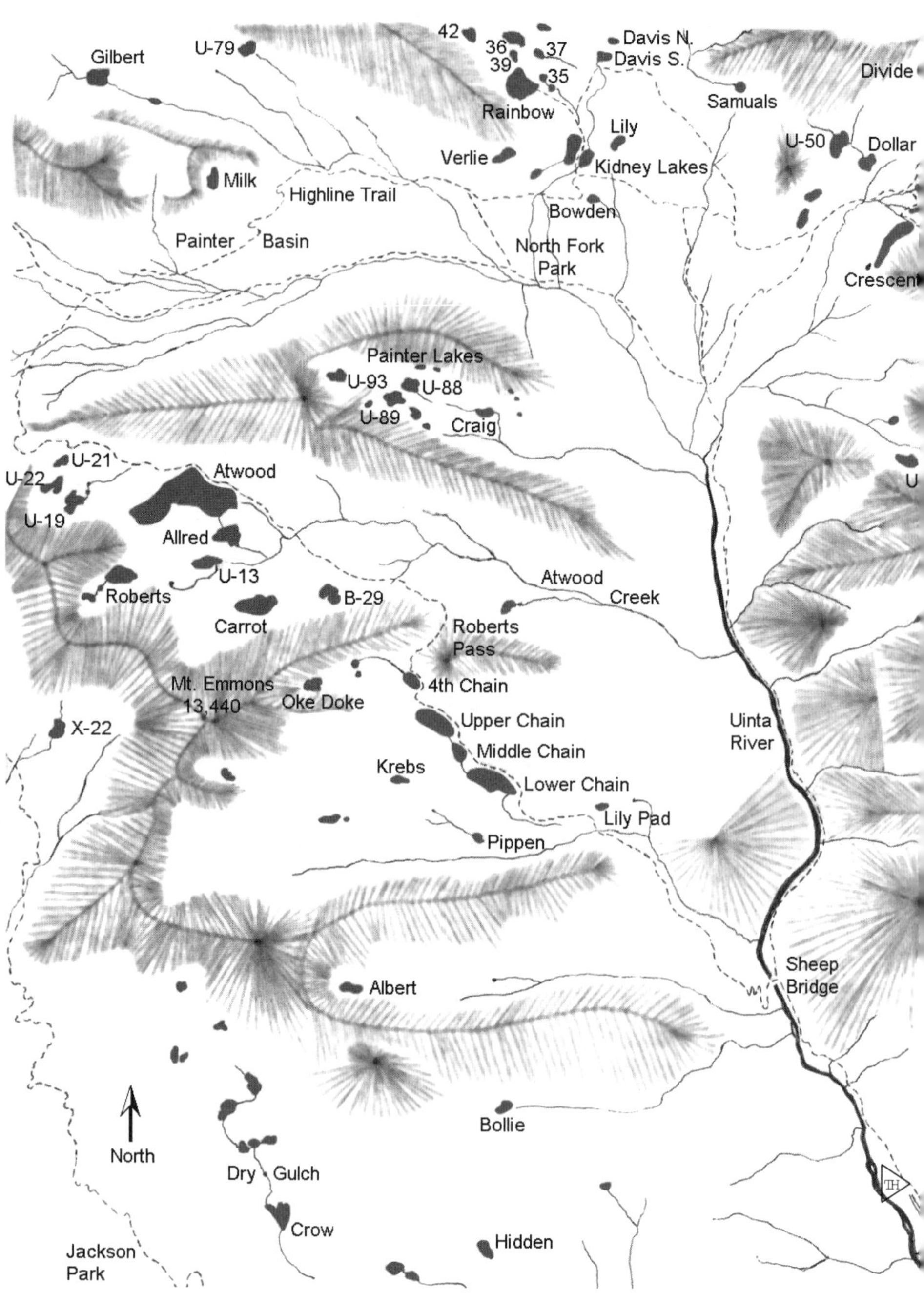

| Lake | Ref # | Elev. | Miles | Acres | Dee | Fish | Us | Cmp | Spr | Fd |
|---|---|---|---|---|---|---|---|---|---|---|
| Albert | U-94 | 10,826 | 9 | 7 | 8 | C | VL | P | | P |
| Allred | U-14 | 10,995 | 13.8 | 34 | 30 | B | M | G | | E |
| Atwood | U-16 | 11,030 | 13.6 | 250 | 40 | B | M | G | | G |
| B-29 Lake | U-18 | 10,740 | 12.5 | 19 | 7 | B | L | G | | E |
| Beard | U-74 | 11,740 | 16.3 | 9.2 | 15 | B | L | P | | P |
| Bollie | U-96 | 10,660 | 6 | 10 | 15 | C | L | E | | E |
| Bowden | U-32 | 10,693 | 13.5 | 4.5 | 14 | B | M | G | | G |
| Brook | U-54 | 10,950 | 10.3 | 10 | 8 | B,C | L | F | | F |
| Carrot | U-17 | 10,830 | 14.5 | 31 | 31 | B | L | G | | G |
| Chain 1 (Lower) | U-3 | 10,580 | 8 | 62 | 30 | B | H | F | | F |
| Chain 2 (Middle) | U-2 | 10,605 | 8.7 | 14.4 | 13 | B | H | F | | G |
| Chain 3 (Upper) | U-1 | 10,623 | 8.9 | 51 | 44 | B | M | F | | F |
| Chain 4 | U-4 | 10,870 | 9.7 | 13.5 | 31 | C | L | F | | P |
| Craig | U-85 | 10,848 | 14.3 | 9.3 | 14 | B,C | L | G | | G |
| Crescent | U-48 | 10,830 | 8.2 | 31 | 23 | B,C | H | G | | F |
| Davis, North | U-46 | 11,060 | 14.1 | 3.7 | 7 | B | L | G | Y | F |
| Davis, South | U-34 | 11,020 | 13.8 | 6.1 | 4 | B | L | G | Y | G |
| Divide | U-59 | 11,217 | 10.5 | 18.9 | 39 | C | L | P | | P |
| Dollar (alias Dime) | U-49 | 10,704 | 9.5 | 11.5 | 6 | B | M | E | | E |
| Fox | U-47 | 10,790 | 8.5 | 102 | 47 | B,C | H | G | | G |
| George Beard | U-21 | 11,420 | 16 | 7.4 | 15 | B | L | P | | P |
| Gilbert | U-82 | 11,459 | 20.5 | 14.6 | 20 | B | L | P | | F |
| Kidney, East | U-25 | 10,850 | 13.5 | 13.7 | 12 | B,R | H | G | N | G |
| Kidney, West | U-26 | 10,850 | 13.5 | 20 | 4 | B,C,R | H | G | N | G |
| Krebs | U-10 | 10,600 | 9.5 | | | | | | | |
| Lily | U-23 | 10,919 | 14.5 | 5.3 | 15 | B | L | F | | F |
| Lily Pad | U-8 | 10,180 | 7 | 3.7 | 7 | B,R | M | F | | F |
| Milk | U-73 | 11,236 | 19.5 | 13.1 | 35 | B,C | VL | P | | P |
| Mt. Emmons | U-13 | 10,990 | 14 | 15.5 | 21 | B,Go | M | P | | F |
| Oke Doke | U-5 | 11,320 | 10.5 | 12.9 | 38 | C | L | P | | F |

***Continued on next page***

# Uinta Drainage (continued)

| Lake | Ref # | Elev. | Miles | Acres | Dee | Fish | Us | Cmp | Spr | Fd |
|---|---|---|---|---|---|---|---|---|---|---|
| Penny Nickell | U-98 | 10,710 | 12.5 | 11.5 | 43 | C | L | P | | F |
| Pippen (alias Island) | U-9 | 10,450 | 9 | 3.2 | 3 | B | M | E | | E |
| Rainbow | U-33 | 11,130 | 14 | 35.1 | 20 | B,R | M | P | | P |
| Roberts | U-15 | 11,550 | 15.5 | 23.3 | 38 | B,C | L | P | | P |
| Samuals | U-27 | 10,995 | 13 | 4.8 | 7 | B | L | G | | E |
| Verlie | U-41 | 10,906 | 14 | 10.6 | 12 | B,C | M | F | | P |
| | U-19 | 11,420 | 16.4 | 15 | 8 | B | L | P | | P |
| | U-35 | 11,110 | 14 | 4.4 | 5 | B,C | M | P | | P |
| | U-36 | 11,100 | 13 | 4.6 | 7 | B | M | P | | P |
| | U-37 | 11,180 | 14.8 | 6.3 | 12 | B | L | P | | P |
| | U-38 | 11,218 | 14.8 | 15.7 | 13 | C | L | P | | F |
| | U-39 | 11,160 | 14.7 | 5.3 | 9 | B | M | P | | P |
| | U-42 | 11,350 | 15.2 | 7.6 | 7 | C | L | P | | P |
| | U-45 | 11,425 | 15.4 | 5 | 5 | C | L | P | | P |
| | U-50 | 10,832 | 9.8 | 18 | 8 | B | M | F | | G |
| | U-75 | 11,390 | 23.3 | 6.9 | 18 | B | VL | P | | P |
| | U-76 | 11,475 | 24.5 | 6 | 15 | B,C | VL | P | | P |
| | U-88 | 11,030 | 15.3 | 14 | 18 | B | L | E | | F |
| | U-89 | 11,037 | 15.4 | 11.5 | 15 | B | L | E | | F |
| | U-93 | 11,402 | 16.2 | 11.1 | 8 | C | VL | P | | P |

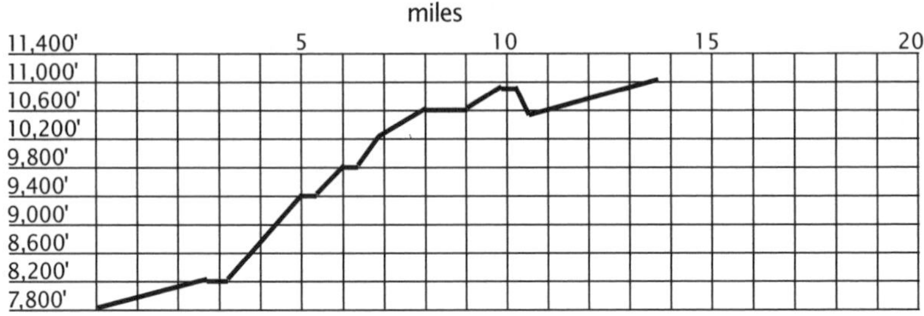


**U-Bar Ranch to Lake Atwood**

# Notes:

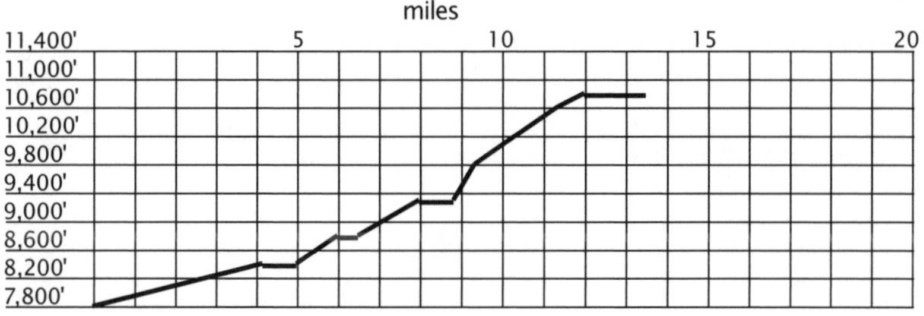


***U-Bar Ranch to Kidney Lakes***

# Whiterocks Drainage

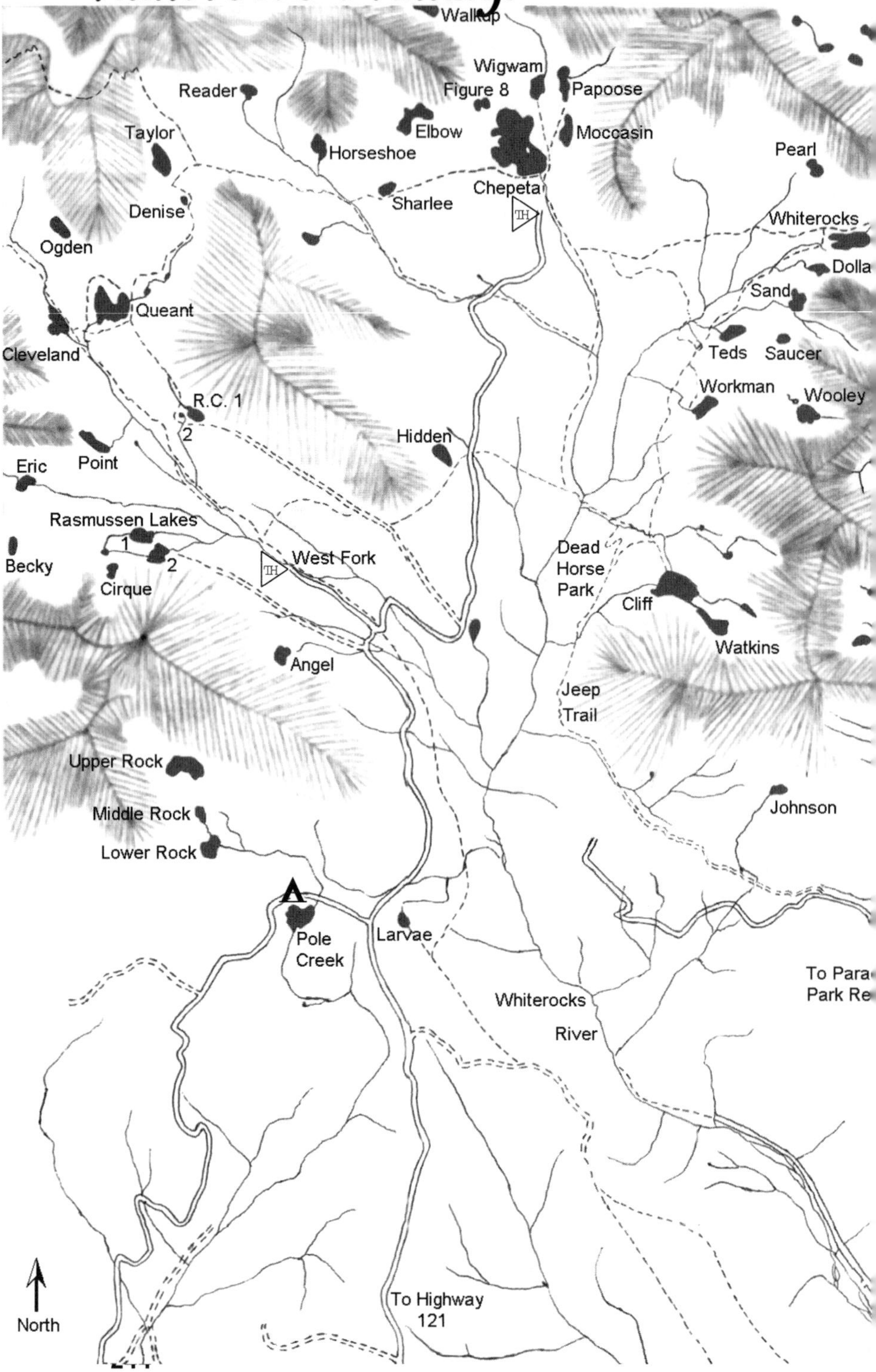

Walkup
Wigwam
Reader
Figure 8
Papoose
Taylor
Elbow
Moccasin
Horseshoe
Pearl
Chepeta
Denise
Sharlee
TH
Whiterocks
Ogden
Dolla
Sand
Queant
Cleveland
Teds
Saucer
Workman
R.C. 1
Wooley
2
Hidden
Eric
Point
Rasmussen Lakes
1
Dead
Horse
Park
Becky
2
West Fork
TH
Cirque
Cliff
Watkins
Angel
Jeep
Trail
Upper Rock
Johnson
Middle Rock
Lower Rock
Pole
Creek
Larvae
To Para
Park Re
Whiterocks
River
To Highway
121
North

| Lake | Ref # | Elev. | Miles | Acres | Deep | Fish | Use | Cmp | Spr | Fd |
|---|---|---|---|---|---|---|---|---|---|---|
| Angel | WR-19 | 10,407 | 0.7 | 10.4 | 17 | C | L | P | Y | P |
| Ann | WR-74 | 10,910 | 4 | 3.4 | 14 | C | VL | F | Y | F |
| Becky | WR-14 | 10,960 | 3.3 | 6.5 | 24 | B | VL | P | N | P |
| Chepeta | WR-64 | 10,560 | 0 | 135 | 55 | C | VH | G | Y | E |
| Cirque | WR-33 | 10,652 | 2.1 | 6.8 | 10 | G | VL | F | N | P |
| Cleveland | WR-7 | 10,640 | 4 | 23.9 | 6 | B,C | M | G | N | E |
| Cliff | WR-49 | 10,348 | 5.6 | 68 | 55 | B,C | L | P | N | P |
| Dead | WR-29 | 10,075 | 0.2 | 9.7 | 15 | N | H | G | N | P |
| Denise | WR-9 | 11,160 | 5.9 | 3 | 9 | B | L | G | Y | G |
| Dollar | WR-43 | 10,500 | 5 | 7.3 | 15 | B,C | M | P | N | P |
| Elbow | WR-58 | 10,910 | 2 | 26 | 27 | B | M | G | Y | P |
| Eric | WR-76 | 10,610 | 3.7 | 4.2 | 6 | B,C | L | G | Y | G |
| Figure-Eight | WR-56 | 10,660 | 0.3 | 3.6 | 5 | C | L | F | Y | F |
| Hidden | WR-63 | 10,350 | 0.3 | 13.2 | 45 | B | L | F | Y | P |
| Horseshoe | WR-67 | 10,860 | 3.2 | 12 | 14 | B,C | M | G | Y | G |
| Katy | WR-34 | 11,200 | 4.8 | 9 | 45 | C | VL | P | N | P |
| Larvae | WR-12 | 10,030 | 0.3 | 5.8 | 29 | B | M | G | N | G |
| Lower Rock | WR-17 | 10,550 | 1.5 | 18.7 | 39 | B | L | F | Y | F |
| Middle Rock | WR-16 | 10,580 | 1.6 | 7.3 | 10 | B | L | P | N | F |
| Moccasin | WR-53 | 10,620 | 1.2 | 11.1 | 27 | B,C | H | G | N | F |
| Nellie | WR-75 | 10,691 | 3.7 | 2.7 | 8 | C | L | P | Y | P |
| Ogden | WR-5 | 10,900 | 5.5 | 13.9 | 21 | C | M | G | Y | E |
| Papoose | WR-52 | 10,635 | 2 | 14.9 | 21 | B,C | M | G | Y | G |

***Continued on next page***

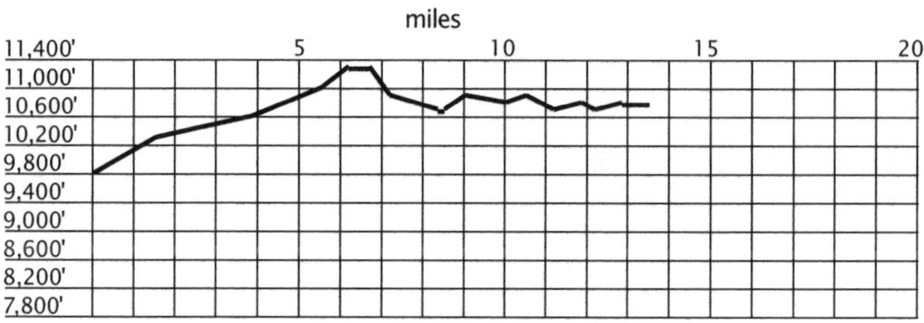


***West Fork Whiterocks to Kidney Lakes***

# Whiterocks Drainage (continued)

| Lake | Ref # | Elev. | Miles | Acres | Dee | Fish | Us | Cmp | Spr | Fd |
|---|---|---|---|---|---|---|---|---|---|---|
| Paradise Park Res. | WR-18 | 9,900 | 0 | | | R,B | VH | E | Y | F |
| Pearl | WR-45 | 10,700 | 5.5 | 7.9 | 15 | B,C | VL | G | Y | G |
| Point | WR-6 | 10,720 | 3.2 | 16.1 | 21 | B | M | F | Y | G |
| Pole Creek | WR-13 | 10,150 | 0 | | | R | VH | E | Y | F |
| Queant | WR-4 | 10,652 | 5 | 57 | 44 | B | H | G | Y | E |
| Rasmussen 1 | WR-35 | 10,473 | 1.8 | 17 | 5 | B | L | G | N | F |
| Rasmussen 2 | WR-36 | 10,620 | 1.6 | 15.6 | 8 | B | L | G | N | P |
| R.C. No. 1 | WR-2 | 10,630 | 2.6 | 10.2 | 16 | C | L | G | N | P |
| R.C. No. 2 | WR-3 | 10,620 | 2.5 | 1.7 | 7 | C | L | G | N | P |
| Reader | WR-66 | 10,960 | 4.2 | 10 | 10 | N | L | G | Y | F |
| Robb | WR-1 | 11,060 | 5.7 | 4.2 | 5 | B | L | P | N | P |
| Sand | WR-42 | 10,435 | 5.9 | 4.9 | 5 | B,C | M | G | Y | E |
| Saucer | WR-41 | 10,500 | 6 | 4.5 | 5 | B | VL | P | Y | F |
| Sharlee | WR-57 | 10,740 | 2 | 9.4 | 4 | B,C | M | G | N | E |
| Tamara | WR-73 | 10,960 | 4.2 | 6.9 | 18 | C | L | P | N | P |
| Taylor | WR-8 | 11,220 | 5 | 22.4 | 53 | B | M | P | Y | P |
| Ted's | WR-44 | 10,336 | 5 | 13.9 | 20 | B,C | H | G | N | E |
| Upper Rock | WR-14 | 10,592 | 2 | 33.4 | 33 | C | L | P | N | P |
| Walk-Up | WR-55 | 11,114 | 3.8 | 18.4 | 55 | B | VL | F | Y | P |
| Watkins | WR-48 | 10,390 | 6 | 18.4 | 36 | B | L | P | Y | P |
| Whiterocks | WR-46 | 10,607 | 3.1 | 67 | | N | L | G | Y | G |
| Wigwam | WR-54 | 10,607 | 2.2 | 13.5 | 11 | B,C | M | G | Y | P |
| Wooley | WR-40 | 10,680 | 6 | 20.5 | 42 | B | L | F | Y | F |
| Workman | WR-50 | 10,460 | 5.1 | 16.3 | 12 | B,C | M | G | Y | F |

# Notes:

# Ashley Creek Drainage

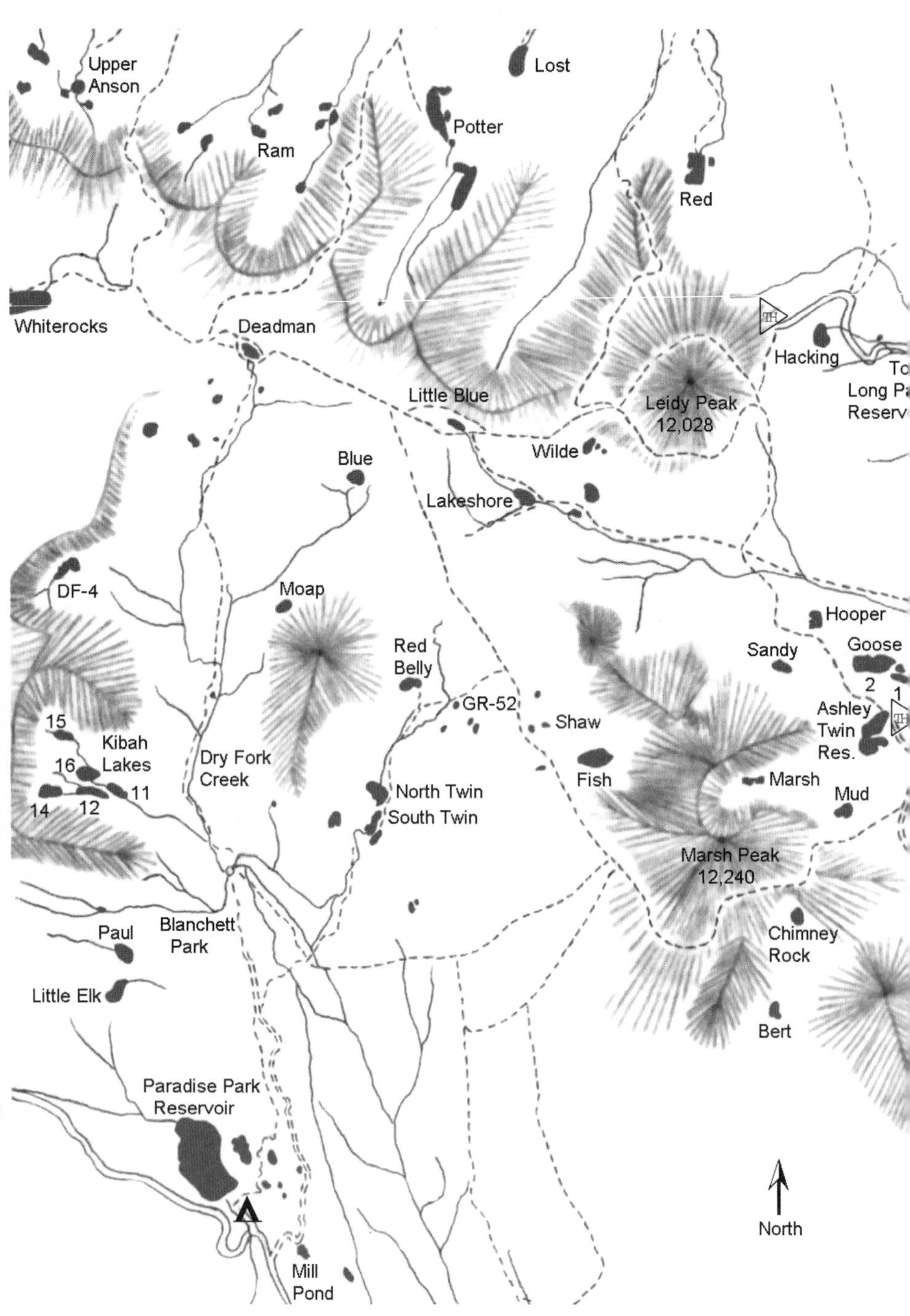

# Ashley Creek Drainage

| Lake | Ref # | Elev. | Miles | Acres | Deep | Fish | Use | Cmp | Spr | Fd |
|---|---|---|---|---|---|---|---|---|---|---|
| Ashley Twins Res. | GR-35 | 10,332 | 0 | 30.3 | 18 | B,C | H | F | Y | F |
| Bert | GR-62 | 10,220 | 3 | 3.7 | 11 | B | VL | F | Y | P |
| Blue | DF-1 | 11,160 | 6.8 | 6.5 | 16 | B | M | P | Y | F |
| Chimney Rock | GR-63 | 10,540 | 2 | 6.5 | 16 | N | VL | F | N | P |
| Deadman | GR-38 | 10,790 | 5 | 7 | 9 | B,C | H | F | | F |
| Fish | GR-57 | 10,745 | 8.3 | 17.5 | 40 | C | H | G | Y | F |
| Goose #1 | GR-42 | 10,240 | 0.5 | 3.8 | 13 | C | L | P | N | P |
| Goose #2 | GR-43 | 10,252 | 0.5 | 19.4 | 15 | C | L | F | N | F |
| Hacking | GR-40 | 10,625 | 0 | 7.4 | 15 | R,B | H | F | Y | P |
| Hooper | GR-46 | 10,305 | 1.3 | 4.5 | 4 | C | M | F | Y | E |
| Kibah, East | DF-11 | 10,495 | 1.3 | 2.9 | 12 | R,B | M | P | N | P |
| Kibah, Finger | DF-12 | 10,515 | 1.3 | 4.7 | 9 | B | M | P | N | P |
| Kibah, Island | DF-16 | 10,540 | 1.5 | 8 | 14 | B | M | F | N | P |
| Kibah, North | DF-15 | 10,750 | 2 | 4.5 | 12 | N | L | P | N | P |
| Kibah, West | DF-14 | 10,580 | 1.8 | 7.8 | 15 | B | M | F | N | P |
| Lakeshore | GR-34 | 10,792 | 4.5 | 11.1 | 18 | B,C | M | G | Y | E |
| Little Blue | GR-48 | 11,215 | 5.5 | 3.2 | 6 | B | VL | P | Y | F |
| Little Elk | DF-17 | 10,550 | 1.8 | 7.4 | 10 | N | L | F | N | P |
| Marsh | GR-39 | 10,820 | 1 | 12.6 | 21 | B | M | P | Y | P |
| Moap | DF-2 | 10,740 | 3 | 2.7 | 5 | N | VL | F | | P |
| Mud | GR-47 | 10,582 | 0.5 | 4.2 | 15 | C | L | F | Y | P |
| North Twin | GR-50 | 10,305 | 6 | 10.3 | 24 | B,C | H | G | Y | G |
| Paul | DF-18 | 10,630 | 2.3 | 11.1 | 17 | B | L | G | | P |
| Red Belly | GR-51 | 10,540 | 7.3 | 6.3 | 8 | C | M | G | Y | G |
| Sandy | GR-45 | 10,500 | 1.2 | 5.6 | 10 | C | L | F | N | P |
| Shaw | GR-59 | 10,700 | 7.8 | 2.8 | 5 | C | L | G | Y | G |
| South Twin | GR-49 | 10,300 | 5 | 6.2 | 8 | B,C | H | G | N | G |
| Wilde | GR-36 | 10,950 | 5 | 4.3 | 13 | N | VL | P | N | P |
| | DF-4 | 10,830 | 4 | 10 | 23 | C | VL | P | N | P |
| | GR-52 | 10,515 | 7.3 | 2.1 | 4 | B | M | G | Y | G |

***See page 277 for Elevation Grid***

# Weber River Drainage (West)

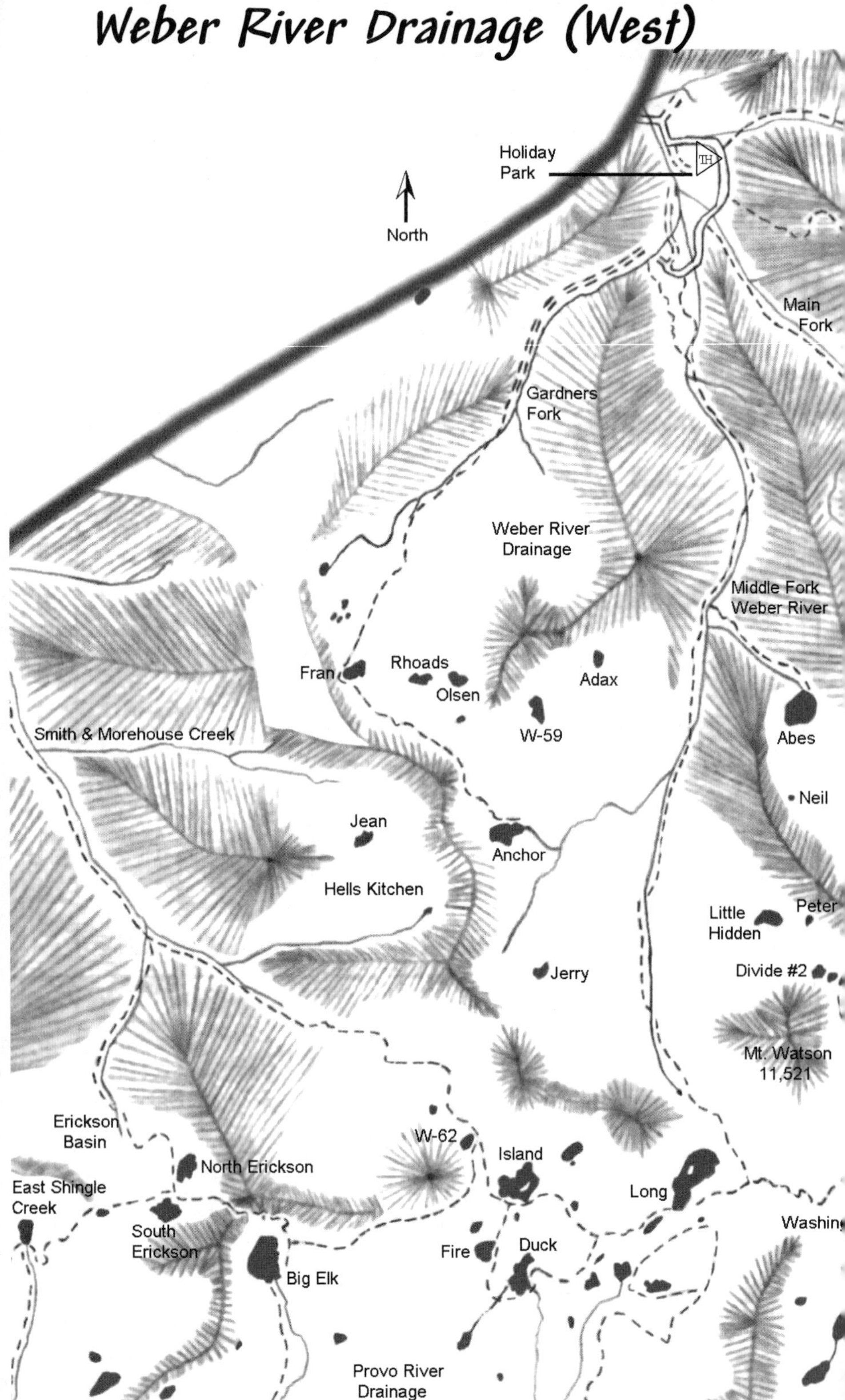

# Weber River Drainage (West)

| Lake | Ref # | Elev. | Miles | Acres | Deep | Fish | Use | Cmp | Spr | Fd |
|---|---|---|---|---|---|---|---|---|---|---|
| Abes | W-30 | 9,820 | 3.5 | 21.6 | 62 | C | L | G | Y | P |
| Adax | W-34 | 9,700 | 3.5 | 5 | 10 | B,C | L | G | N | G |
| Anchor | W-29 | 10,380 | 3.5 | 15 | 58 | B | L | G | N | P |
| Divide #2 | W-20 | 10,460 | 2.5 | 3.5 | 10 | N | M | G | Y | F |
| Erickson, South | W-25 | 10,100 | 2.5 | 10 | 12 | B | L | F | N | F |
| Erickson, North | W-26 | 10,020 | 2.8 | 9 | 12 | B | M | E | Y | F |
| Fran | W-39 | 10,060 | 1 | 3 | 8 | B | M | G | Y | G |
| Ibantik | W-24 | 10,100 | 3 | 10.2 | 37 | B | H | G | N | P |
| Jean | W-58 | 10,100 | 4 | 3 | 25 | C | L | F | Y | F |
| Jerry | W-28 | 10,220 | 5.5 | 3.2 | | B | L | P | N | P |
| Little Hidden | W-21 | 10,280 | 3 | 8 | 28 | B | M | G | Y | F |
| Lovenia | W-23 | 10,300 | 2.8 | 2.5 | 11 | B | H | F | Y | F |
| Meadow | W-27 | 9,820 | 4.3 | 29 | 46 | C | M | F | N | P |
| Neil | W-31 | 10,140 | 4 | 1.1 | 20 | B | L | P | N | P |
| Olsen | W-32 | 10,220 | 1.5 | 7 | 13 | B | L | G | N | F |
| Peter | W-22 | 10,460 | 2.8 | 3 | 13 | N | L | P | N | P |
| Rhoads | W-33 | 10,140 | 1.3 | 7.5 | 32 | B | M | E | Y | P |
| | W-59 | 10,140 | 4 | 4 | 10 | B | L | F | N | P |
| | W-62 | 10,340 | 4 | 2.1 | 18 | B | L | G | Y | G |

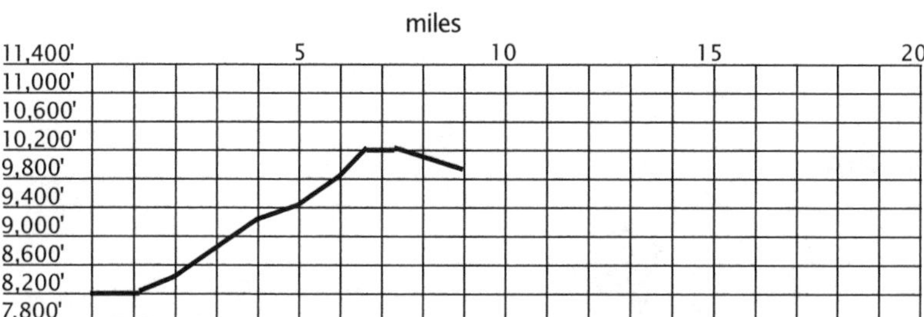


***Holiday Park to Crystal Lake***

# Weber River Drainage (East)

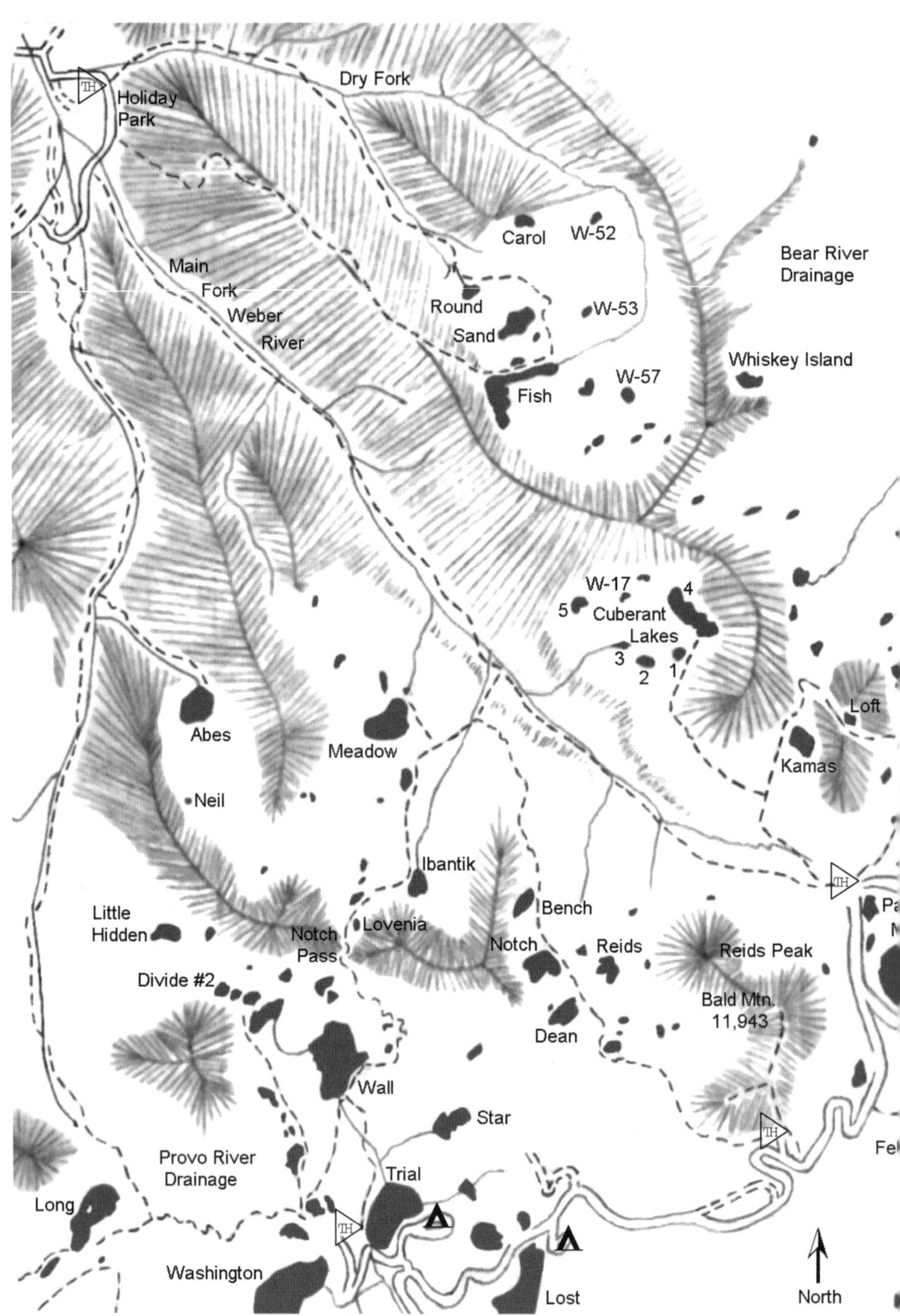

# Weber River Drainage (East)

| Lake | Ref # | Elev. | Miles | Acres | Deep | Fish | Use | Cmp | Spr | Fd |
|---|---|---|---|---|---|---|---|---|---|---|
| Abes | W-30 | 9,820 | 3.5 | 21.6 | 62 | C | L | G | Y | P |
| Bench | W-37 | 10,260 | 2.8 | 7 | 10 | B | M | G | N | F |
| Carol | W-51 | 9,860 | 4 | 3 | 25 | B | L | F | N | F |
| Cuberant #1 | W-42 | 10,360 | 2.5 | 3.5 | 18 | B,C | M | P | N | P |
| Cuberant #2 | W-43 | 10,220 | 2.5 | 3.2 | 6 | B | M | E | N | G |
| Cuberant #3 | W-44 | 10,180 | 2.7 | 3.5 | 24 | B | M | G | Y | P |
| Cuberant #4 | W-45 | 10,420 | 2.7 | 22 | 25 | C | M | G | N | G |
| Cuberant #5 | W-46 | 10,060 | 3.1 | 3 | 15 | N | VL | P | N | F |
| Dean | W-35 | 10,340 | 2 | 12 | 16 | B,C | H | G | N | E |
| Divide #2 | W-20 | 10,460 | 2.5 | 3.5 | 10 | N | M | G | Y | F |
| Fish | W-47 | 10,180 | 4.5 | 59 | 57 | G,B | H | F | N | F |
| Ibantik | W-24 | 10,100 | 3.3 | 10.2 | 37 | B | H | G | N | P |
| Kamas | W-40 | 10,500 | 1.5 | 17.1 | 42 | C | H | G | N | P |
| Little Hidden | W-21 | 10,280 | 3 | 8 | 28 | B | M | G | Y | F |
| Lofty | W-41 | 10,820 | 2.3 | 4 | 20 | C | H | G | N | F |
| Lovenia | W-23 | 10,300 | 2.8 | 2.5 | 11 | B | H | F | Y | F |
| Meadow | W-27 | 9,820 | 4.3 | 29 | 46 | C | M | F | N | P |
| Neil | W-31 | 10,140 | 4 | 1.1 | 20 | B | L | P | N | P |
| Notch | W-36 | 10,300 | 2.3 | 20.2 | 58 | B | H | G | Y | F |
| Peter | W-22 | 10,460 | 2.8 | 3 | 13 | N | L | P | N | P |
| Reids | W-38 | 10,340 | 2.3 | 3 | 8 | B | M | P | Y | F |
| Round | W-48 | 9,940 | 3.5 | 5 | 36 | G | H | G | Y | G |
| Sand | W-49 | 10,140 | 4 | 19.3 | 51 | G | H | G | Y | G |
|  | W-17 | 10,340 | 3 | 1.7 | 15 | B | L | G | N | P |
|  | W-52 | 9,780 | 4.8 | 4 | 25 | B | L | P | N | P |
|  | W-53 | 10,060 | 4.3 | 2.2 | 11 | B | L | G | Y | F |
|  | W-57 | 10,340 | 5.3 | 3 | 8 | B | M | P | N | F |

***See page 277 for Elevation Grid***

# Bear River Drainage (West)

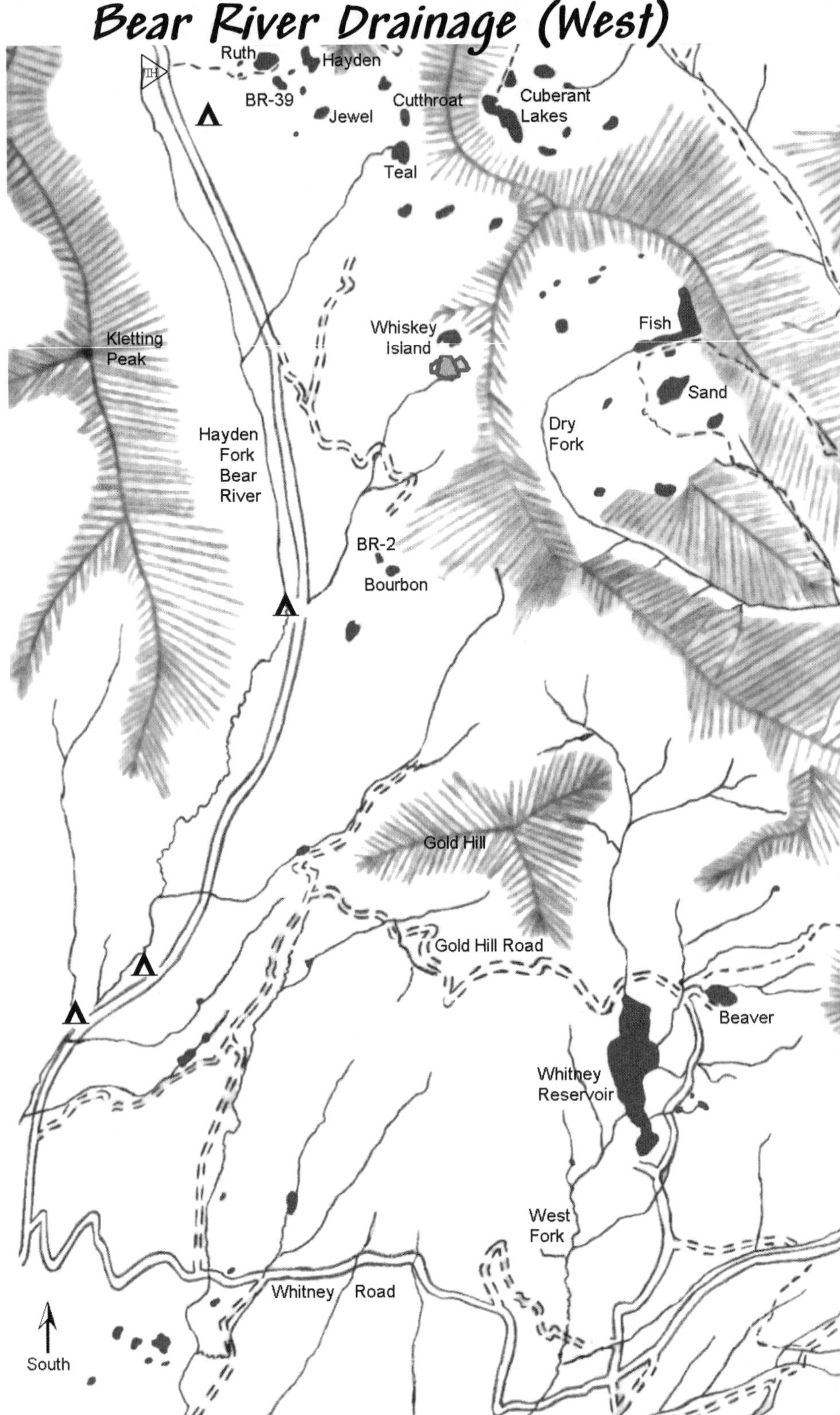

# Bear River Drainage (West)

| Lake | Ref # | Elev. | Miles | Acres | Deep | Fish | Use | Cmp | Spr | Fd |
|---|---|---|---|---|---|---|---|---|---|---|
| Beaver | BR-10 | 9,420 | 0 | 13.2 | 32 | R,B,C | M | E | N | G |
| Bourbon (Gold Hill) | BR-1 | 9,820 | 0.3 | 1.9 | 8 | B | H | P | Y | F |
| Cutthroat | BR-37 | 10,390 | 1.8 | 3.8 | 16 | B,C | M | P | Y | P |
| Hayden | BR-36 | 10,420 | 1 | 4.4 | 5 | C | M | G | Y | F |
| Jewel | BR-38 | 10,300 | 1.3 | 2.4 | 13 | C | M | G | N | G |
| Ruth | BR-40 | 10,340 | 0.8 | 9.7 | 30 | B | H | G | Y | F |
| Teal | BR-32 | 10,260 | 2 | 6.9 | 14 | C | M | F | N | P |
| Whiskey Island | BR-3 | 10,340 | 1.3 | 5 | 19 | G | L | F | N | P |
|  | BR-2 | 9,780 | 0.4 | 0.7 | 5 | B | L | F | N | F |

# Bear River Drainage (Central)

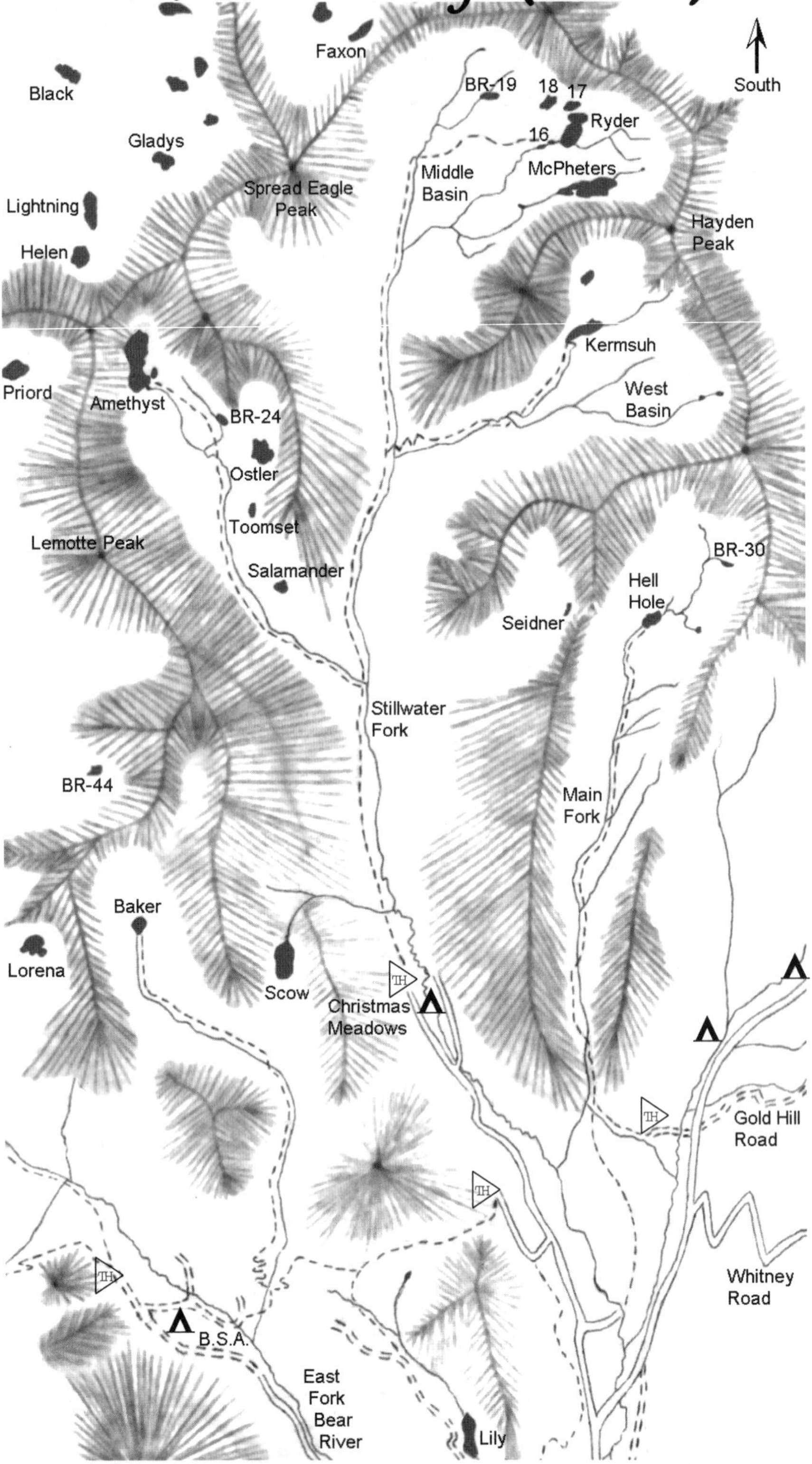

Faxon
BR-19
18
17
South
Black
Ryder
16
Gladys
Middle Basin
McPheters
Spread Eagle Peak
Lightning
Hayden Peak
Helen
Kermsuh
Priord
Amethyst
West Basin
BR-24
Ostler
Toomset
Lemotte Peak
BR-30
Salamander
Hell Hole
Seidner
Stillwater Fork
BR-44
Main Fork
Baker
Lorena
Scow
TH
Christmas Meadows
TH
Gold Hill Road
TH
TH
Whitney Road
B.S.A.
East Fork Bear River
Lily

# Bear River Drainage (Central)

| Lake | Ref # | Elev. | Miles | Acres | Deep | Fish | Use | Cmp | Spr | Fd |
|---|---|---|---|---|---|---|---|---|---|---|
| Amethyst | BR-28 | 10,750 | 5.8 | 42.5 | 59 | B,C | M | F | Y | F |
| Baker | BR-45 | 10,420 | 4.5 | 3.6 | 8 | B | M | G | Y | G |
| Hell Hole | BR-29 | 10,340 | 5 | 8.5 | 9 | C | M | E | Y | G |
| Kermsuh | BR-20 | 10,300 | 6.8 | 12.4 | 14 | C | L | P | Y | F |
| Lily | BR-11 | 8,890 | 0 | 12.6 | 20 | R | M | F | N | F |
| Lorena | BR-46 | 10,580 | 3.5 | 12 | 20 | B | L | P | N | P |
| McPheters | BR-14 | 10,860 | 8.5 | 28.8 | 45 | C | M | F | Y | F |
| Meadow | BR-19 | 10,470 | 7.8 | 2.9 | 5 | B | L | G | Y | F |
| Ostler | BR-27 | 10,540 | 5.5 | 14 | 14 | B,C | M | F | Y | F |
| Priord | BR-48 | 10,860 | 9.3 | 12 | 20 | C | M | G | Y | F |
| Ryder | BR-15 | 10,620 | 8 | 23.7 | 55 | B | M | G | Y | G |
| Salamander | BR-26 | 10,020 | 4 | 4.1 | 13 | B | L | P | N | P |
| Scow | BR-12 | 10,100 | 3.3 | 22.9 | 6 | B | M | G | Y | F |
| Seidner | BR-31 | 10,460 | 4.5 | 3.2 | 8 | B | VL | G | Y | G |
| Toomset | BR-25 | 10,300 | 5.8 | 2.1 | 11 | B | L | P | N | P |
|  | BR-16 | 10,610 | 8 | 1 | 5 | B,C | M | G | N | F |
|  | BR-17 | 10,630 | 8.3 | 2.8 | 7 | B | M | G | Y | F |
|  | BR-18 | 10,610 | 8.4 | 4.8 | 12 | B | L | G | Y | F |
|  | BR-24 | 10,460 | 5.3 | 2.4 | 10 | C | M | E | Y | G |
|  | BR-30 | 10,580 | 5.8 | 1.2 | 6 | N | L | F | Y | F |
|  | BR-44 | 10,900 | 7 | 3.6 | 15 | C | VL | F | N | P |

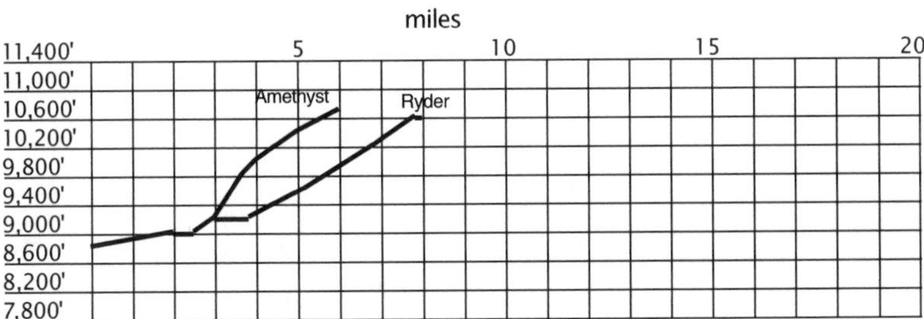


**Christmas Meadows to Ryder Lake**

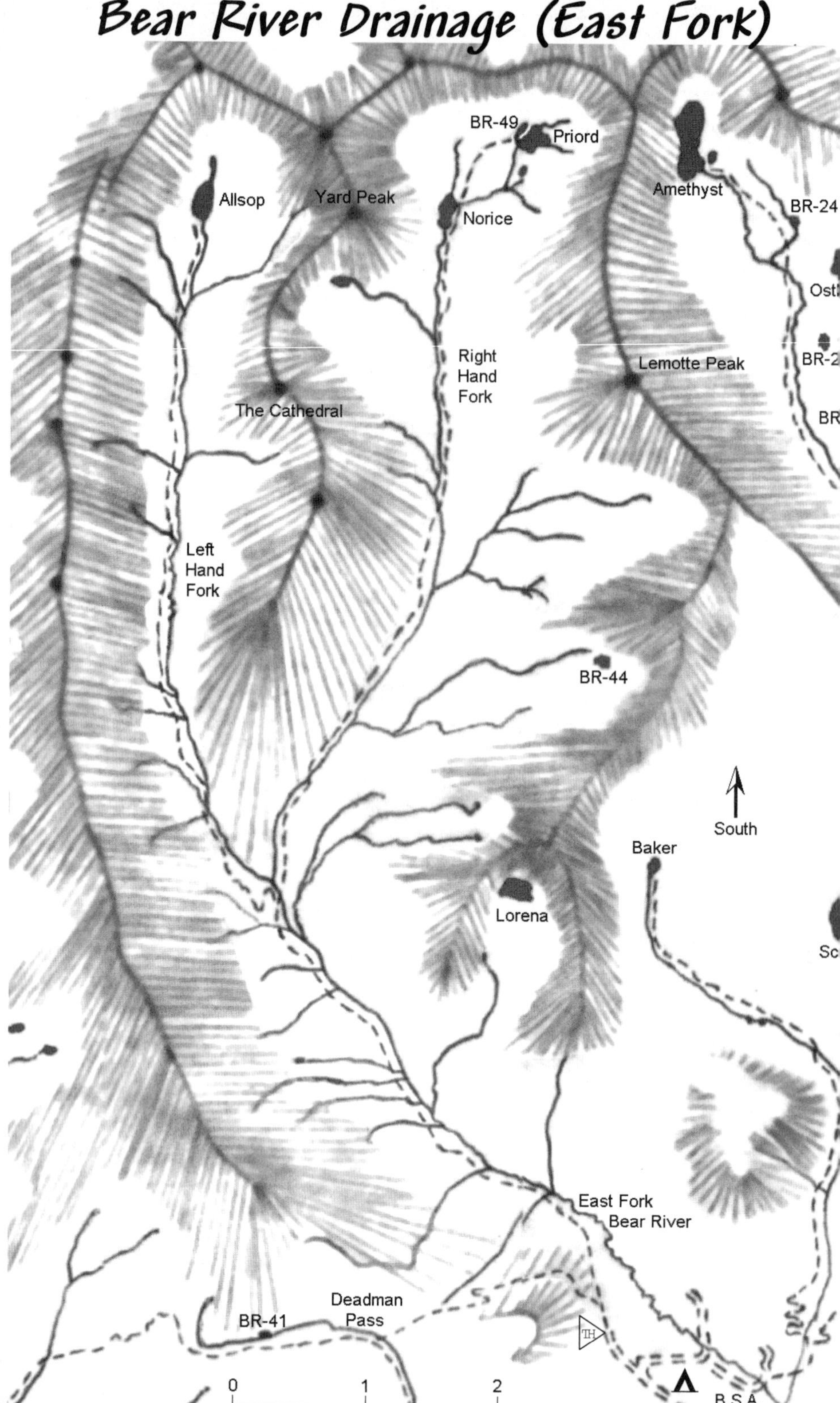

Bear River Drainage (East Fork)
BR-49
Priord
Allsop
Yard Peak
Norice
Amethyst
BR-24
Right
Hand
Fork
Lemotte Peak
The Cathedral
Left
Hand
Fork
BR-44
South
Baker
Lorena
East Fork
Bear River
Deadman
Pass
BR-41
TH
0
1
2
B.S.A.

# Bear River Drainage (East Fork)

| Lake | Ref # | Elev. | Miles | Acres | Deep | Fish | Use | Cmp | Spr | Fd |
|---|---|---|---|---|---|---|---|---|---|---|
| Allsop | BR-42 | 10,580 | 8.5 | 12.3 | 22 | C | M | G | Y | G |
| Amethyst | BR-28 | 10,750 | 5.8 | 42.5 | 59 | B,C | M | F | Y | P |
| Baker | BR-45 | 10,420 | 4.5 | 3.6 | 8 | B | M | G | Y | G |
| Lorena | BR-46 | 10,580 | 3.5 | 12 | 20 | B | L | P | N | P |
| Norice | BR-47 | 10,470 | 8.3 | 4.8 | 3 | C | M | G | N | F |
| Ostler | BR-27 | 10,540 | 5.5 | 14 | 14 | B,C | M | F | Y | F |
| Priord | BR-48 | 10,860 | 9.3 | 12 | 20 | C | M | G | Y | F |
| Salamander | BR-26 | 10,020 | 4 | 4.1 | 13 | B | L | P | N | P |
| Scow | BR-12 | 10,100 | 3.3 | 22.9 | 6 | B | M | G | Y | F |
| Toomset | BR-25 | 10,300 | 5.8 | 2.1 | 11 | B | L | P | N | P |
|  | BR-24 | 10,460 | 5.3 | 2.4 | 10 | C | M | E | Y | G |
|  | BR-41 | 10,412 | 1.5 | 3.4 | 19 | N | L | F | N | P |
|  | BR-44 | 10,900 | 7 | 3.6 | 15 | C | VL | F | N | P |

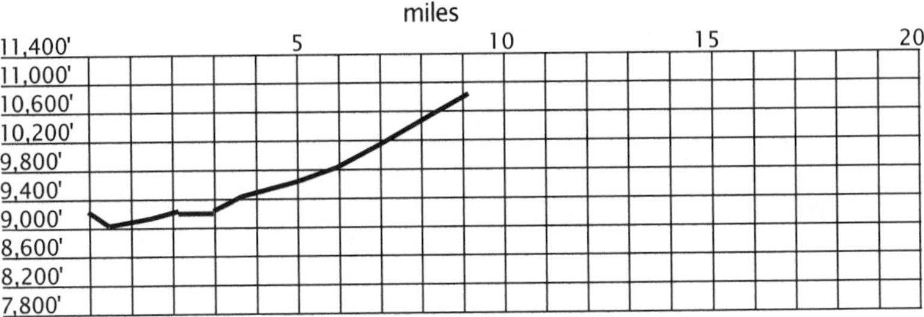


***East Fork Bear River to Priord Lake***

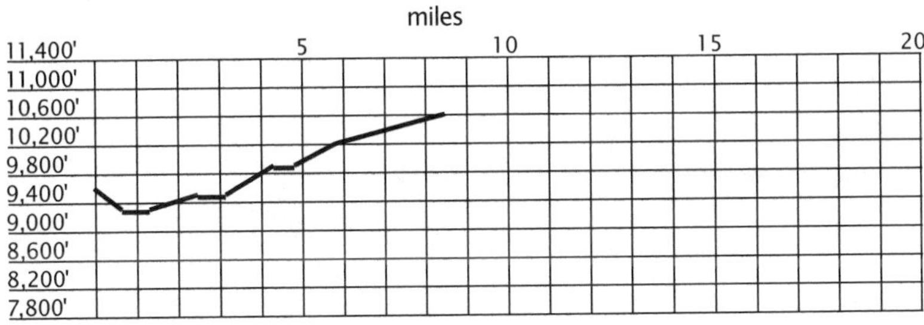


***East Fork Bear River to Allsop Lake***

# Blacks Fork Drainage (West Fork)

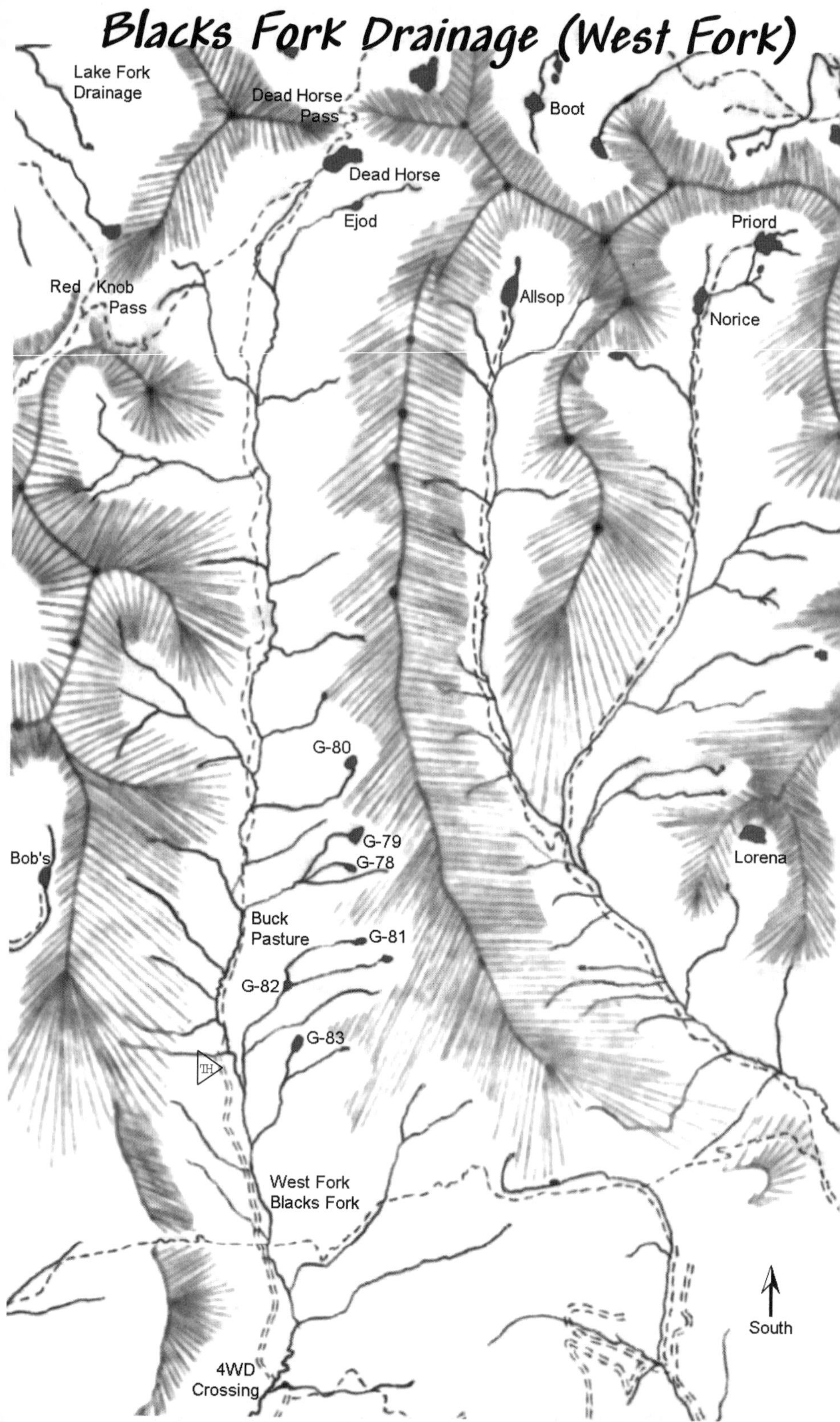

# Blacks Fork Drainage (West Fork)

| Lake | Ref # | Elev. | Miles | Acres | Deep | Fish | Use | Cmp | Spr | Fd |
|---|---|---|---|---|---|---|---|---|---|---|
| Bobs | G-73 | 11,150 | 10.3 | 6.6 | 30 | C | L | P | Y | F |
| Dead Horse | G-77 | 10,878 | 7.5 | 16 | 41 | C | M | F | N | F |
| Ejod | G-76 | 10,900 | 7.8 | 6.7 | 12 | C | L | P | N | F |
| | G-72 | 11,198 | 9.8 | 1.3 | 6 | B | VL | P | Y | P |
| | G-74 | 10,934 | 9.5 | 3.4 | 3 | B | VL | G | Y | G |
| | G-78 | 10,660 | 2.3 | 3.2 | 9 | B | L | F | N | F |
| | G-79 | 10,820 | 2.8 | 2.5 | 5 | B | VL | F | Y | P |
| | G-80 | 10,580 | 3.3 | 1.8 | 8 | B | L | F | Y | P |
| | G-81 | 10,665 | 4 | 1.6 | 5 | C | VL | F | Y | P |
| | G-82 | 10,140 | 0.5 | 3.8 | 6 | B | M | G | N | P |

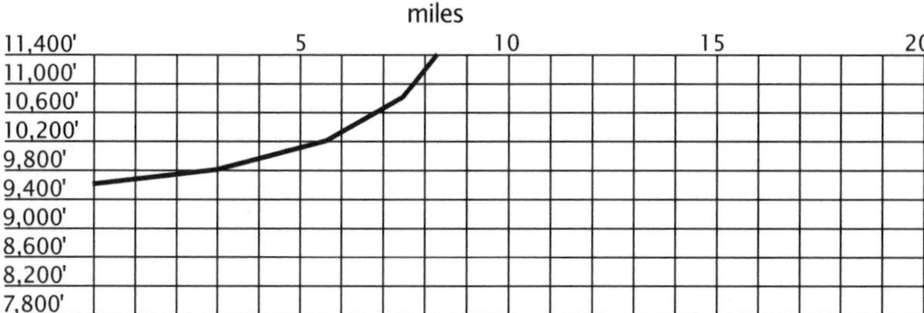


***West Fork Blacks Fork to Dead Horse Pass***

# East Fork Blacks Fork Drainage

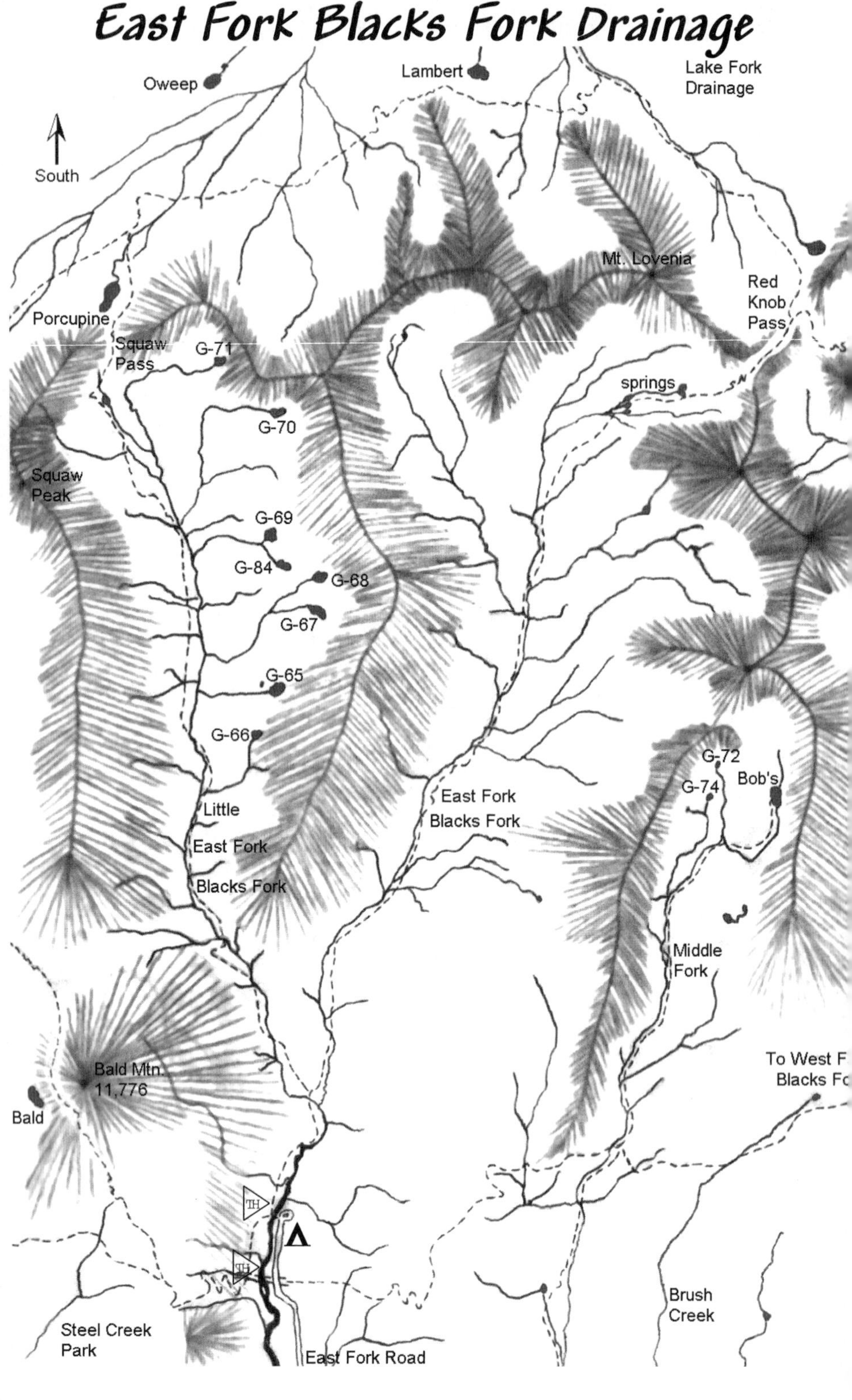

# Blacks Fork Drainage (East Fork)

| Lake | Ref # | Elev. | Miles | Acres | Deep | Fish | Use | Cmp | Spr | Fd |
|---|---|---|---|---|---|---|---|---|---|---|
| | G-65 | 10,900 | 6.8 | 5 | 5 | B | L | F | N | F |
| | G-66 | 10,561 | 5.8 | 4 | 12 | B | M | G | Y | P |
| | G-67 | 11,158 | 7.8 | 7.7 | 25 | B | L | P | Y | P |
| | G-68 | 11,421 | 8 | 4.1 | 6 | N | L | P | N | P |
| | G-69 | 11,109 | 8.5 | 4.8 | 13 | C | L | P | N | P |
| | G-70 | 11,450 | 9.8 | 3.8 | 4 | C | VL | P | Y | P |
| | G-71 | 11,527 | 10.3 | 4.8 | 14 | B | VL | P | Y | P |
| | G-72 | 11,198 | 10.3 | 1.3 | 6 | B | VL | P | Y | P |
| Bobs | G-73 | 11,150 | 10.3 | 6.6 | 30 | C | L | P | Y | F |
| | G-74 | 10,934 | 10.1 | 3.4 | 3 | B | VL | G | Y | G |

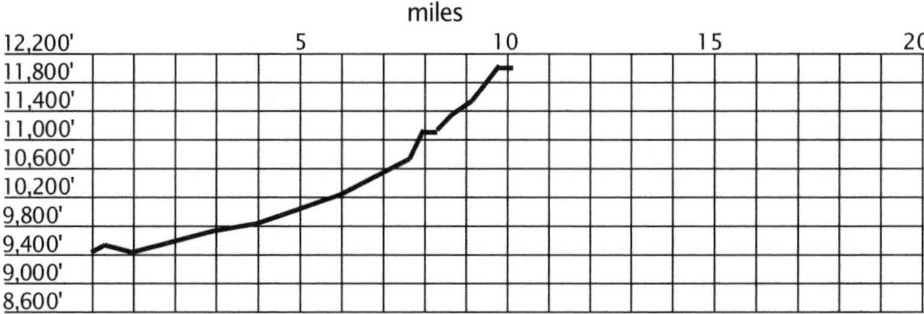


***East Fork Blacks Fork to Red Knob Pass***

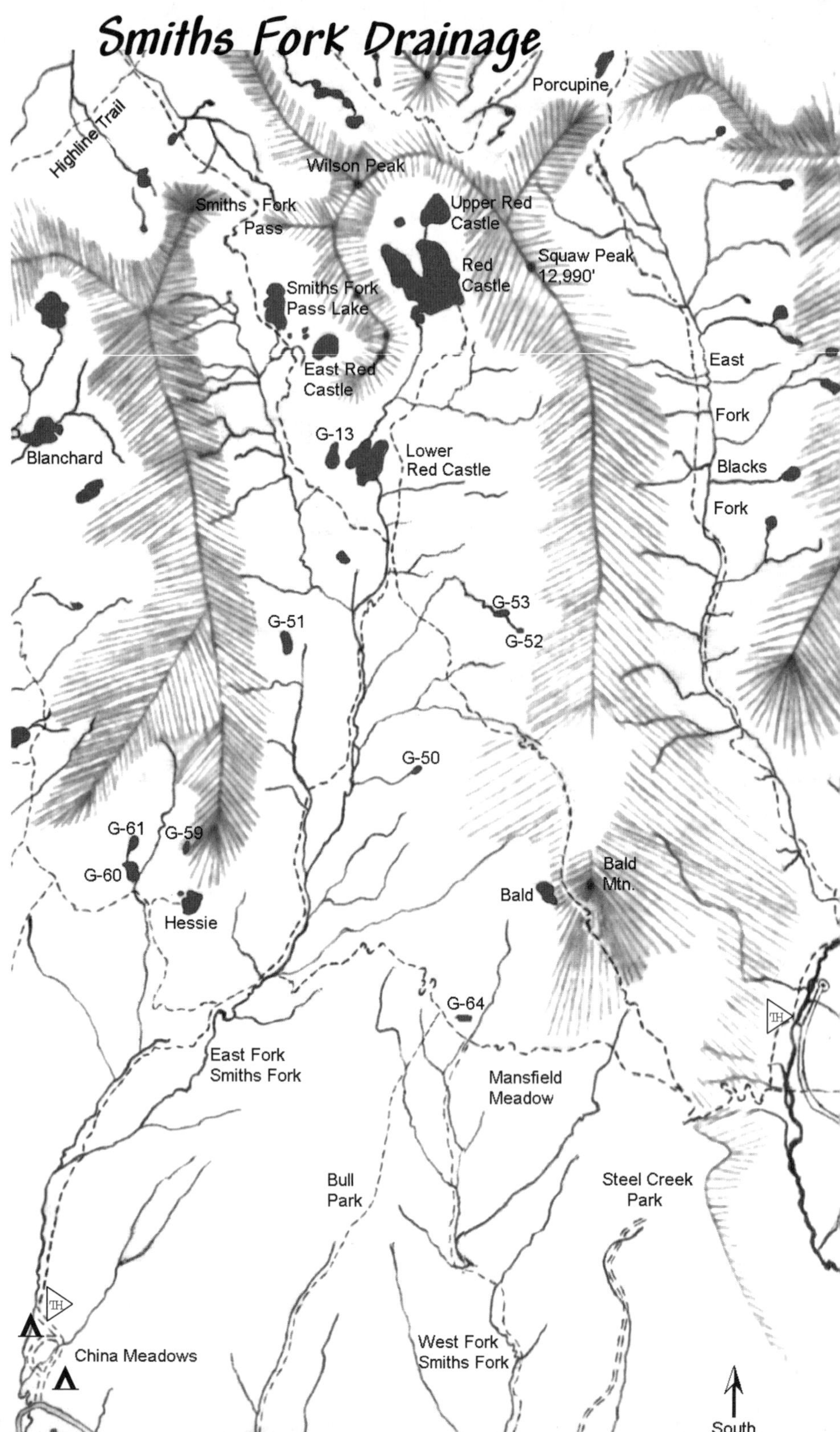
Smiths Fork Drainage
Porcupine
Highline Trail
Wilson Peak
Smiths Fork
Pass
Upper Red
Castle
Squaw Peak
12,990'
Red
Castle
Smiths Fork
Pass Lake
East Red
Castle
East
Fork
Blacks
Fork
G-13
Lower
Red Castle
Blanchard
G-53
G-52
G-51
G-50
G-61
G-59
G-60
Hessie
Bald
Mtn.
Bald
G-64
TH
East Fork
Smiths Fork
Mansfield
Meadow
Bull
Park
Steel Creek
Park
TH
China Meadows
West Fork
Smiths Fork
South

# Smiths Fork Drainage

| Lake | Ref # | Elev. | Miles | Acres | Deep | Fish | Use | Cmp | Spr | Fd |
|---|---|---|---|---|---|---|---|---|---|---|
| Bald | G-63 | 11,030 | 5 | 6.4 | 23 | B | L | G | N | P |
| Bridger | G-20 | 9,350 | 0 | 21 | 15 | R,B | VH | E | Y | F |
| China | G-21 | 9,408 | 0.2 | 31.2 | 45 | B,G | VH | E | N | F |
| Grahams | G-32 | 9,210 | 0.8 | 18.5 | 25 | N | M | G | N | F |
| Hessie | G-18 | 10,620 | 5.8 | 13.2 | 18 | C | H | G | Y | G |
| Marsh | G-19 | 9,335 | 0 | 33.6 | 35 | R,B | VH | E | Y | F |
| Red Castle | G-15 | 11,295 | 11 | 168.2 | 103 | C | H | P | N | P |
| Red Castle, East | G-17 | 11,190 | 11 | 21.1 | 58 | C | M | P | Y | P |
| Red Castle, Lower | G-12 | 10,758 | 9 | 45 | 28 | R,B,C | H | G | Y | G |
| Red Castle, Upper | G-16 | 11,542 | 11.8 | 25.6 | 72 | C | M | P | Y | P |
| Sargent | G-35 | 9,690 | 1 | 8.3 | 22 | ? | L | G | N | F |
| Smiths Fork Pass | G-14 | 11,152 | 11 | 26.1 | 17 | C | L | P | Y | P |
| | G-13 | 10,860 | 9.5 | 7.9 | 17 | B | M | F | N | F |
| | G-34 | 9,390 | 0 | 1 | 6 | R,B | H | F | Y | F |
| | G-36 | 9,430 | 0.2 | 4.7 | 11 | ? | L | F | N | F |
| | G-45 | 11,220 | 10.5 | 3.1 | 12 | B | L | P | Y | P |
| | G-49 | 10,830 | 9.8 | 3.9 | 11 | R,B,C | L | G | N | G |
| | G-50 | 10,639 | 6.8 | 3.7 | 5 | B | L | G | N | F |
| | G-51 | 10,620 | 8.3 | 8.1 | 5 | B | M | E | Y | E |
| | G-52 | 11,340 | 10.2 | 2.6 | 4 | C | VL | P | N | P |
| | G-53 | 11,180 | 10 | 5.5 | 17 | B,C | M | E | Y | G |
| | G-56 | 11,460 | 10.5 | 1.5 | 12 | B | VL | P | N | P |
| | G-58 | 10,620 | 5.4 | 1.3 | 5 | C | M | G | N | F |
| | G-59 | 10,740 | 6 | 3.2 | 24 | B | L | G | N | F |
| | G-60 | 10,500 | 5.3 | 2.5 | 9 | B | M | E | Y | E |
| | G-61 | 10,669 | 5.5 | 3.1 | 6 | B | L | G | N | G |
| | G-64 | 10,470 | 3 | 3.4 | 5 | C | VL | G | Y | G |

***See page 277 for Elevation Grid***

# Henrys Fork Drainage

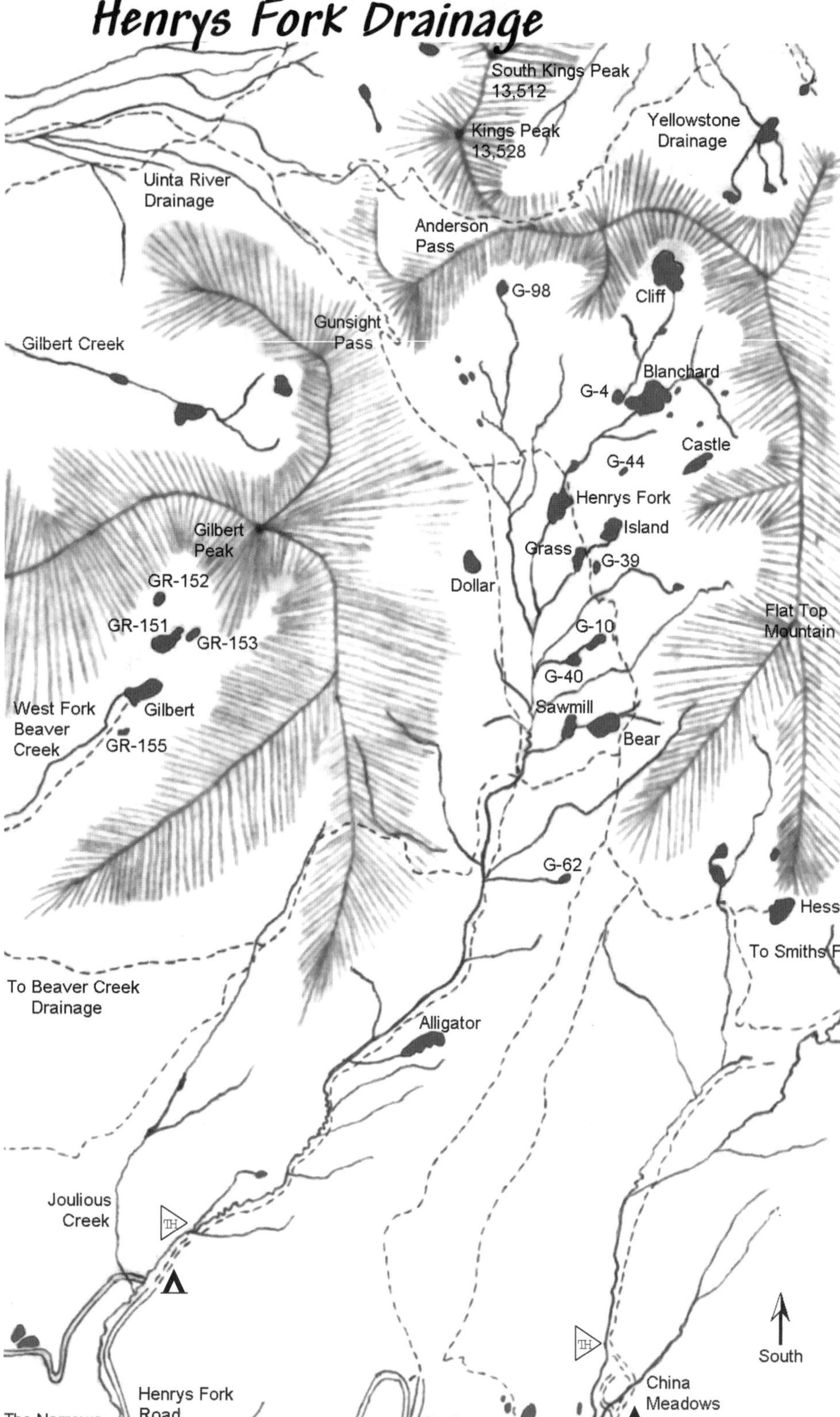

# Henrys Fork Drainage

| Lake | Ref # | Elev. | Miles | Acres | Deep | Fish | Use | Cmp | Spr | Fd |
|---|---|---|---|---|---|---|---|---|---|---|
| Alligator | G-38 | 10,033 | 2.7 | 14.5 | 26 | B | H | G | N | F |
| Bear | G-7 | 10,767 | 6.5 | 16.9 | 37 | B,C | M | G | N | P |
| Blanchard | G-3 | 11,164 | 8.7 | 31.3 | 29 | C | M | P | N | P |
| Castle | G-11 | 11,363 | 9.2 | 11.5 | 10 | B | L | P | Y | P |
| Cliff | G-5 | 11,443 | 10 | 33.1 | 69 | C | L | P | Y | P |
| Dollar | G-2 | 10,785 | 7 | 9.7 | 18 | B,C | M | E | Y | G |
| Grass | G-8 | 10,740 | 8 | 5.5 | 4 | B,C | M | G | Y | G |
| Henrys Fork | G-1 | 10,830 | 7.5 | 19.7 | 19 | C | H | G | Y | G |
| Island | G-9 | 10,830 | 8.1 | 10.4 | 5 | B,C | L | F | Y | G |
| Little Blanchard | G-4 | 11,169 | 8.7 | 3.6 | 8 | C | L | P | N | P |
| Sawmill | G-6 | 10,661 | 6.3 | 7.2 | 21 | B,C | H | G | Y | P |
| | G-10 | 10,772 | 7.5 | 5.4 | 12 | B | L | G | Y | F |
| | G-39 | 10,820 | 8 | 2.6 | 7 | B | L | F | N | F |
| | G-42 | 10,900 | 8.5 | 4.6 | 2 | B,C | L | P | N | E |
| | G-44 | 11,140 | 9 | 1.5 | 7 | C | L | P | N | P |
| | G-62 | 10,630 | 5 | 2.2 | 7 | B | L | F | N | F |
| | G-98 | 11,208 | 9.5 | 5.4 | 10 | N | VL | P | Y | F |

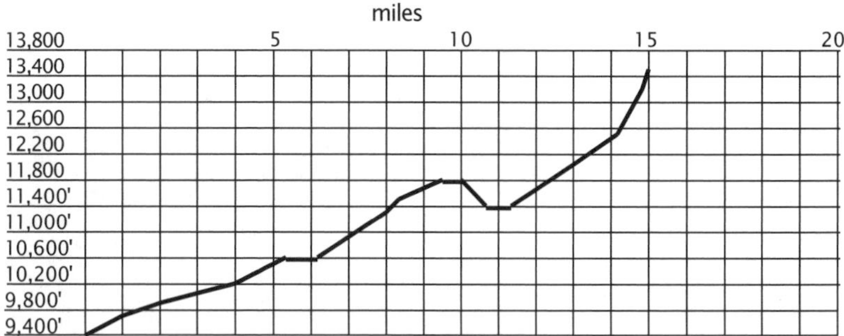


***Henrys Fork to Kings Peak***

# Beaver Creek Drainage

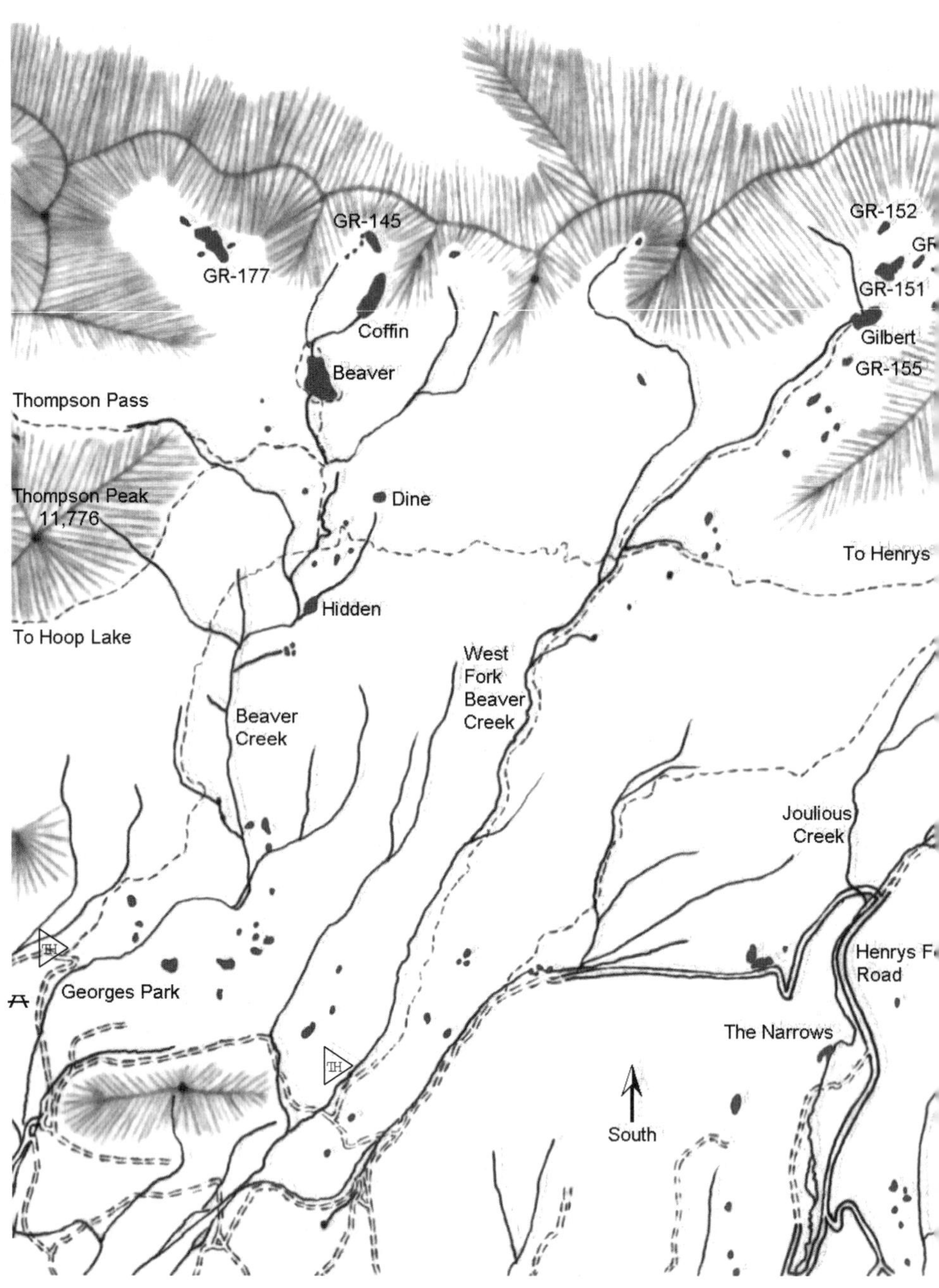

# Beaver Creek Drainage

| Lake | Ref # | Elev. | Miles | Acres | Deep | Fish | Use | Cmp | Spr | Fd |
|---|---|---|---|---|---|---|---|---|---|---|
| Beaver | GR-147 | 10,505 | 6.8 | 38.3 | 30 | B,C | H | E | Y | G |
| Coffin | GR-144 | 10,853 | 7.8 | 25.8 | 28 | C | L | F | Y | P |
| Dine | GR-148 | 10,460 | 5.5 | 5.1 | 15 | B | L | F | Y | P |
| Gilbert | GR-150 | 10,905 | 8 | 15.2 | 2 | B,C | M | G | Y | E |
| Hidden | GR-149 | 10,148 | 5.5 | 6.5 | 18 | B | L | G | N | F |
| | GR-145 | 11,020 | 8.3 | 5.6 | 11 | C | L | F | Y | P |
| | GR-151 | 11,033 | 8.5 | 12.6 | 11 | B | L | P | Y | G |
| | GR-152 | 11,295 | 9 | 4.8 | 13 | B | VL | P | Y | P |
| | GR-153 | 11,060 | 8.6 | 3.6 | 2 | B,C | VL | F | Y | E |
| | GR-155 | 10,860 | 7.8 | 1.6 | 6 | B | L | F | Y | E |
| | GR-177 | 10,860 | 8.3 | 18.3 | 11 | C | L | F | Y | G |

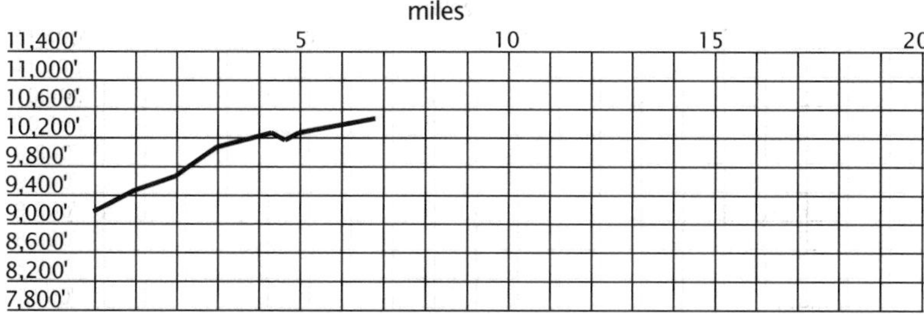


**Georges Park to Beaver Lake**

# Burnt Fork Drainage

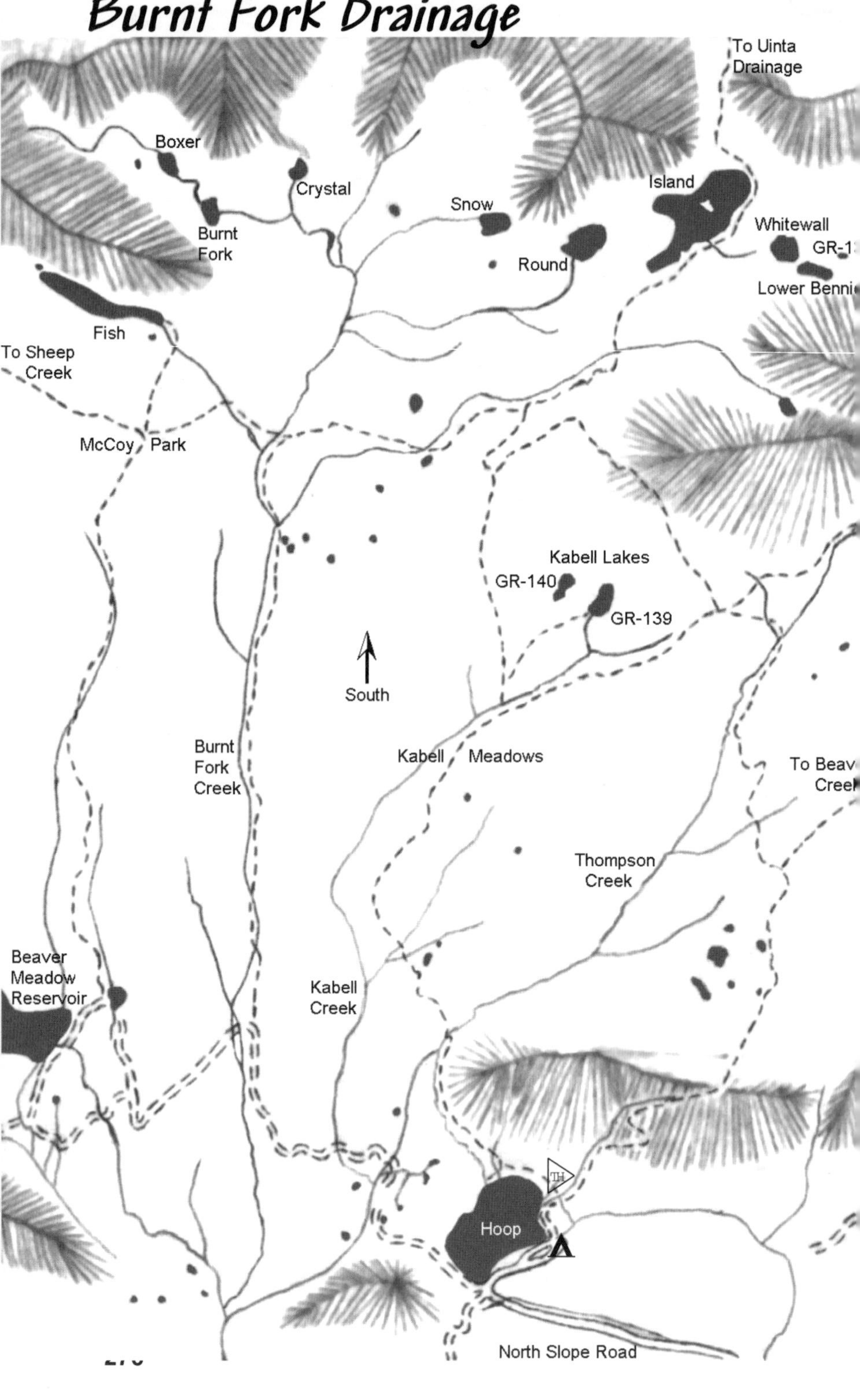

# Burnt Fork Drainage

| Lake | Ref # | Elev. | Miles | Acres | Deep | Fish | Use | Cmp | Spr | Fd |
|---|---|---|---|---|---|---|---|---|---|---|
| Bennion, Lower | GR-134 | 10,950 | 8.3 | 7.7 | 13 | B,C | L | G | Y | F |
| Bennion, Upper | GR-135 | 10,970 | 8.4 | 2 | 3 | B,C | L | G | Y | F |
| Boxer | GR-126 | 10,700 | 6.5 | 6 | 11 | C | M | G | Y | E |
| Burnt Fork | GR-127 | 10,630 | 6.1 | 9.8 | 25 | C | M | F | N | F |
| Crystal | GR-128 | 10,380 | 6.7 | 5.4 | 5 | B,C | VL | P | Y | P |
| Fish | GR-125 | 10,685 | 5.1 | 38.3 | 23 | B,C | H | G | Y | F |
| Island | GR-132 | 10,777 | 7.8 | 117.8 | 34 | B,C | H | E | Y | F |
| Kabell | GR-140 | 10,348 | 5.2 | 14.7 | 23 | C | M | P | Y | F |
| Round | GR-131 | 10,662 | 8 | 24.3 | 38 | C | M | E | Y | G |
| Snow (alias Andrea) | GR-130 | 10,550 | 8.7 | 9.4 | 35 | C | L | P | Y | F |
| Whitewall | GR-133 | 10,900 | 8.1 | 14.5 | 3 | B,C | L | G | Y | E |

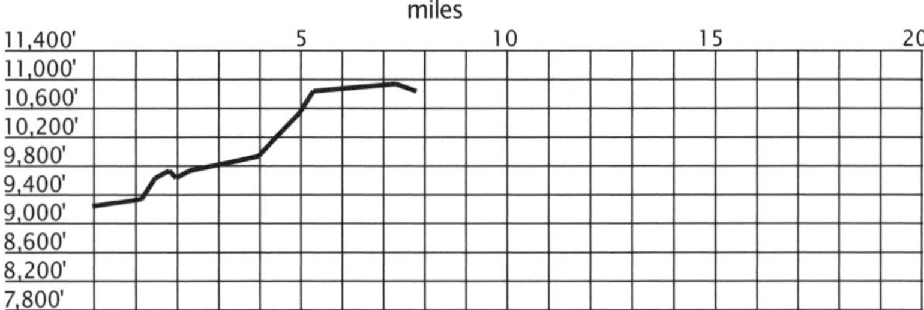


***Hoop Lake to Island Lake***

# Sheep Creek Drainage

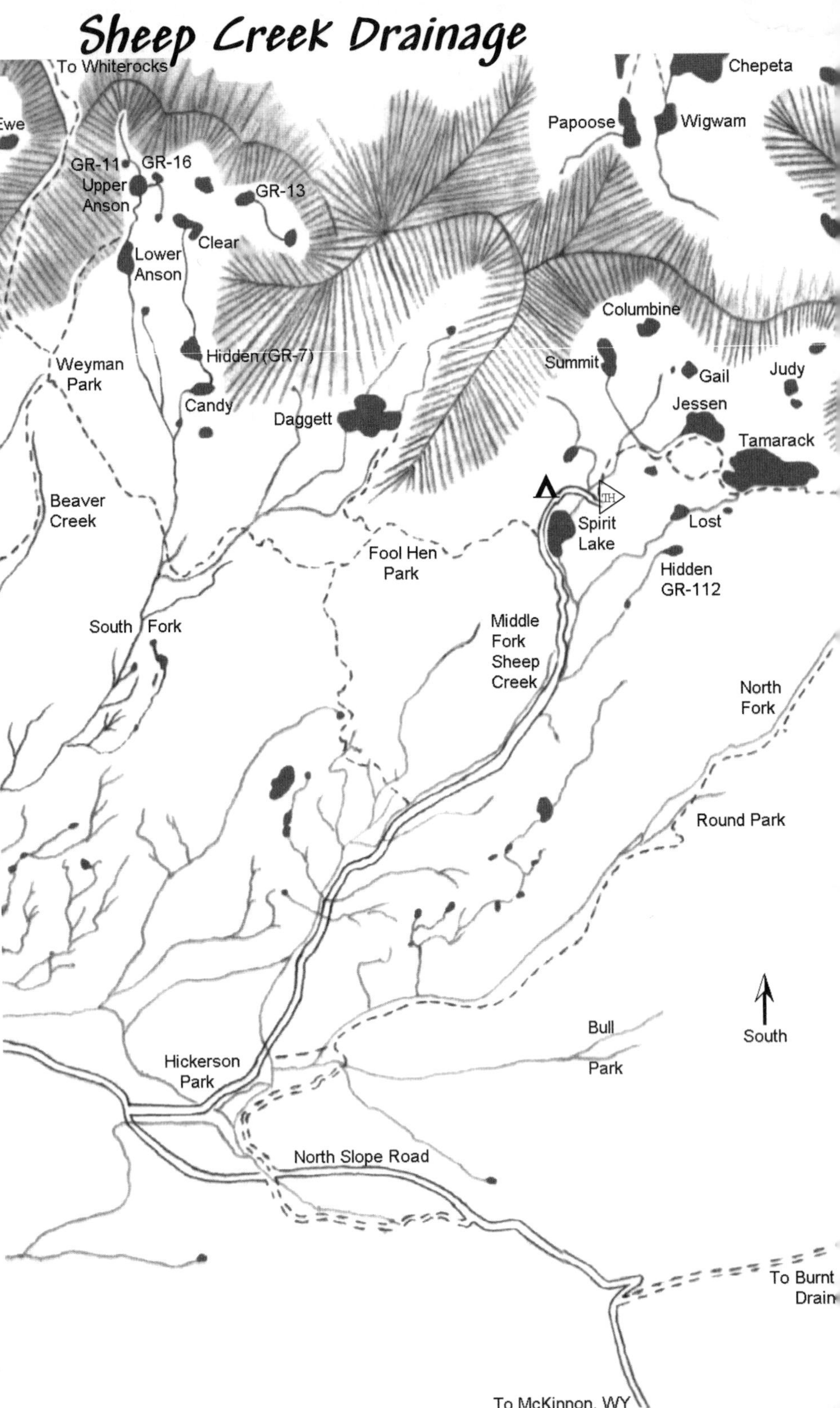

# Sheep Creek Drainage

| Lake | Ref # | Elev. | Miles | Acres | Dee | Fish | Us | Cmp | Spr | Fd |
|---|---|---|---|---|---|---|---|---|---|---|
| Anson, Lower | GR-9 | 10,575 | 6.5 | 14.5 | 20 | B | M | F | N | F |
| Anson, Upper | GR-10 | 10,660 | 6.9 | 7.7 | 58 | B | M | N | Y | F |
| Candy | GR-17 | 10,290 | 7.9 | 5.5 | 29 | N | L | P | Y | P |
| Clear | GR-12 | 10,780 | 7.5 | 10.2 | 25 | C | L | P | N | P |
| Columbine | GR-116 | 10,550 | 1.3 | 5.7 | 5 | B | L | F | Y | P |
| Dagget | GR-6 | 10,462 | 2.8 | 42.6 | 29 | R,C | H | G | Y | F |
| Gail | GR-115 | 10,420 | 1.1 | 4.5 | 25 | C | VL | P | N | P |
| Hidden | GR-7 | 10,780 | 7.6 | 8.5 | 26 | B,C | L | F | Y | P |
| Hidden | GR-112 | 10,270 | 1.3 | 4.3 | 8 | B,C | L | P | N | F |
| Jesson | GR-1 | 10,392 | 1 | 25.5 | 56 | B,C | H | F | Y | P |
| Judy | GR-25 | 10,830 | 1.8 | 4.7 | 24 | B | L | P | N | P |
| Lost | GR-4 | 10,300 | 1.1 | 3.2 | 7 | C | L | G | N | P |
| Penguin | GR-16 | 10,665 | 7.1 | 2.1 | 20 | B | M | P | N | P |
| Sesame | GR-15 | 10,780 | 7.4 | 6 | 7 | B | VL | P | N | P |
| Summit | GR-5 | 10,460 | 1 | 9.9 | 7 | N | VL | G | N | G |
| Tamarack | GR-2 | 10,429 | 1.4 | 79.1 | 90 | B,C | H | G | Y | G |
|  | GR-11 | 10,635 | 7 | 2.6 | 8 | B | L | P | N | P |
|  | GR-13 | 10,820 | 7.8 | 9.2 |  | B | VL | P | N | P |

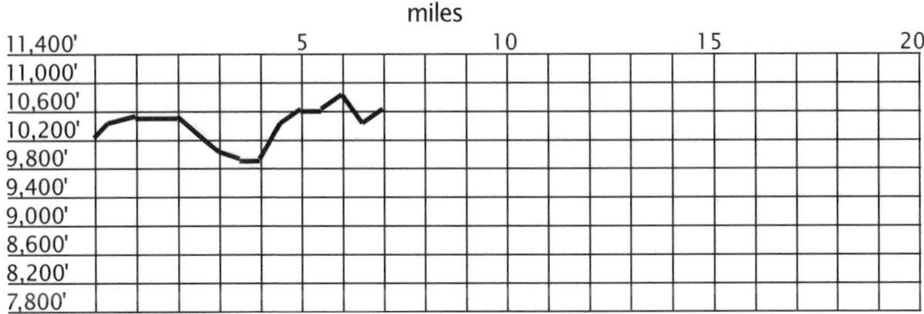


**Spirit Lake to Upper Anson Lake**

# Carter Creek Drainage

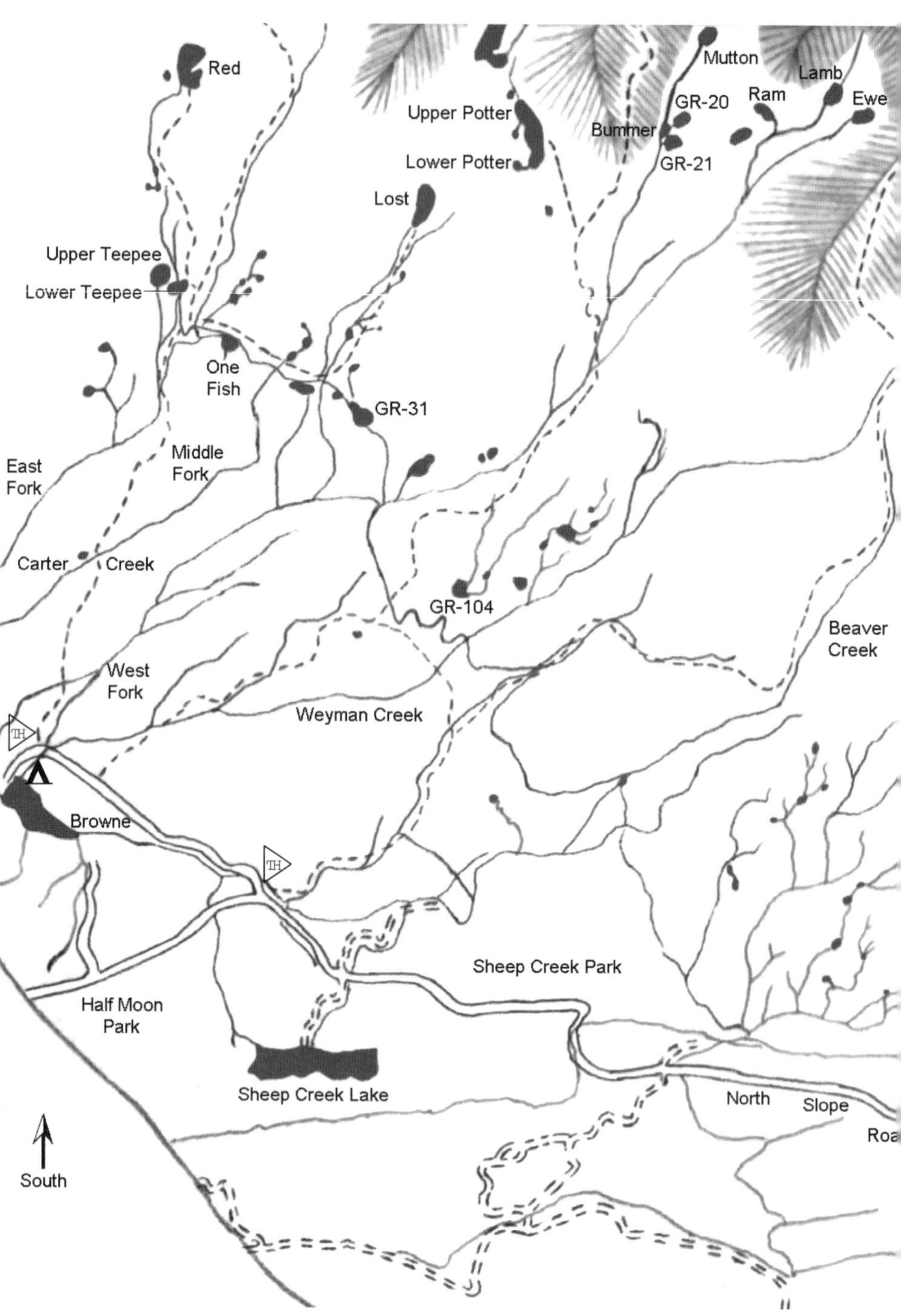

# Carter Creek Drainage

| Lake | Ref # | Elev. | Miles | Acres | Deep | Fish | Use | Cmp | Spr | Fd |
|---|---|---|---|---|---|---|---|---|---|---|
| Bummer | GR-22 | 10,350 | 6.5 | 1.9 | 6 | B | L | F | N | F |
| Ewe | GR-18 | 10,750 | 7.3 | 3 | 10 | N | L | P | Y | P |
| Lamb | GR-19 | 10,540 | 7.5 | 6 | 10 | C | L | P | Y | P |
| Lost (alias Mystery) | GR-101 | 9,750 | 4.9 | 10.2 | 25 | C | M | P | Y | P |
| Mutton | GR-23 | 10,570 | 7 | 3.8 | 10 | B | VL | F | Y | P |
| One Fish | GR-32 | 9,350 | 3.5 | 4.5 | 35 | B | L | F | Y | G |
| Potter, Lower | GR-27 | 10,130 | 6.5 | 3.4 | 16 | B | L | P | N | P |
| Potter, Upper | GR-27 | 10,130 | 6.5 | 21.3 | 75 | B | L | P | N | P |
| Ram | GR-24 | 10,380 | 6.9 | 7 | 27 | C | L | F | Y | G |
| Red | GR-33 | 9,850 | 5 | 20.9 | 57 | B | L | P | N | F |
| Teepee, Lower | GR-28 | 9,410 | 3.5 | 4.3 | 6 | B | H | G | Y | G |
| Teepee, Upper | GR-30 | 9,430 | 3.6 | 6.5 | 28 | C | M | F | N | P |
|  | GR-20 | 10,355 | 6.5 | 5.7 | 8 | B | VL | F | N | F |
|  | GR-21 | 10,355 | 6.5 | 3.7 | 7 | B | VL | F | N | F |
|  | GR-31 | 9,270 | 4.1 | 6 | 6 | B | VL | P | N | P |
|  | GR-104 | 9,290 | 3.1 | 4.3 | 19 | N | VL | P | N | P |

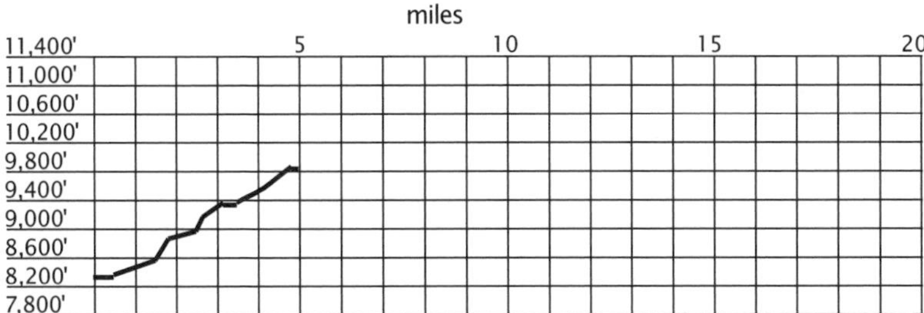


**Browne Lake to Red Lake**

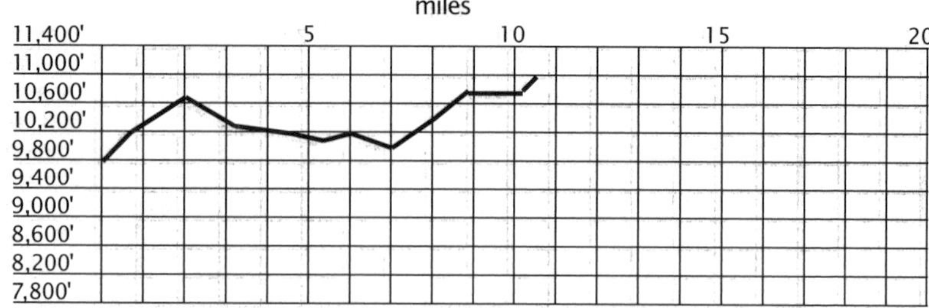


***Grandview to Cyclone Pass***

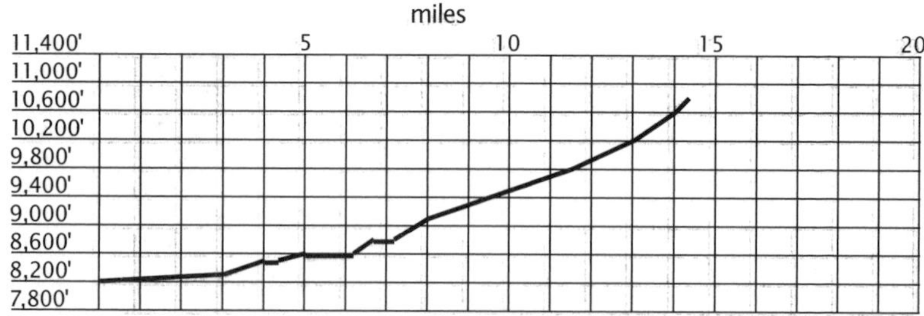


***Upper Stillwater to Lightning Lake***

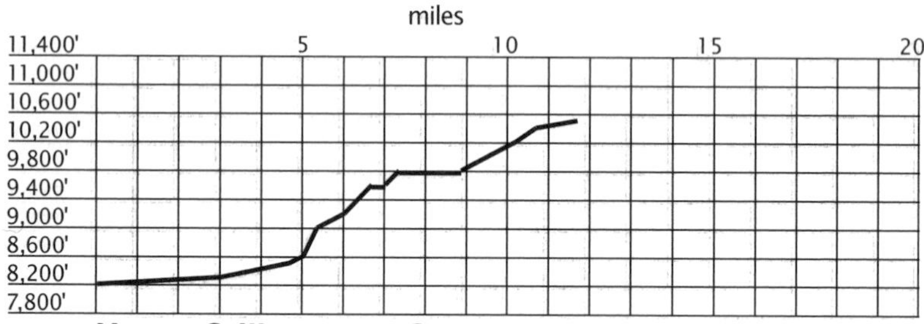


***Upper Stillwater to Squaw Lake***

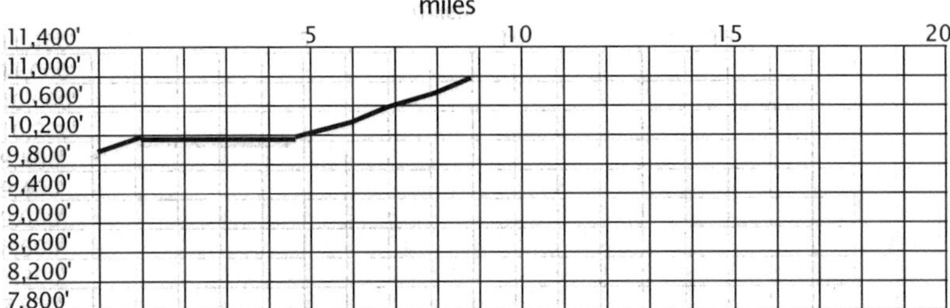


**Paradise Park to Deadman Lake**

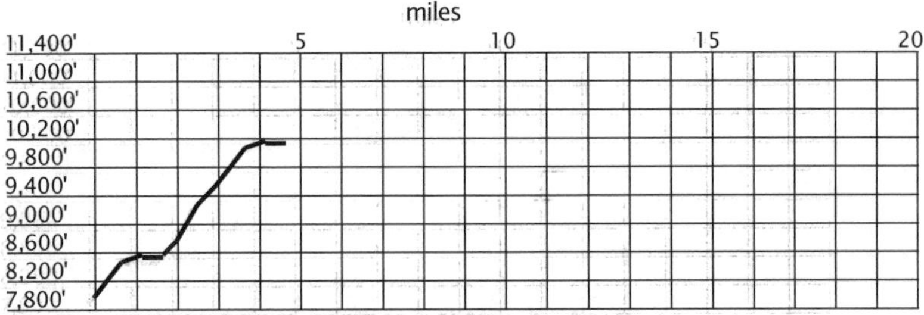


**Holiday Park to Fish Lake**

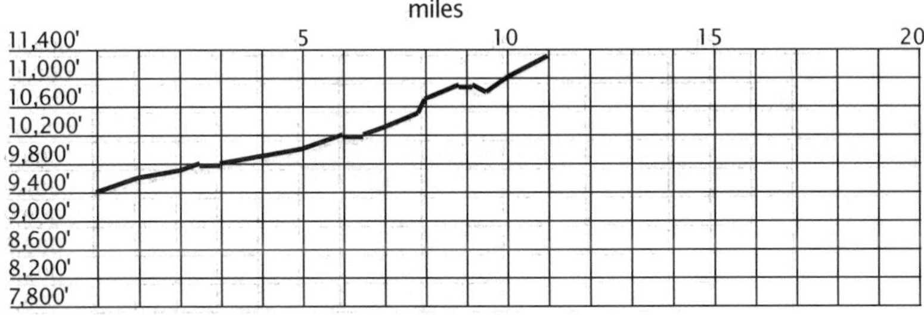


**China Meadows to Red Castle Lake**

# Uinta Mountain Campgrounds

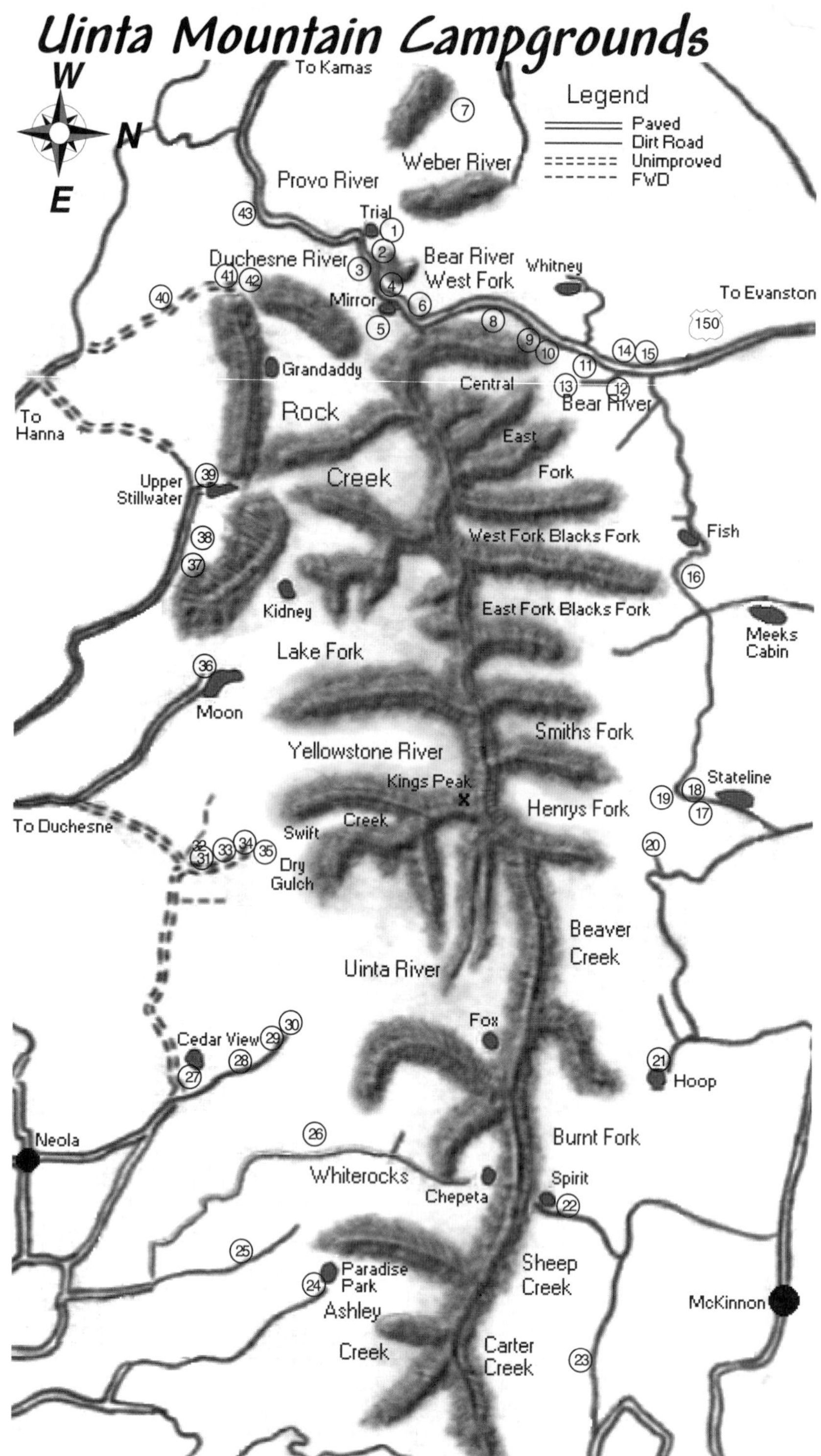

# Uinta Mountain Campgrounds

| # | Campground | Sites |
|---|---|---|
| 1 | Trial Lake | 63 |
| 2 | Lilly Lake | 14 |
| 3 | Lost Creek | 37 |
| 4 | Moosehorn | 35 |
| 5 | Mirror Lake | 99 |
| 6 | Butterfly Lake | 16 |
| 7 | Ledgefork | 75 |
| 8 | Sulpher | 23 |
| 9 | Beaver View | 20 |
| 10 | Hayden Fork | 9 |
| 11 | Stillwater | 22 |
| 12 | Wolverine | ? |
| 13 | Xmas Meadows | 12 |
| 14 | Bear River | 5 |
| 15 | East Fork | 8 |
| 16 | Little Lyman | 10 |
| 17 | Bridger Lake | 25 |
| 18 | Marsh Lake | 38 |
| 19 | China Meadows | 9 |
| 20 | Henrys Fork | ? |
| 21 | Hoop Lake | 44 |
| 22 | Spirit Lake | 23 |
| 23 | Browne Lake | 8 |

| # | Campground | Sites |
|---|---|---|
| 24 | Paradise Park | 14 |
| 25 | Whiterocks | 21 |
| 26 | Pole Creek Lake | 18 |
| 27 | Cedar View | ? |
| 28 | Big Springs | ? |
| 29 | Uinta Canyon | 25 |
| 30 | Wandin | 7 |
| 31 | Yellowstone | 14 |
| 32 | Bridge | 5 |
| 33 | Reservoir | 5 |
| 34 | River View | 20 |
| 35 | Swift Creek | 13 |
| 36 | Moon Lake | 59 |
| 37 | Miners Gulch | ? |
| 38 | Yellow Pine | 6 |
| 39 | Upper Stillwater | 6 |
| 40 | Hades | 17 |
| 41 | Iron Mine | 17 |
| 42 | Mill Flat | ? |
| 43 | Cobblerest | 17 |

# High Uintas Trailheads

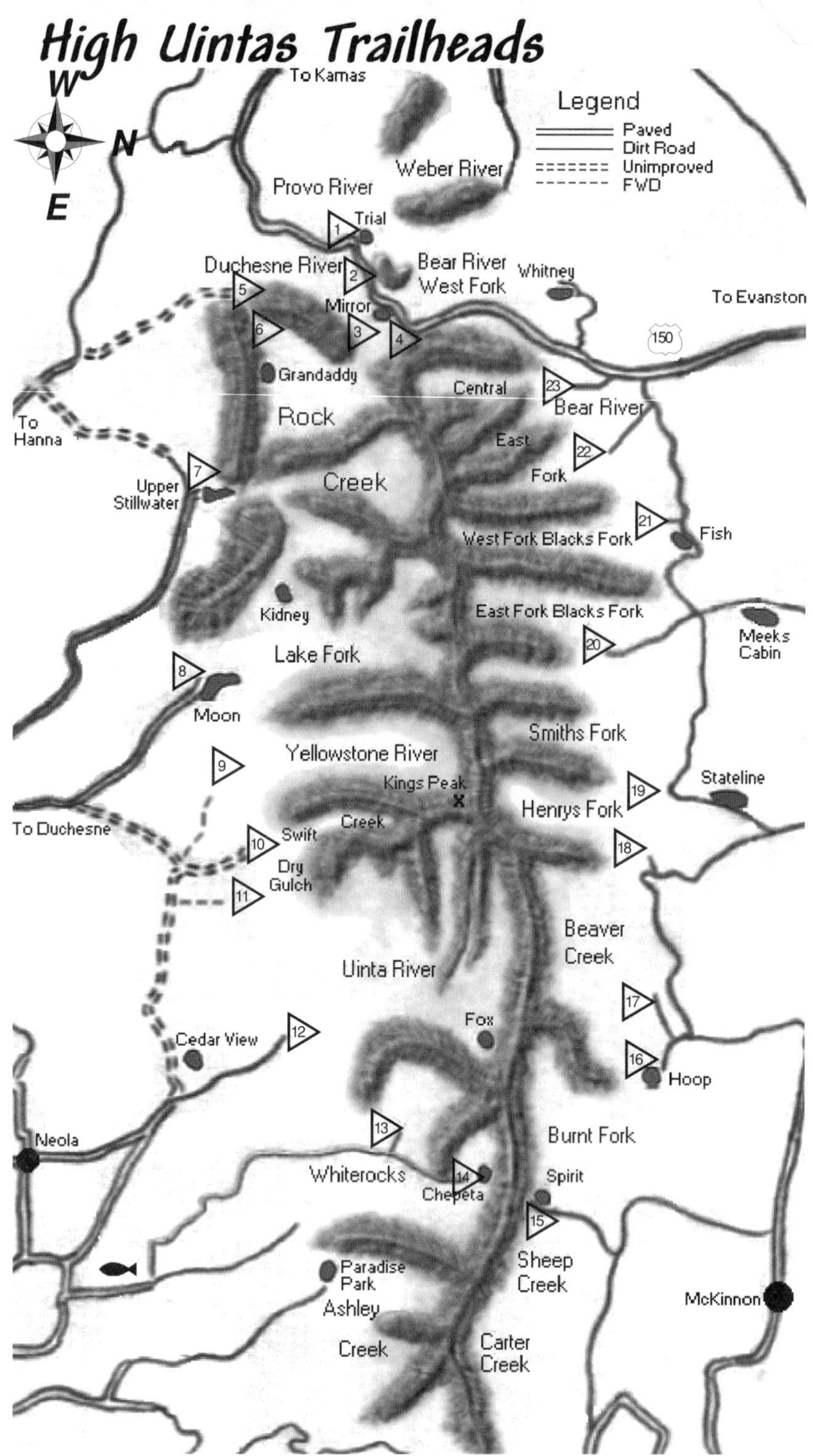

## Trailheads

| # | Trailhead Name | Miles | To Town | # Vehicles | Stock Ramp | Water | Toilets | Developed Campsites | Information |
|---|---|---|---|---|---|---|---|---|---|
| 1 | **Crystal Lake** | 27 | Kamas | 57 | | | X | | |
| 2 | **Bald Mountain** | 30 | Kamas | 25 | | | X | | X |
| 3 | **Mirror Lake** | 31 | Kamas | 18 | X | X | X | X | X |
| 4 | **Highline Trail** | 34 | Kamas | 24 | X | X | X | X | X |
| 5 | **Mill Flat** | 12 | Hanna | 10 | | | | | |
| 6 | **Grandview** | 14 | Hanna | 50 | X | | X | | X |
| 7 | **Rock Creek** | 22 | Mountain Home | 25 | X | X | X | X | X |
| 8 | **Lake Fork** | 29 | Duchesne | 40 | | | X | X | X |
| 9 | **Center Park** | 33 | Duchesne | 15 | | | | | |
| 10 | **Swift Creek** | 31 | Duchesne | 10 | X | X | X | X | X |
| 11 | **Jackson Park** | 32 | Roosevelt | 3 | | | | | |
| 12 | **Uinta** | 28 | Roosevelt | 20 | X | | X | X | X |
| 13 | **West Fork Whiterocks** | 24 | Whiterocks | 10 | X | | X | X | X |
| 14 | **Chepeta** | 30 | Whiterocks | 10 | | | | | X |
| 15 | **Spirit Lake** | 27 | Lonetree | 5 | | X | X | X | |
| 16 | **Hoop Lake** | 10 | Lonetree | 30 | X | | X | X | X |
| 17 | **Georges Park** | 10 | Lonetree | 5 | | | | | |
| 18 | **Henry's Fork** | 23 | Mountain View | 50 | X | | X | X | X |
| 19 | **China Meadows** | 22 | Mountain View | 50 | X | X | X | X | X |
| 20 | **East Fork Blacks Fork** | 22 | Evanston | 10 | X | | X | X | |
| 21 | **West Fork Blacks Fork** | 20 | Evanston | 15 | | | | | |
| 22 | **East Fork Bear River** | 36 | Evanston | 5 | X | | X | | |
| 23 | **Christmas Meadows** | 37 | Evanston | 15 | X | X | X | X | X |

# Trailhead Directions and Info

The South slope of the High Uinta Mountains is characterized by steep, rocky trails that lead into vast, open tundra in the upper basins. The North slope trails are generally not as steep, but are still rugged. These trails venture into small canyons surrounded by high vertical cliffs. These cliffs and glacial cirques make up some of the most spectacular formations in the High Uintas.

Regardless of which slope you choose, an excellent trail system exists to lead the way. This section will help you locate the trailheads. Pick one, and let your adventure begin there.

**#1 - Crystal Lake Trailhead**

From Kamas, take the Mirror Lake Highway (150) 27 miles to Trial Lake. Exit west on a good dirt road, and travel about a mile to a fork in the road. Then turn north for another mile to the trailhead.

This is a popular trailhead with room for 57 vehicles and has nice toilet facilities. Water and other amenities can be found at Trial Lake Campground. Crystal Lake Trailhead is the main take off point to many lakes only 1 to 5 miles away. Nearby lakes include Wall, Ibantik, Meadow, Cliff, Watson, Clyde, Long, Island, Big Elk, Fire, Duck, Weir, and the breath-taking Lovenia.

**#2 - Bald Mountain Trailhead**

From Kamas, take the Mirror Lake Highway (150) 30 miles to Bald Mountain overlook. About 1/2 mile north of the overlook is the turnoff to Bald Mountain.

Bald Mountain has space for 25 cars, and offers picnic tables and toilets. Water is not present. Bald Mountain trailhead is heavily used by hikers making the 2.5 mile trek to the top of Bald Mountain, where you can peer into four major drainages.

**#3 - Mirror Lake Trailhead**

From Kamas, take the Mirror Lake Highway (150) 31 miles to Mirror Lake. About 1/2 mile west of the Mirror Lake entrance you will find the trailhead.

This trailhead has 18 parking places, and offers a very popular and well-maintained campground with water, toilets, and a stock unloading ramp.

**#4 - Highline Trailhead**

The Highline is the most popular trailhead of the High Uintas. From Kamas, take the Mirror Lake Highway (150) 34 miles to a large sign on the east side of the road that says "Highline Trail." You can't get lost finding this one.

This trailhead has a listed capacity of 24 vehicles, but there are often considerably more parked here on busy weekends. This over-crowded trailhead is equipped with toilets, water, stock ramp, and nearby campsites. This is the main take off point for popular treks ranging from 6 to 50 miles in length.

Many of the lakes in the West Fork of the Rock Creek Drainage are accessible from the Highline Trailhead, but most of these lakes are easier to reach from the Grandview Trailhead.

**#5 - Mill Flat Trailhead**

From Heber City take Highway 40 east to State Route 208, which is east of Fruitland about 6 miles. Head north on 208 for 10 miles to Route 35. Follow 35 northeast 10 miles to Hanna. From Hanna, take a dirt road 12 miles northwest to Mill Flat Trailhead.

Mill Flat has 10 vehicle parking places, but no facilities. Campsites, water, and toilets can be found at Iron Mine Campground, just half a mile south.

**#6 - Grandview Trailhead**

(See directions to Hanna - Mill Flat Trailhead) From Hanna, follow a dirt road 11 miles northwest to Hades Campground. Stay on the same road another half a mile to a junction. One road takes off to Mill Flat, and the other road ventures northeast about 5 steep miles to Grandview Trailhead.

Grandview has 50 parking places, and accommodations include toilets and a stock unloading ramp. Sorry, no water here. Grandview is the starting point for lakes in the West Fork of the Rock Creek Drainage. This area is perhaps the most heavily used area in the High Uintas.

**#7 - Rock Creek Trailhead**

From Heber City, take Highway 40 east 69 miles to Duchesne. Then take State Route 87 north 14 miles to Mountain Home. Rock Creek Trailhead is 22 miles northwest of Mountain Home; mostly on a good dirt road.

Rock Creek has space for 25 vehicles, and offers campsites, toilets, water, and a stock ramp. This is a popular take-off point for horsemen heading into the Fall Creek or Squaw Basin areas. It's a long steep hike to any lakes from here. Some lakes at the head of the Rock Creek Drainage are easier reached via the Highline Trail over Rocky Sea Pass. For lakes in the West Fork of Rock Creek use the Grandview Trailhead.

**#8 - Lake Fork Trailhead**

From Heber City, take Highway 40 east 69 miles to Duchesne. Turn north on State Route 87 and travel 14 miles to Mountain Home. Take the Moon Lake Road north about 15 miles to the Lake Fork Trailhead.

Lake Fork has 40 vehicle parking places, and offers campsites and toilets. All other facilities can be found 1/4 mile northwest at Moon Lake Campground. Lake Fork is the main take off point for Brown Duck Basin, East Basin, Ottoson Basin, and is an optional trailhead for Squaw Basin.

**#9 - Center Park Trailhead**

From Heber City, take Highway 40 east 69 miles to Duchesne. Turn north on State Route 87 and travel 14 miles to Mountain Home. Follow the Moon Lake Road north 4 miles to where the Yellowstone River Road intersects on the east side. From this point, follow the Yellowstone River Road another 4 miles to the Hell's Canyon Road. Center Park is 7 miles northwest up Hell's Canyon Road, or stay on the Yellowstone River Road to go to the Swift Creek Trailhead (6 miles from fork).

Center Park has room for 15 vehicles to park, but no facilities. Hell's Canyon Road fits its name perfectly, as it is a road from hell. It is well defined, but is steep and very rocky. A truck/jeep is recommended, and may require 4-wheel drive when wet.

**#10 - Swift Creek Trailhead**

See directions for Center Park. The Swift Creek Trailhead can handle parking for 10 vehicles, and is equipped with campsites, toilets, water, and a stock ramp. Most of the high lakes are 10 to 15 miles away, up steep and rocky terrain. Swift Creek also serves as an optional trailhead for the Yellowstone River Drainage.

**#11 - Jackson Park and Dry Gulch**

From the Center Park / Swift Creek junction follow the Yellowstone River Road northeast about 3 miles to a 4WD road (#119) that winds southeast then east about 5 miles to Jackson Park Road (#120). About 3 miles northwest up road 120 it turns into a rough jeep road, but it is really quite inaccessible even with four-wheel drive. This is Jackson Park Trailhead. The Dry Gulch Trailhead is 2 miles east of the Jackson Park Road turnoff to Dry Gulch Road (#122), and another 4 miles to Dry Gulch Trailhead. There are no facilities at either of these trailheads.

**#12 - Uinta Trailhead**

From Heber City, take Highway 40 east 99 miles to Roosevelt. Then take State Route 121 north for 11 miles to Neola. Head north 17 miles on road #118 to Wandin and Uinta Campgrounds. The trailhead is located 1/2 mile north of Wandin, near the U-Bar Ranch.

The Uinta Trailhead has room for 20 vehicles, and accommodations include campsites, toilets, and a stock ramp. There is no water at the trailhead, but you can fill up at any of the campgrounds.

**#13 - West Fork Whiterocks Trailhead**

From Heber City take Highway 40 east 99 miles to Roosevelt. Then take State Route 121 north for 11 miles to Neola. Follow 121 east about 5 miles to a junction. From the junction, follow a paved road north 3 miles to the town of Whiterocks. Keep on the road heading north for 4 miles to another junction. At this point, follow road (#117) which winds east then north 18 miles to Pole Creek Junction. Then take road (#110) about 4 miles north to the West Fork junction. From here it's about 1 mile northwest to the West Fork Trailhead, or the road continues north another 7 miles to the Chepeta Trailhead. Total distances from Whiterocks to West Fork and Chepeta are 24 and 30 miles respectively. There are numerous 4WD roads in the area, so stay on the road most travelled.

West Fork Whiterocks has 20 vehicle parking places, campsites, toilets, corrals, and a stock unloading ramp. There's no water, but four separate springs can be found along the trail to Larvae Lake.

**#14 - Chepeta Trailhead**

See the directions to West Fork Whiterocks

Chepeta has 10 vehicle parking places, but has no toilets or water, and camping is limited. This trailhead is the take off point for a number of popular lakes ranging from 1/2 to 5 miles in distance. The lakes include Chepeta, Moccasin, Papoose, Wigwam, Elbow, Walk-up, and Reader Lakes. Because of their easy access, these lakes receive substantial camping and fishing pressure. For more solitude visit the eastern side of the Whiterocks Drainage, and try out Pearl, Whiterocks, Dollar, Sand, Teds, Saucer, Workman, and Wooley

Lakes. Chepeta is an optional trailhead for Dead Horse Park or Fox Lake Basin.

**#15 - Spirit Lake Trailhead**

From Evanston, take Interstate Highway 80 east 28 miles to the turn towards Fort Bridger. At this point, stay with the highway another 5 miles to a junction. Then take the south paved road about 3 miles to Mountain View, Wyoming. Take Highway 414 east then south about 20 miles to Lonetree. After about 10 miles east on Highway 414 is a 3 way junction that provides access to Spirit Lake and Browne Lake. At this junction, take the south dirt road (#221) 13 miles to a junction with a posted sign. Browne Lake is 8 miles east (road #221), or road #001 winds west then south 7 miles to Spirit Lake.

The Spirit Lake Trailhead has only 5 parking places, and can accommodate you with excellent campsites, toilets, water, cafe, horse rentals, and stock ramp. Spirit Lake Trailhead also serves as an optional trailhead for the Burnt Fork Drainage if you're heading to Island, Round, or Bennion Lake.

**Browne Lake Trailhead**

See the directions to Spirit Lake.

Campsites, toilets, and water are located at Browne Lake along with three different trailheads. Two of the three trailheads are the take off points for East Fork Carter Creek and West Fork Carter Creek. Lakes in the Carter Creek Drainage are from 5 to 8 miles south of Browne. Promising lakes include Red, Tepee, Lost, Potter, and Lamb Lakes. These lakes receive only light to moderate camping pressure, due partly to rough and rocky terrain.

**#16 - Hoop Lake Trailhead**

From Lonetree, take the dirt road south about 6 miles to a junction where one road ventures west to Henry's Fork, and another road takes off south about 1/2 miles to another junction. At this point road #058 winds south then east about 3 miles to Hoop Lake. The other road winds west then south about 3 miles to Georges Park Trailhead or Middle Beaver Trailhead. Access to West Fork Beaver Creek or Bullocks Park is 3 and 5 miles respectively on a rough 4WD road out of Georges Park.

Hoop Lake Trailhead has 30 vehicle parking places next to an excellent Forest Service campground that provides toilets, water, and a stock unloading ramp.

**#17 - Georges Park**

See directions to Hoop Lake.

Georges Park and Middle Beaver both service one trailhead for the Middle Fork of Beaver Creek Drainage. Georges Park has 5 parking places, while Middle Beaver has 10. Neither has campsites or any facilities.

The West Fork Trailhead can be reached from Georges Park or Henrys Fork on a rough road. West Fork has room for 8 vehicles, but no accommodations. West Fork is the main take off point for Gilbert Lake, which is 9 miles southwest.

**#18 - Henrys Fork Trailhead**

See directions to Mountain View (Spirit Lake Trailhead). From Mountain View, take Highway 410 south about 6 miles to a junction. Then take a well maintained gravel road south about 12 miles to a fork in the road. The east road #077 heads south about 5 miles to Henrys Fork. The west road #072 winds about 4 miles to China Meadows.

Henrys Fork Trailhead has 50 parking places, and is equipped with toilets, campsites, corrals, and a stock ramp. No water can be obtained at the trailhead, but is present at Henrys Fork Campground.

Henrys Fork Trailhead is the best starting point for Kings Peak, the highest point in Utah at an elevation of 13,528 feet. Kings Peak can be reached by following an excellent trail about 15 miles.

**#19 - China Meadows**

See the directions to Henrys Fork.

China Meadows has 50 parking places, and offers campsites, water, toilets, corrals, and a stock ramp. This is a very popular trail for Boy Scouts and naturalists seeking the unique red-rock scenery around Red Castle Lakes.

**#20 - East Fork Blacks Fork Trailhead**

From Evanston, take the Mirror Lake Highway 150 south about 30 miles to the East Fork of the Bear turnoff. This road is often referred to as the North Slope Road. Follow this road east about 20 miles to a junction just past Lyman Lakes. Then take the south road (#065) just a little over 5 miles to East Fork Blacks Fork Trailhead.

This trailhead has 10 parking places at the upper trailhead and 20 at the lower trailhead. Good campsites and toilets are located at the upper trailhead.

East Fork Blacks Fork is the take off point for East Fork and

Little East Fork Drainages. East Fork has no real lakes, but reaches deep into the wilderness to Red Knob Pass where you can continue on to either the Lake Fork Drainage or the West Fork Blacks Fork Drainage. The East Fork is a major trail used to get sheep in and out of the high country.

**#21 - West Fork Blacks Fork Trailhead**

From Evanston take the Mirror Lake Highway 150 south about 30 miles to the East Fork of the Bear turnoff. This road is often referred to as the North Slope Road. Follow this road east 15 miles to a 4 way junction. At this point, follow a good dirt road (#063) until you come to a stream crossing. You'll need a 4WD vehicle to safely cross the river, and to negotiate the rocks and mud holes that lie ahead.

West Fork Blacks Fork has room for 15 vehicles, but no campsites, toilets, or drinking water. This is the trailhead for Dead Horse Lake (8 miles) and Dead Horse Pass, which provides access to the upper regions of the Rock Creek Drainage.

**#22 - East Fork Bear River Trailhead**

From Evanston take the Mirror Lake Highway 150 south about 30 miles to the East Fork of the Bear turnoff. This road is often referred to as the North Slope Road. Follow this road east 1.5 miles to a junction. Take road #059 south about 4 miles to East Fork of the Bear River Trailhead. You may need a 4WD vehicle for the last mile when wet.

This trailhead has space for only 5 vehicles. It is located by a Boy Scout camp that has toilets, water, and campsites. This is the main take off point for Allsop Lake located 9 miles away in the Left Hand Fork. Priord and Norice Lakes are 9 miles away following the Right Hand Fork. All are popular scout lakes.

**#23 - Christmas Meadows Trailhead**

From Evanston, take the Mirror Lake Highway 150 south about 33 miles to the Christmas Meadows turnoff. Follow a good dirt road south about 4 miles to the trailhead.

Christmas Meadows has 15 parking places and a stock ramp. The nearby campgrounds have toilets and water. This popular trail leads into some of the most spectacular scenery in the High Uintas.

# U.S.G.S. Topographical Maps

W
N
E

To Kamas

| Soapstone Basin | Erickson Basin | Slater Basin | Legend |
|---|---|---|---|
| Iron Mine Mountain | Mirror Lake | Whitney Reservoir | Seven Tree Flat |
| Grandaddy Lake | Hayden Peak | Christmas Meadows | Deadman Mountain |
| Tworoose Pass | Explorer Peak | Red Knob | Elizabeth Mtn. |
| Kidney Lake | Oweep Creek | Mt. Lovenia | Lyman Lake |
| Lake Fork Mountain | Garfield Basin | Mt. Powell | Bridger Lake |
| Burnt Mill Spring | Mt. Emmons | Kings Peak | Gilbert Peak |
| Heller Lake | Bollie Lake | Fox Lake | Hole in the Rock |
| Pole Creek Cave | Rasmussen Lakes | Chepeta Lake | Hoop Lake |
| Ice Cave Peak | Paradise Park | Whiterocks Lake | Phil Pico Mountain |
| Lake Mtn. | Marsh Peak | Leidy Peak | Jessen Butte |

Legend:
Paved
Dirt Road
Unimproved
FWD

To Evanston
To Hanna
To Duchesne
Neola
McKinnon

# Index

## A



## B



## C



## D

## E



## F



## G



## H



## I



## J



## K

## S



## T



## U



## W



## Y

**Jeffrey Probst** is a life-long resident of the state of Utah. His favorite place to backpack is the High Uinta Mountains. Fishing, solitude, and photography are his main reasons for packing into the backcountry.

Outdoor writing is a preferred activity, but Jeff also spends a lot of time programming computers. That's how he makes ends meet. Writing books about the sport he loves (backpacking) provides plenty of excuses to combine his interests of computing and outdoor writing. He has also authored occasional articles for outdoor magazines.

Having backpacked in the High Uintas for over thirty years, he has admiration and a deep respect for the wonders of nature. He realizes that we all have a part to play in keeping our wilderness unspoiled. Jeff hopes that many will join in his awareness of the great outdoors, enjoy it as he does, and preserve it for generations to come. But mostly he wishes we can all just have a great time exploring. He'll see you out there!

Being native to northern Utah, **Brad Probst** has voyaged into many of its regions. However, none fulfills his needs like the lakes of the High Uintas. For over 25 years, Brad and his brother, Jeff, have dedicated at least one trip a year to visit a new and different vicinity. In doing so, most of their facts have been orchestrated throughout this book.

Sometimes solo expeditions attract Brad's attention. He loves being isolated from the outside world, while connecting inner thoughts within himself. Believing nature rates high among the elite of delights, Brad spends much of his spare time exploring the wilderness with his dog. Special friends enhance these exciting getaways, and family brings warmth and comfort on return trips.

During the winter months, Brad plans a variety of new adventures. He also spends time drawing maps and writing outdoor literature. Other inspirations include fishing, photography, sketching, and preparing gourmet meals while watching football or the Utah Jazz.